Women and Men
of the States

Bureaucracies, Public Administration, and Public Policy

Kenneth J. Meier
Series Editor

Bureaucracies, Public Administration,
and Public Policy

Women and Men of the States

Public Administrators at the State Level

M. Frances Branch	Mary M. Hale
Georgia Duerst-Lahti	Cathy Marie Johnson
Lois Lovelace Duke	Rita Mae Kelly
Mary E. Guy	Phoebe Morgan Stambaugh

MARY E. GUY, EDITOR

M.E. Sharpe Inc.
Armonk, New York
London, England

Library of Congress Cataloging-in-Publication Data

Women and men of the states : public administrators at the state level /
edited by Mary E. Guy
p.   cm.
Includes bibliographical references and index.
ISBN 1-56324-051-3—ISBN 1-56324-052-1 (pbk.)
1. Government executives—United States—States/
2. Women government executives—United States—States.
I. Guy, Mary E. (Mary Ellen)
JK2482.E94W66   1992
353.9′174—dc20
91-9035
CIP

Printed in the United States of America

The paper used in this publication meets the minimum requirements of
American National Standard for Information Sciences—
Permanence of Paper for Printed Library Materials,
ANSI Z39.48–1984.

BM   10 9 8 7 6 5 4 3 2 1

Dedicated to those women and men in public service
who strive to make a difference

Contents

━━━━━━━ List of Tables and Figures

Tables

ix

Figures

Preface and Acknowledgments

This book describes the status of women compared with that of men in managerial positions in state governments. Chapters add to theory building in regard to the types of positions that men and women hold in state governments, how they arrive at their positions, and what structural characteristics contribute to helping or hindering career advancement, especially as it differs between the sexes.

The book compares and contrasts women's positions with those held by men in order to tease out both the contrasts and the commonalities. Each chapter captures the state of employment for men and women from a unique perspective: career advancement, personal background, personal life, mentoring, sexual harassment, management styles, agency culture, and policy preferences. The themes of each chapter reinforce each other. Each chapter is based on empirical data, but the emphasis in the text is on using the data as a springboard for discussion, not as the focus of discussion. In other words, the chapters present empirical data to lend credibility and highlight patterns. Each chapter introduces its subject, followed by a presentation of survey data, and then the bulk of the discussion focuses on what the findings mean for women and men in state government careers, and what normative issues arise from the information presented. Prevailing patterns are explained by the structure of the system, that is, cultural expectations, societally imposed barriers, democracy in practice rather than theory, personnel system requirements, the role of work in peoples' lives, the breach/bridge between personal lives and public work, and agency norms versus sex role norms.

Hundreds of managers in Alabama, Arizona, California, Texas,

Utah, and Wisconsin have made this book possible. They completed lengthy questionnaires, gave interviews, and, above all, tested hypotheses with their feet. Were it not for them, the insights provided in this book would never have been uncovered. Likewise, to all those gatekeepers who allowed access to these managers, I say thank you. Without respondents, there would have been no survey.

I would be remiss not to thank Norma Ann Dodd, who produced the questionnaire for distribution to the Alabama respondents. Research assistants Michele Slay, Becky Liscum, M. Frances Branch, Beth Bracewell, and Scott Nafte assisted with the preparation of this book by analyzing data, reviewing the literature, editing drafts, providing useful criticisms, and generally keeping the process on track. I thank each of you for your unique contribution. To Cindy Michelson, I say thank you for, once again, giving your good humor and support to one more writing project.

I owe an intellectual debt to Rita Mae Kelly who persistently pursued a vision of cross-state comparisons of women and men in management positions. Without her vision and perseverance, this work would never have come to fruition.

I also wish to acknowledge the following for granting permission to reproduce or cite specific items: The American Society for Public Administration (ASPA) for permission to use material from *Public Administration Review*, vol. 51(5), "Public managers in the states: A comparison of career advancement by sex," including Table 1, p. 407 in its entirety and discussion on pp. 407–408; Table 2, p. 408 in its entirety and discussion on pp. 408–409; a portion of the contents of Table 3, p. 409; and material from the highlighted area on p. 406 entitled "State Sample Designs." Permission granted from ASPA, 1120 G Street NW, Suite 500, Washington, DC 20005.

The Haworth Press, Inc., for release of Figure 1, pp. 78–79, and Table 2, pp. 80–83, used in *Women & Politics*, vol. 10(4), 1990.

Sage Publications, Inc., for release of Table 6.1 used in *The Gendered Economy* by Rita Mae Kelly, 1991, p. 111.

About the Contributors

M. Frances Branch is a research assistant and graduate student in the public administration program at the University of Alabama at Birmingham. Her interests include social, environmental, and health policies, particularly those with global effects.

Georgia Duerst-Lahti is Associate Professor of Government and member of the Women's Studies Faculty at Beloit College. Her research interests focus on gender, power, and leadership in public bureaucracies. Her recent publications have appeared in *Public Administration Review*, *Political Science Quarterly*, *Administration & Society*, and *Women & Politics*.

Lois Lovelace Duke is Associate Professor in the Department of Political Science at Clemson University. In addition to her research in public policy and personnel in the public sector, her work interests include state and local government, American national government, and the mass media and politics. She has most recently edited the volume, *Women in Politics: Have the Outsiders Become Insiders?* (1992).

Mary E. Guy is Professor of Political Science and Public Affairs at the University of Alabama at Birmingham. She has written extensively on subjects related to public management and organization theory and behavior. Her earlier books include *Ethical Decision Making in Everyday Work Situations* (1990), *From Organizational Decline to Organizational Renewal: The Phoenix Syndrome* (1989), and *Professionals in Organizations: Debunking a Myth* (1985).

Mary M. Hale is Assistant Professor in the Division of Social and Policy Sciences at the University of Texas at San Antonio. Her research interests include health policy, social policy, public management, and administrative behavior. She has published in the fields of public administration and women in politics. She is co-editor of *Gender, Bureaucracy, and Democracy: Careers and Equal Opportunity in the Public Sector* (1989). Her recent work has appeared in *Public Administration Review*, among other journals.

Cathy Marie Johnson is Assistant Professor of Political Science at Williams College. She teaches and researches the ways American institutions make public policy. She is the author of *The Dynamics of Conflict between Bureaucrats and Legislators* (1992). Other publications have appeared in *Public Administration Review*, *Western Political Quarterly*, and *Women & Politics*.

Rita Mae Kelly is Director and Chair of the School of Justice Studies, and Professor of Justice Studies, Political Science, and Women's Studies at Arizona State University. She has written widely in the field of women and politics, including *The Gendered Economy: Work, Careers, and Success* (1991); *Gender, Bureaucracy, and Democracy: Careers and Equal Opportunity in the Public Sector* (with Mary M. Hale, 1989); *Women in the Arizona Political Process* (1988); and *The Making of Political Women* (with Mary Boutilier, 1978).

Phoebe Morgan Stambaugh is pursuing her doctorate in the School of Justice Studies at Arizona State University. She teaches courses on the intersection of women, law, and social control. Her research interests involve issues of sexual harassment and violence against women. She assisted in the research and publication of the Arizona women's 1990 Town Hall Project, which focused on women's career opportunities.

Foreword

The M.E. Sharpe, Inc., series "Bureaucracies, Public Policy, and Public Administration" is designed as a forum for the best work on bureaucracy and its role in public policy and governance. Although the series is open with regard to approach, methods, and perspectives, especially sought are three types of research. First, the series hopes to attract theoretically informed, empirical studies of bureaucracy. Public administration has long been viewed as a theoretical and methodological backwater of political science. This view persists despite a recent accumulation of first-rate research. The series seeks to place public administration at the forefront of empirical analysis within political science. Second, the series is interested in conceptual work that attempts to clarify theoretical issues, set an agenda for research, or provide a focus for professional debates. Third, the series seeks work that challenges the conventional wisdom about how bureaucracies influence public policy or the role of public administration in governance.

Women and Men of the States: Public Administrators at the State Level is a cutting-edge empirical study of gender in state bureaucracies that both describes the current situation and presents policy prescriptions for change. I read *Women and Men of the States* expecting to learn of much meaningful improvement. After all, Title IX prohibiting sex discrimination in employment has been law for twenty years, sex-segregated job recruitment is illegal, admissions to professional schools have become more equitable in terms of gender so that law school traditions such as "ladies day" are no longer acceptable, and so on. Surely an empirical study of gender and bureaucracy would reveal significant progress for women in management positions. But although some progress has been made, I am struck by the lack of progress along several dimensions. The career patterns of women managers described in this book are little different from those described in the *American Federal Executive* for 1959. There are more women in management positions today, but women managers remain as different from male managers as they did in days when management was almost exclusively a male vocation. Perhaps equally important, *Women and Men of the States* demonstrates that male managers perceive female managers differently from the ways female managers perceive themselves and their careers. A common ground of shared perceptions would generate optimism that current differences could be eliminated at some future time.

Professor Guy and her colleagues make a major contribution to the literature on organization theory with their explanation of the persistence of these differences. State agencies, similar to other bureaucracies, are open systems that have to adapt to their environment. The sexual division of labor in American society creates a dual role for women managers by assigning them the primary responsibility for the family in addition to their managerial function in their organization. Women who break out of societally defined sex roles and become upper-level managers generally have different role models, frequently have better access to other resources such as education, and often forgo family and children.

Because women managers are different from male managers, equity in access to management positions has a significant impact on the organization. Gender and organizations interact to influence the values held by women managers. The research in this volume will force the theory of representative bureaucracy to give gender attention equal to race, class, and other factors that have been the mainstays of this theory. This research provides a foundation that others can use to develop additional empirical studies in this area.

The issues addressed in *Women and Men of the States*—affirmative action, sexual harassment, flextime, effective recruitment, mentoring, and the rest—are not going to disappear. Given the trends in government employment, we can expect that more women will pursue careers in government and that such issues will become even more salient. Public managers will need to know the reasons why these issues are important to people and will need to know how to address them. The policy proposals in this book comprise a blueprint for action. *Women and Men of the States* should be required reading in all public personnel management classes and will be of great interest to everyone concerned with gender issues in public administration and with organization and management theory generally.

Kenneth J. Meier
University of Wisconsin,
Milwaukee

Introduction

Until recently, the study of public administrators has been largely a study of the achievements and activities of men. In 1985 the members of the Committee on Sex Roles of the International Political Science Association decided to collaborate on a cross-national project to remedy this absence of knowledge about women in the public service. After several years of study, a symposium edited by Jane Bayes summarizing the results of this worldwide effort appeared in *Women & Politics* (1992, vol. 11, no. 4). Also in 1985, within the United States, a subgroup of scholars from the IPSA Committee decided that the fifty U.S. states provided a useful testing ground for examining gender differences in career advancement, behavior, managerial styles, and other related phenomena. Surveying employees in state governments would permit a systematic comparison across organizational and political units.

Using the more qualitative analyses and interview results completed in the international project, several U.S. scholars (Jane Bayes, Dail Neugarten, Dorothy Riddle, Nancy Felipe Russo, Beverly Springer, and Jeanie Stanley) joined with Rita Mae Kelly and Mary M. Hale to develop a survey instrument that would be applicable at the state level of government. This questionnaire was comprehensive, dealing with career patterns, perceptions of career success, factors promoting and impeding career advancement, managerial/leadership styles, and sexual harassment, among other topics. Pretested with public servants at the federal training center in Colorado and with a randomly selected group as well as a focus group of public administrators in the state of Arizona, the questionnaire became the basis for comparable studies across six states: Alabama, Arizona, California, Texas, Utah, and Wisconsin. It is currently being replicated in Florida.

This particular volume is the second book-length work reporting the results of these studies across several states. The first, *Gender, Bureaucracy, and Democracy: Careers and Equal Opportunity in the Public Sector*, edited by Mary M. Hale and Rita Mae Kelly (1989), examined the theoretical arguments for a representative bureaucracy that would incorporate women as equal partners at all levels of the public service. It also presented four case studies of the impact of gender on public sector careers in four states: Arizona, California, Texas, and Utah. A chapter reviewing the position of women in municipal bureaucracies in the Southwest was included as an addendum, providing the reader with an overview of the progress, or lack of it, of women in the public service in state and local government in the southwestern part of the United States.

This volume continues the work begun earlier but expands the themes and foci in several ways. First, data from six states are included (Alabama, Arizona, California, Texas, Utah, and Wisconsin). Second, thematic issues are systematically explored across the states. The key issues emphasized in this volume include career development and affirmative action, background characteristics as a determinant of careers and status, the link between public work and private roles, mentoring, sexual harassment, management styles, agency cultures and gender, and policy preferences regarding workplace reform. This volume advances our knowledge systematically in these areas and lays a foundation for generalizations about progress to date and for areas of research in the future.

It is hoped that the research reported herein and the data bases developed will be used not only for teaching but also for longitudinal projects in the future. I commend Mary Ellen Guy and the other contributors for their hard and excellent efforts. We all hope that practitioners as well as scholars will find the material useful and stimulating.

Rita Mae Kelly

Women and Men
of the States

1

The Context of Public Management in the States

Mary E. Guy

Middle and upper-level managers who work in state agencies control the programs and services of the states. Because of the large numbers of personnel employed at the state level, coupled with the importance of policies and programs developed and governed by the states, this segment of the work force constitutes an important part of the public service. This chapter provides an introduction to public management in the states and explains why a focus on women and men in managerial positions is beneficial. — Editor's Note

Governmental agencies are the hands and feet of important public purposes (DiIulio 1989). How agencies go about implementing those purposes hinges on the people who are responsible for breathing life into policies and programs. In other words, managers matter because management matters. This is especially true at the state level for three reasons: first, state governments function as distinct entities with their own constitutions, laws, elected officials, and independently raised revenues. Second, in the context of American federalism, states remain vigorous administrative machines upon which Congress depends for policy implementation (Derthick 1987). Third, they employ a lot of people. In 1989, state and local governments employed over 3 million people (U.S. EEOC 1990). Of those working in state governments, 33.3 percent of full-time workers were employed in higher education;

14.4 percent were employed in hospitals; 8.2 percent were employed in corrections; 7.7 percent were employed in administration; 6.9 percent were employed in highways; 5.4 percent were employed in public welfare; 4 percent were employed in health; and 20.1 percent were employed in other programs (*Governing* 1991). This variety of programs and services represent a plethora of policy areas, jobs, skills, and responsibilities.

The responsibilities of public managers in the states are many and the results of their work are far-reaching. It is their responsibility to make sure that education equips a state's citizens with the skills and knowledge necessary to contribute to the economy and to society in general. Likewise, it is the responsibility of public managers to ensure that adequate health care is provided, that correctional systems rehabilitate those incarcerated, that taxes are collected and allocated, that highways and bridges are maintained, and that the work of government is handled as efficiently, effectively, and responsively as possible.

In 1990 the National Commission on the Public Service, more commonly called "The Volcker Commission," issued a report arguing that it is essential that government employ well-trained, experienced executives who are capable of adapting to the demands of a changing society and an interconnected world (National Commission on the Public Service 1990). Although the commission was focusing its recommendations on public service at the federal level, its concerns are equally true at the state level. Innovative management is essential if states are to implement programs and deliver services in a way that maximizes access by citizens, efficiently coordinates services, and stretches resources. Management matters more than any other organizational factor because innovative public managers have a bias toward action. And it is action that makes the difference (Sanger and Levin 1991).

Survey of Managers

So, who are the managers in the states? Who make the difference? This book uses data gathered from surveys conducted in Alabama, Arizona, California, Texas, Utah, and Wisconsin to answer these questions. The surveys were conducted to discover the backgrounds of middle and upper-level managers in state agencies, to find how they had achieved their posts, and to learn about the career helps and hindrances they encountered. Their managerial styles were also explored to learn how they view themselves and their work. They were selected according to criteria based on salary levels, duties performed, and personnel grade schedules. (See appendix A for an explanation of the research design and appendix B for a list of the survey questions.)

Because of the different personnel systems in each state, the precise definition of the upper echelon managers varied somewhat from state to state. The six surveys include responses from 1,289 respondents, of whom 870 are men and 419 are women. Because it was important to the researchers to learn whether or how gender affects women and men differently in their managerial careers, results are analyzed by sex of respondents. The chapters in this book are based upon the data from the surveys and identify factors that either unite or differentiate women and men in managerial positions. These factors are then discussed in terms of the normative issues that they raise regarding structures within public agencies that affect the employment of women and men in administrative positions.

The Status of Women and Men in State and Local Public Administration

In the business sector of the economy, women have made significant inroads into boardrooms and corporate office-holding over the past few decades, but they still trail far behind men in terms of their overall representation in important posts and in salary attainment (Dreher, Dougherty, and Whitely 1989). An examination of data supplied by the U.S. Equal Employment Opportunity Commission shows a similar finding in state and local government. There is a significant difference in the rate at which women enter managerial positions and the rate at which men enter similar positions in state government.

National data provide a backdrop that enlightens the discussions in the following chapters. These national data collected from all state and local governments show significant disparities between the status of women and the status of men in terms of their employment (U.S. EEOC 1982, 1985, 1990). Tables 1.1 through 1.5 display these data.

Table 1.1 indicates that the wage gap between women and men employed full-time in state and local government has increased from 1980 to 1990 and that women are increasingly landing part-time positions and entering the public service in greater numbers than men. A comparison of the median salary for all full-time employees working

Table 1.1

Full-Time Median Salary, Part-Time Employment, and New Hires

	Women	Men	Difference
Median salary ($)			
1980	11,414	15,159	−3,745
1985	17,262	22,332	−5,070
1990	20,631	26,070	−5,439
Part-time employment (%)			
1980	51.0	49.0	+2.0
1985	53.4	46.6	+6.8
1990	55.3	44.7	+10.6
New hires (%)			
1980	50.5	49.5	+1.0
1985	49.0	51.0	−2.0
1990	51.4	48.6	+2.8

for state and local government in the United States in 1980, 1985, and 1990 is telling. While men, on average, made $3,745 more than women in 1980, they made $5,439 more by 1990. Likewise, part-time employment has fallen more and more to women. Of all those who held part-time employment in 1980, there were 2 percent more women than men. After a decade of gradual change, women held 10.6 percent of the part-time jobs. Over the course of the 1980s these numbers show that more doors have opened for women. In 1980, there were 1 percent more women among new hires and by 1990 there were 2.8 percent more women among new hires.

Table 1.2 shows the median salary of full-time employees working in state and local governments according to their type of employment. A comparison of the median salaries of women and men employed full-time in state and local governments is enlightening when job categories are broken down into "officials/administrators," "professionals," and "office/clerical/administrative support." The table shows that the wage gap has increased from 1980 to 1990 for officials/administrators. While men made $5,657 more than women in 1980, they made $7,783 more in 1990. The wage gap did not progress as steadily for either of the other two categories, although it remained ever-present. While male professionals made $4,246 more than women in 1980, they made

Table 1.2

Full-Time Median Salary by Occupation ($)

	Women	Men	Difference
Officials/ administrators			
1980	17,493	23,150	−5,657
1985	26,440	33,370	−6,930
1990	32,686	40,469	−7,783
Professionals			
1980	15,738	19,984	−4,246
1985	23,306	28,750	−5,444
1990	28,291	33,033	−4,742
Office/clerical/ administrative support			
1980	10,429	11,858	−1,429
1985	15,135	17,140	−2,005
1990	18,082	19,672	−1,590

$4,742 more in 1990. While men in clerical positions made $1,429 more than women in 1980, they made $1,590 more than women in 1990.

Table 1.3 shows the median salary of full-time employees in state and local governments in 1980, 1985, and 1990 in the six states that were surveyed for this study. When the wage gap is examined in these six states, the evidence is that it is nowhere close to disappearing. In all states, regardless of geographic region, political context, or comparable-worth initiatives, the gap remained. And in all but Alabama, the gap was larger by 1990 than it was in 1980. Even in Alabama the gap had only closed by slightly more than $300. The largest gap that developed over the decade of the 1980s was in California, with an increase of $3,337.

Table 1.4 shows the distribution of part-time employment by sex in 1980, 1985, and 1990 in the six states that were surveyed. The pattern that emerges when one examines part-time employment is that women increasingly hold a higher percentage of part-time jobs, except in Utah, where men have held over 54 percent of these jobs throughout the 1980s. The most dramatic growth in the percentage of part-time jobs held by women occurred in Alabama with a growth from 55 percent of

Table 1.3

Full-Time Median Salary by State ($)

	Women	Men	Difference
Alabama			
1980	9,835	11,914	−2,079
1985	14,986	16,872	−1,886
1990	19,563	21,334	−1,771
Arizona			
1980	11,793	16,110	−4,317
1985	16,678	23,052	−6,374
1990	19,592	26,639	−7,047
California			
1980	13,672	20,099	−6,427
1985	23,592	30,764	−7,172
1990	26,088	35,852	−9,764
Texas			
1980	9,986	13,527	−3,541
1985	15,532	19,966	−4,434
1990	17,917	21,859	−3,942
Utah			
1980	11,785	17,500	−5,715
1985	16,368	23,181	−6,813
1990	18,168	25,088	−6,920
Wisconsin			
1980	12,713	17,166	−4,453
1985	17,096	22,955	−5,859
1990	19,876	26,382	−6,506

all such jobs to over 62 percent. Arizona also reflected this pattern, with women increasing their share of part-time jobs from almost 47 percent to almost 58 percent.

Table 1.5 shows the number of new hires in state and local government by sex in 1980, 1985, and 1990 in the six states surveyed. Just as the Volcker Commission report suggested, women are moving into the public work force at a higher rate than men. While men represented almost 51 percent of all new hires in Alabama in 1980, they represented only 45 percent by 1990. This trend is repeated in each state

Table 1.4

Percentage of Part-Time Employment by Sex

	Women	Men	Difference
Alabama			
1980	54.9	45.1	9.8
1985	57.5	42.5	15.0
1990	62.4	37.6	24.8
Arizona			
1980	46.7	53.3	−6.6
1985	51.3	48.7	2.6
1990	57.8	42.2	15.6
California			
1980	54.2	45.8	8.4
1985	56.0	44.0	12.0
1990	55.9	44.1	11.8
Texas			
1980	51.9	48.1	3.8
1985	51.7	48.3	3.4
1990	53.4	46.6	6.8
Utah			
1980	45.7	54.3	−8.6
1985	45.1	54.9	−9.8
1990	45.2	54.8	−9.6
Wisconsin			
1980	50.2	49.8	0.4
1985	54.5	45.5	9.0
1990	54.2	45.8	8.4

except Utah, where men represented almost 52 percent in 1980 and actually increased to over 52 percent by 1990.

Comparing across States

What do these numbers tell us? Is the public service in the states changing? Can we expect program implementation to reflect the increasing numbers of women in the work force? Can we expect the salience of some issues to change because of the changing work force?

Table 1.5

Percentage of New Hires by Sex

	Women	Men	Difference
Alabama			
1980	49.1	50.9	−1.8
1985	44.5	55.5	−11.0
1990	54.6	45.4	9.2
Arizona			
1980	48.2	51.8	−3.6
1985	47.8	52.2	−4.4
1990	52.3	47.7	4.6
California			
1980	52.5	47.5	5.0
1985	54.1	45.9	8.2
1990	54.5	45.5	9.0
Texas			
1980	47.8	52.2	−4.4
1985	47.1	52.9	−5.8
1990	53.1	46.9	6.2
Utah			
1980	48.4	51.6	−3.2
1985	46.3	53.7	−7.4
1990	47.6	52.4	−4.8
Wisconsin			
1980	48.9	51.1	−2.2
1985	49.1	50.9	−1.8
1990	56.7	43.3	13.4

Or do these numbers mean that, as much as some things change, they still stay much the same? These are tantalizing questions that the following chapters explore. Although the states selected for this study represent a convenience sample, they represent four different regions of the United States: the Southeast, the Southwest, the Far West, and the Upper Midwest. These regions differ in their political contexts, histories, and traditions, yet patterns that emerge in one also emerge in the others.

There are difficulties in making cross-state comparisons because of differences in each state's personnel system, political traditions, and social context. The contextual factors that define each state include, at the least, political, economic, and social variables. States have become more similar in levels of urbanization, industrialization, income, and employment from 1952 through 1984 (Dye 1990). But the trends toward nationalization are tempered by the fact that policy differences among the states do not appear to be decreasing. Dye (1990) cites evidence that per capita state and local tax revenues, total expenditures, and expenditures for education, welfare, health, and highways have remained virtually unchanged over the past thirty years. And political culture differs from state to state and region to region (Elazar 1987), and the political and governmental traditions within the states differs and has differed from the time states created their respective constitutions (Elazar 1988; Lamis 1984). Geographic regions account for additional variables as well, such as institutionalized traditions and size and mix of the minority population.

In spite of all the reasons for differences existing between the states, there are unifying influences as well. The effect of telecommunication, and the mobility and transience from one state to another that is enjoyed by U.S. citizens, make the states mirror images of one another in many ways. Whether one lives in Seattle or in Miami, the same popular television programs can be tuned in and they form the basis of a conversation between two otherwise total strangers. Likewise, the standardization of federal regulations across the states in regard to employment practices and criteria that must be met in order to receive federal funds for programs provides a common thread that makes states similar in many respects.

Kanter's Theory

In her book, *Men and Women of the Corporation*, Rosabeth Moss Kanter (1977) identified structural and systemic characteristics that mitigated against career advancement for women in private sector management. She set forth a theory that focuses on organizational structure to explain why women are disadvantaged, rather than focusing on societal factors or individual factors. The theory includes three sets of variables: the extent to which employees are in a position from which further upward mobility is possible; the extent to which employees possess the power necessary to accomplish their goals; and the relative number of people in a peer group of one's own social type, such as women or men. The basic assumption is that worker commitment and productivity as well as future opportunities for mobility and empowerment are enhanced when workers, at whatever level, are empowered, have mobility opportunity, and are not tokens. This theory assumes that differences in women's and men's attitudes and behaviors are produced by the fact that they play different and unequal roles in the workplace; in turn, the differences produced from this enhance the likelihood that roles will be distributed differentially on the basis of gender to the continuing disadvantage of women.

Whether or not there are structural barriers to the advancement of women into top-level managerial positions is a driving question behind much of the analyses that are conducted in these chapters. Kanter generated a rich set of hypotheses related to structural determinants of behavior in organizations, especially as it related to women's status in the workplace compared with men's. She hypothesized that people low in career opportunity behave differently from people high in career opportunity. Opportunity relates to expectations and future prospects for mobility and growth. Those with high opportunity have high aspirations, are more attracted to high-power people, are competitive, are more committed to the organization and to their careers, value their competence, and become impatient or disaffected if they do not keep moving. On the other hand, those in low-opportunity positions limit their aspirations, seek satisfaction in activities outside of work, have a horizontal orientation rather than a vertical orientation, find ways to create a sense of efficacy and worth through personal relationships, resign themselves to staying put, and are concerned with basic survival and extrinsic rewards. Kanter also developed notions about power, which she defined as the capacity to mobilize resources. People low in organizational power tend to foster lower group morale, behave in more directive, authoritarian ways, use more coercive than persuasive power, and are more insecure, more controlling, and more critical. People high in organizational power foster higher group morale, behave in less rigid, directive, authoritarian ways, delegate more control, allow subordinates more latitude and discretion, and are more often seen as helping rather than hindering.

Kanter called a third characteristic "proportions." This concept relates to the social composition of people in approximately the same situation. It is a quantitative matter of how many people of a kind are present, so that differentness is, or is not, noticeable. People whose type is represented in very small proportion tend to be more visible, that is, they are "on display." They feel more pressure to conform and to make fewer mistakes, find it harder to gain credibility, are more isolated and peripheral, are more likely to be excluded from informal peer networks, and, thus, are limited in their source of power-through-alliance. Furthermore, they face more personal stress, are stereotyped, and are placed in role traps that limit effectiveness. People whose type is represented in very high proportion tend to be seen as "fitting in," are preferred for high-communication managerial jobs, and find it easier to gain credibility for high uncertainty positions. They are more likely to join the informal network and to form peer alliances and learn the ropes from peers. They are also more likely to be sponsored by higher-status organization members and to acquire mentors easily. These three possessions—opportunity, power, and proportion—combine to produce cycles that feed on themselves. Thus, those with opportunity are induced to behave in ways that generate more opportunity, which in turn produces further inducement for the behavior. In other words, power begets power. The relationship between structure and behavior produces upward cycles of advantage or downward cycles of disadvantage. Low opportunity, powerlessness, and tokenism constitute self-perpetuating systems that can only be broken from the outside.

A decade after her original work, Kanter (1987, 1989b) revisited her hypotheses and concluded that they were as sound then as when she had first enumerated them. She argues that they explain why women managers are often stereotyped as being more rigid than men. She argues that it is one's position in the organization, rather than one's sex, that determines one's behavior on the job. She believes that when other things are the same, such as sex, training, and work context, it is the demands of the position that produce what are commonly attributed to sex-specific behaviors. For example, women are often criticized for emphasizing adherence to set policies and procedures. Kanter argues that when women are sticklers for detail, it is because they are in jobs with little discretion, and whatever discretion is allowed is constrained by rigid rules. Thus, their career advancement depends upon the degree to which they adhere to set policies and procedures, rather than the degree to which they practice discretionary authority.

Kanter's work in corporations is germane to this work in state government because it speaks to the status differential between men and women and hints at the structural changes that must occur if there is to be a significant recasting of the status quo. People who are different from the dominant management group tend to be clustered in those parts of management with least uncertainty. They are found in increasing numbers away from the top, in positions of low uncertainty, non-discretionary positions, and in expert, rather than operational roles.

Gender and Organizational Leadership

Gender will be used in this book to denote the social construction of the differences between the sexes. Gender differences have a greater impact on work life than biological differences because of the social definitions that accompany gender. More and more, the literature reflects a growing belief that men and women manage differently (Kanter 1987, 1989a; Rosener 1990). Rosener (1990), for example, classifies the management style of men as being "transactional." By this she means that men view job performance as a series of transactions with subordinates, exchanging rewards for services rendered or punishment for inadequate performance. She believes that men are also more likely to use power that comes from their organizational position and formal authority. On the other hand, she classifies the management style of women as 'interactive." She defines interactive as a style in which managers actively work to make their interactions with subordinates positive for everyone involved. She believes women encourage participation, share power and information, enhance other people's self-worth, and excite others about their work. She pictures this as the preferred style to that of men because she believes that it creates a win–win situation in the workplace that is good for both the employees and the organization. The following chapters explore management styles of men and women and, to some degree, come to a conclusion similar to Rosener's.

Organizational leadership is a key for societal gender equity. Those in decision-making posts affect not only the programs they are responsible for implementing, but also the quality of working life for those women and men whom they supervise. And they affect the attitudes that women and men adopt toward people in authority. If the person in authority is a woman who handles her responsibilities capably, then a positive role model exists for others to emulate. On the other hand, if women are restrained from achieving influential posts, then the role model for women in organizations is to set their sights for career development and empowerment at a lower level than is true for men. Chafetz (1990) makes two basic assumptions regarding gender inequality. The first is that a system of gender stratification implies superior male power resources at the macro level. The second is that a gender division of labor exists in which women are more responsible than men for child rearing and other family and household work. Thus, she uses the two concepts of gender power inequity and gender division of labor as the starting point for explaining the coercive aspects inherent in the typical workplace.

In 1982 Gwen Moore (1987) interviewed men and women managers in two New York state agencies, one an administrative agency and the other a human services agency. The interview queried each respondent's present position, career history, family obligations, and general attitudes. She found that although women comprised about half of the employees in New York state government, they constituted only a tiny proportion of those in top-level positions. She concluded that there is a law of decreasing proportions, in that, as job levels increase, the proportion held by women decreases.

Moore's work in the State of New York also showed that gender stratification in the workplace has generated a segmented work force that interacts with workers' private lives. The women differed from their male counterparts in that women were less likely to be married and, if married, were less likely to have children. This indicates that marriage and children serve as barriers to women who want to rise to management positions. Also, women were more likely than men to hold graduate degrees, which indicates that women require more credentials than men in order for them to attain high-level posts. At the time of the survey, the state's two most recent governors had been strongly committed to affirmative action for women and minorities and had actively pursued the promotion of women into managerial positions. Other than these differences in terms of family obligations, credentials, and impetus for hiring women, Moore found that women and men in management were quite similar. Moore explains this similarity as being a reflection of the winnowing process in which only those women who "fit in well" with their male counterparts are promoted to high ranks.

Hale and Kelly (1989a) have reported studies of women in management positions in California, Texas, Utah, and Arizona. They summarize three reasons why women are represented in much smaller numbers in managerial positions than they are in lower-level positions. These explanations result from obstacles that are related to three kinds of barriers: psychological, support, and structural hurdles. The authors say that there are barriers internal to women, such as self-esteem, and barriers internal to men, such as gender role socialization and role prejudice. They also conclude that barriers exist to support availability such as limited financial resources, education and training, collegial networks, role models and mentors. They also cite structural barriers such as employer biases, sex-segregated jobs, sexual harassment, and pay inequities. On the other hand, there are facilitators, such as distinct career paths, support from one's family, financial, educational, and training supports, informal networks and mentors, promotional opportunities, workplace experience, and employer's commitment to representativeness and affirmative action. Moore's work, along with that of Hale and Kelly, deserves further investigation, especially when considered in light of Kanter's theory. In this context, the following chapters present various aspects of career development for women and men and attempt to discern the patterns that emerge.

Preview of Chapters

The following chapters explore the status of women's and men's careers in management positions in state government. In chapter 2, Lois Lovelace Duke explores the contrasts between women and men in terms of their success at securing positions and the structural barriers that they must overcome. Differences in their personal backgrounds are investigated by Mary E. Guy and Lois Lovelace Duke in chapter 3 in order to identify similarities and contrasts between women and men who achieve management positions. The relationships between employees' work away from home and their lives at home are then explored by Cathy Marie Johnson and Georgia Duerst-Lahti in chapter 4. This is followed by Mary M. Hale's analysis in chapter 5 of how mentoring for women compares with mentoring for men. Rita Mae Kelly and Phoebe Morgan Stambaugh present a discussion in chapter 6 of sexual harassment in the workplace and how this affects the relationship between the sexes. In chapter 7, Georgia Duerst-Lahti and Cathy Marie Johnson investigate the different management styles used by women versus those used by men and discuss the advantages and implications of differences. Mary E. Guy and Georgia Duerst-Lahti then take a look in chapter 8 at organizational culture and how it influences the selection of candidates for managerial positions. Mary M. Hale and M. Frances Branch present a look in chapter 9 at how managerial preferences as related to personnel-related policies differ for women and men. Finally, in the concluding chapter, by Mary E. Guy integrates these diverse yet connected elements into a coherent description of managers in state government.

Summary

This book is an attempt to capture a snapshot of the status of women and men in managerial positions in state government as it is today and to draw inferences about the structural conditions that contribute toward advancing the careers of women and men. Each chapter presents empirical data and then focuses the discussion on what the findings mean for women and men in management careers and what normative issues arise from the analysis. The analyses provide a comparison of the status of women compared to the status of men in managerial positions in state government. When inequities appear between the sexes, they are explored in the context of organizational, structural, and systemic features that contribute to them. The confluence of bureaucracy and gender equity is the focus of attention and I hope the reader will be moved to consider the status quo in a new light. I hope that the reader will be inspired to "think out of the box" about new leadership styles and new personnel structures for enhancing opportunities in state government. The details of life and behavior inside state agencies reflect the culture, language, and style of mainstream American public administration as it approaches the end of the twentieth century. The consequences of high or low opportunity, high or low power, and high or low numerical representation affect program implementation as well as public administrators. The question to keep in mind while reading these chapters is "Can the prevailing patterns be explained by the structure of the cultural expectations, societally imposed barriers, democracy as it is put into practice, personnel system requirements, the role of work in peoples' lives, the breach/bridge between personal lives and public work, and agency norms versus sex role norms?" This is a tantalizing question with many variables intertwined. Although a definitive answer is elusive, the information in the following chapters provides hints of answers.

The unique contribution of these analyses is that they generate a picture of the differential levels of women's participation in the managerial work force in state government. Hypotheses can be generated from this picture about the levers that must be pulled to affect women's ability to secure leadership positions and to ensure that women as well as men have the right to make a difference in implementing important public purposes.

2

Career Development and Affirmative Action

Lois Lovelace Duke

More women have steadily joined the work force since the 1960s. In proportion to their numbers, however, the number in management positions is nowhere close to being representative of their numbers in the work force, in spite of affirmative action initiatives. Surveys indicate that this paradox occurs in both the public and the private sectors. Women managers encounter a number of obstacles blocking their advancement. This chapter details these phenomena.

— Editor's Note

There is a substantial literature that focuses on similarities and differences between women and men in management. Across the board, findings generally show that women are under-represented in top management positions, even though women and men are more similar than they are different in their career patterns and in their management styles and behaviors. Coyle (1989) cites figures for 1988 that show that women occupy about 15 percent of all management or management-related positions (Hammond 1988). This represents a 5 percent increase over the 1970s. However, it is not clear whether there has been any real improvement in women's access to middle and upper management opportunities. There are indications that with the expansion of the service sector, we have had a considerable growth in junior management jobs because more and more women, as new managers, have moved into management at this level (Powell 1988).

Research by the late Linda Keller Brown, a social scientist who was a pioneer in the study of women in management, revealed that in the generation since 1960 the proportion of women managers doubled, reaching 30 percent (Adler and Izraeli 1988; Brown 1988). This statistic is misleading, however, when the number of women in the work force is considered, coupled with the facts that less than one-third hold management positions and that this progress has been achieved over a thirty-year period. Obviously, Brown's assessment does not reflect real advancement. Instead, the increase of women managers has failed to keep pace with the rapid influx of women into the labor force (Maital 1989). For example, at the state and local level, the numbers of women employed from 1973 to 1980 increased by 320,000 (Moore and Mazey 1986). The number of women nationally in public administration almost doubled from 1.2 million in 1970 to 2.1 million in 1980. These figures represent a proportional increase from 34 percent of the public work force to 41 percent (Bremer and Howe 1988; U.S. Department of Commerce, Bureau of the Census 1980).

The data presented in this volume, as well as those of prior studies, reveal a paradox that should be of concern to both public and private sector administrators at all levels. Research that spans about twenty years shows that women continue to remain at the lower levels of management and earn on the average about 60 to 64 percent of what men earn (Kelly and Bayes 1988). During this same period, more and more women have entered the work force. In the early 1970s, Congress, the president, and the courts intervened actively to promote affirmative action and equal opportunity employment practices. Therefore, with more women working and the federal government actively advocating change, one would expect to see women making significant advances in salary and management positions. However, as the data in this volume confirm, women have not advanced to the higher levels of management. Instead, the proportion of women managers is greatest at the lower levels of management, smaller at the middle management levels, and smallest at the top management levels. If there are no barriers to advancement for female managers, the numbers of women in middle and top management positions should have increased much more than it has (Powell 1988).

Past studies have attempted to explain women's limited advancement in management in terms of psychological, sociological, or structural barriers (Harlan and Weiss 1981). The psychological barriers focus on the differences between women and men managers based on their personal background, such as education or life experiences. The sociological approach focuses on the organizational environment in which women must work. The two issues that have been examined most closely using this second approach are sex role stereotypes and organizational structure and policies (Stewart 1976). Sex role stereotypes, as well as certain organizational structures, place women at a disadvantage and lead to women's inequitable experiences. Rosabeth Moss Kanter has examined barriers from a structural perspective. She has argued that women's limited success can be traced to the extremely low proportion of women in power positions and the fact that opportunities for advancement are more often closed to women than to men. This leads to women being seen and responded to in stereotypical ways. Kanter maintains that these inequities will not be changed until the approach shifts from looking at intrapsychic differences between women and men to looking at structural components that limit upward movement (Kanter 1977, 1979).

Managers in the States and Their Characteristics

What are some of the characteristics of the women who do move into management positions? The data from surveys of women and men in Arizona, Texas, Wisconsin, and Alabama basically show that women tend to move into management at a younger age than their male counterparts. This finding is also confirmed in a study that examined the work experiences of white and non-white males and females to identify patterns that contribute to influence and promotion. Miller (1986) and Bremer and Howe (1988) report that they found no single set of strategies for gaining workplace advantages that worked for all participants. Instead, they cite four different types of techniques for dealing with work settings, one for each race/gender category. For white males, the successful strategy approximated a classical bureaucratic career pattern that favors official rank and high client contact positions. For white women, only age (youth) correlated positively with organizational advantage; for non-white women, only education correlated positively with organizational advantage. Laura Vertz (1985) found that men tend to work their way up through the ranks, whereas women have entered at higher levels in the organization at a younger age and with experience gained from work outside the organization. This finding is also revealed in other studies that show that young, white, middle-class, college graduates who are female are much more likely to succeed (Coyle 1989).

Do women then end up "leapfrogging" over more qualified male incumbents? Apparently not. There is no empirical evidence to show that women are promoted over equally qualified men. There is evidence, however, to show that women are fast-tracked when compared to men. They are promoted from one position to another in less time than men are. Women also tend to be younger and have fewer years of service within each position they have held as contrasted with men. Table 2.1 illustrates this observation, showing that women assumed their current positions at a younger age than men; they held their positions for shorter lengths of time, and they are younger than their male peers. The surveys also confirm previous research (Hale and Kelly 1989a), which found that women receive lower pay and often do not supervise as many employees as men.

Table 2.1 shows the pattern of career advancement for women and men in managerial positions in Alabama, Arizona, Texas, and Wisconsin. Although these four states represent three distinctly different regions of the United States—the Southeast, the Southwest, and the Upper Midwest—there are remarkable similarities in the patterns that emerge between the sexes. Across all four states, women have held each of their last four positions for shorter lengths of time than men have. In terms of salary differences, women always earn less than men, but the salary gap between the sexes is growing narrower in managerial positions. In their current positions, women's salaries represent 91.9 percent of men's salaries in Alabama, 93 percent in Arizona, 90.2 percent in Texas, and 90.5 percent in Wisconsin. In their earlier jobs four positions ago, the gap was wider for respondents in Arizona, Texas, and Wisconsin, ranging from 83.5 percent in Arizona to 84.8 percent in Texas. Alabama is the only state where the gap has widened rather than narrowed: in their fourth most recent position, Alabama women's salaries represented 93.8 percent of men's, representing a gap that was 1.9 percent closer four jobs ago than in their current positions.

Although not shown in the table, salary differences between women and men in Utah are more pronounced. The average salary for managerial-level women in 1987 was $37,821 compared to $43,627 for men, representing a salary gap of 13 percent. Cultural norms and religious values help to explain this. In Utah, female political and work force participation has been affected by the strength of the Church of Jesus Christ of Latter-Day Saints (Mormons). Historically, the Mormon church has taken the view that men should be the leaders, the providers, and the public spokespersons for the family, and that women should emphasize reproductive labor and homemaking (Austin 1972). These factors combine to provide a strong disincentive for women to seek positions of public leadership, and when they do, their public work is devalued in favor of their private lives as wives and mothers.

California has seen an overall improvement of its average salary differences between men and women between 1975 and 1985. In 1975 women earned 60.4 percent of what men in the state civil service earned, whereas in 1985 they earned, on the average, 74.3 percent of what men earned. Case studies of the California Departments of Finance and Social Services indicate that substantial variation exists by department (Bayes 1989). In the Department of Finance the women who held the higher positions earned more on the average than the men did. In the Department of Social Services women earned only 88 percent of the men's salaries.

Judging from the age at which women and men have assumed their positions, there is evidence that women are fast-tracked into their positions. In the states shown in Table 2.1, as well as in Utah and California, women holding the higher level positions were younger on average than were the men and they were moving faster through the ranks. Only Wisconsin provides evidence contrary to this. In the third and fourth most recent positions for Wisconsin's managers, women were older than men. This pattern does not hold, however, for the two more recent positions.

Thus, in terms of salary, age, and mobility, the trends are fairly uniform across states. The pattern changes, however, when the average number of employees supervised is examined. In Alabama and Wisconsin, women and men have supervised about the same number of employees in their two most recent positions. Prior to that, men tended to supervise more employees than women. But in Arizona and Texas, women tended to supervise significantly fewer employees than men in their current positions. A possible explanation for this is that women in Arizona and Texas may hold more staff positions than they do in the other states that were surveyed, and staff positions typically do not have supervisory responsibilities. (Survey responses do not reveal whether the positions that respondents hold are classified as line or staff positions. The closest indicator is the number of employees they supervise.)

Table 2.1

Career Advancement for Last Four Positions

State	Sex	Current	Second recent	Third recent	Fourth recent
Average number of years in position					
Alabama					
	Women	5.54	4.31	4.48	3.66
	Men	5.72	5.13	4.41	3.99
Arizona					
	Women	2.63*	2.34*	2.19*	2.63*
	Men	3.96*	4.57*	3.58*	4.29*
Texas					
	Women	3.83*	3.34*	2.63*	2.75*
	Men	5.17*	4.50*	3.80*	3.87*
Wisconsin					
	Women	4.20*	4.50	3.10*	3.10
	Men	6.30*	5.30	4.60*	4.00
Salary					
Alabama					
	Women	$41,411*	$30,281	$24,090	$18,001
	Men	$45,045*	$33,052	$26,224	$19,195
Arizona					
	Women	$47,192*	$34,425	$26,961	$21,244
	Men	$50,738*	$38,428	$29,790	$25,451
Texas					
	Women	$37,773	$29,200	$23,435	$18,000
	Men	$41,887	$32,931	$25,745	$21,221
Wisconsin					
	Women	$41,061*	$31,736*	$25,885*	$20,901*
	Men	$45,356*	$38,126*	$31,110*	$24,817*

(continued)

Table 2.1 *(continued)*

State	Sex	Current	Second recent	Third recent	Fourth recent
Average age when taking positions					
Alabama					
	Women	39.53	34.72	31.20	28.61
	Men	41.57	36.06	32.43	29.40
Arizona					
	Women	37.80*	34.70*	32.80	30.00
	Men	43.30*	38.70*	34.70	31.70
Texas					
	Women	36.80*	33.50*	31.00	28.30
	Men	40.70*	36.30*	32.20	29.40
Wisconsin					
	Women	39.50	35.50	32.40	31.20
	Men	40.70	36.00	32.00	29.00
Average number of employees supervised					
Alabama					
	Women	22.42	14.31	6.43	3.46
	Men	22.43	14.95	8.56	7.54
Arizona					
	Women	11.90*	14.50	10.60	5.90
	Men	20.00*	13.20	11.50	11.00
Texas					
	Women	12.40	11.80*	2.90*	4.00
	Men	22.20	15.90*	12.10	5.80
Wisconsin					
	Women	23.30	8.80	5.20	6.10
	Men	20.00	9.50	4.90	7.10

*$p < 0.05$

Source: Rita Mae Kelly, Mary E. Guy, et al. (1991), Public managers in the states: A comparison of career advancement by sex. *Public Administration Review* 51(5): 409.

From the data in the table it appears that women are not forced to remain in lower positions longer than men before having "proved themselves," as has been found in federal jobs (Lewis and Park 1989). Rather, they appear to be promoted faster and at younger ages than men. The salary differential, which is consistent across all states, may be due to several factors. For instance, the fact that women are in positions for shorter lengths of time and are younger than men may account for their lower salaries. Also, it is likely that women are concentrated in the helping agencies, such as human resources, welfare, and education, where managerial positions are compensated at lower wages than similar positions would be in male-dominated agencies, such as highway departments. Women also continue to be under-represented in traditionally "male" occupations, such as engineering. Women tend to be clustered in public welfare, hospitals, health, and employment security, while they are under-represented in highways, transportation, and corrections.

These findings are consistent with a study done in 1980 and reported by Moore and Mazey (1986). At that time, women were very much under-represented in a number of functional categories—streets and highways, police protection, fire protection, natural resources, housing, corrections, utilities, transportation, sanitation, and sewage. Most of these categories involve manual labor, the perception of danger, or both, and have been viewed traditionally as occupations in which only men should work. In the 1980 study, women continued to be most over-represented in public welfare, health care, and employment security. These categories contain jobs that traditionally have been viewed as women's work: social work, nursing, and clerical work. Thus, even though the number of women working has increased, more women are still working in the traditionally "female" occupations (Moore and Mazey 1986).

Generally, there are more similarities than there are differences in the male and female managers surveyed in the states. Both men and women view their career advancement and their behavioral patterns on the job similarly. These findings parallel other studies that reveal that men and women managers have few attitudinal differences and utilize similar tactics when exercising power (Harlan and Weiss 1981; Kipnis, Schmidt, and Wilkinson 1980; Vertz 1985). Donnell and Hall (1980) also found that female and male managers did not differ in their behavior toward subordinates and showed practically no difference in their behavior toward colleagues and superiors. Still other studies reveal little or no significant gender differences in the use of conflict resolution styles at work (Renwick 1977; Revilla 1984; Shockley-Zalabak 1981; Sone 1982). However, despite these findings and the emergence of such management concepts as the "androgynous manager," the "feminization of management," and the demise of macho management styles (Coyle 1989; Sargent 1983), there are other studies that verify Kanter's thesis. These findings confirm sex bias and stereotyping of women as a part of the organizational environment. Managerial competence is still heavily associated with masculinity, specifically with white, middle-class, male authority, power, and control. This means that no matter how well qualified and experienced women are, they are not considered to be of management potential in many circumstances. As a result, proportionately few women are recruited into management and, for those who do get there, their daily experience is one where their competence is continually challenged (Coyle 1989).

Women and Men in the Federal Public Sector

How are these findings about managers in state government similar to what we know about public managers who work at the federal level? The numbers, as far as salaries and positions are concerned, form a similar pattern. The 1980 U.S. Census indicated that despite representing 31 percent of all government managerial workers, women continued to occupy disproportionately lower salary ranges. Women constituted 50 percent of the lowest salary range, but only 4 percent of the highest managerial range. The median salary for female managers was only 60 percent of the median salary for males (Bremer and Howe 1988; U.S. Department of Commerce, Bureau of the Census 1980).

An analysis of employment gains for federal employees at level GS–13 and above for the period 1976 to 1986 indicated that women more than doubled their representation in that work force (from 5 percent to 13 percent), although their overall share continued to be low (Lewis 1988b). On the other hand, a study of clerical workers over the period 1973–1982 revealed that women were three times as likely as men to be placed into federal clerical positions, while men were much more likely than women to shift from clerical work into professional, administrative, or technical occupations (Kelly and Bayes 1988; Lewis 1988). Therefore, one can conclude that women generally have not fared much better at the federal level than they have at the state level when it comes to advancing in management.

The equal employment opportunity (EEO) process is complex, whether the enforcement is at the federal or state level. How have affirmative action and equal employment opportunity programs worked for the federal female manager? In a report by Florence Perman (1988), who was formerly director of the Federal Women's Program in the U.S. Department of Health and Human Services, three major players are identified at the federal level: (1) the Equal Employment Opportunity Commission (EEOC), (2) the Office of Federal Contract Compliance Program (OFCCP) in the U.S. Department of Labor, and (3) the Employment Litigation Section of the Civil Rights Division of the U.S. Department of Justice (DOJ). The EEOC enforces a policy of nondiscrimination in the federal and private sectors; OFCCP enforces nondiscrimination in companies that have been awarded federal contracts; and the DOJ enforces nondiscrimination in state and local governments. To add further complexity to the matter, the enforcement responsibilities of the three agencies are based on a variety of empowering statutes (Perman 1988). The EEOC enforces Title VII of the Civil Rights Act of 1964, which prohibits discrimination on the basis of race, color, religion, sex, and national origin. It also enforces the Age Discrimination in Employment Act of 1967, the Equal Pay Act of 1964, and Sections 501 and 505 of the Rehabilitation Act of 1973, which prohibits discrimination because of handicap in the federal sector. The OFCCP is empowered by Executive Order 11246 and extends Title VII prohibitions and requirements for affirmative action to companies with federal contracts. It is also empowered by Section 503 of the Rehabilitation Act of 1973 and by the Vietnam Era Veterans Readjustment Assistance Act of 1974. The DOJ enforces Title VII.

Until 1979, EEOC was only responsible for enforcing Title VII in private business. The U.S. Civil Service Commission (CSC), now the U.S. Office of Personnel Management (OPM), was responsible for enforcing Title VII (Sec. 717), which provides for enforcement in the federal sector. The President's Reorganization Plan No. 1 of 1978 transferred enforcement of Title VII from the U.S. CSC to the EEOC and also transferred from the Department of Labor to EEOC the responsibility for enforcing nondiscrimination based on age, equal pay, and handicap (Perman 1988).

In assuming responsibility for the Equal Employment Opportunity program for federal employees, EEOC retained the CSC procedures of having agencies investigate EEOC complaints in which they were the defendants. In order for EEOC to perform its expanded role, positions and employees were transferred to EEOC from CSC and the Department of Labor. The EEOC also investigates individual complaints of alleged discrimination referred from OFCCP for disposition under Title VII (Perman 1988; U.S. Commission on Civil Rights 1987).

How has this complex maze of overlapping bureaucracy advanced affirmative action and equal employment opportunity for women working in the federal government? Perhaps this question can best be addressed by examining written testimony by Virginia Shiehl Delgado, an ex-Navy employee whose complaint of sexual harassment and sex discrimination was finally resolved by a court decision in her favor—after almost five years. Her written testimony concluded:

> A system that so delays relief, that entrusts to the same agency that I sued the responsibility for processing and judging my claim and that entrusts responsibility for processing my claim to people with little knowledge of the law and little incentive to move my claim promptly should not be tolerated. I hope that you will make changes to the administrative process in which I have suffered so that others may be spared this pain and inconvenience.

In this same case, Clarence Thomas, then Chair of the EEOC, testified that the federal EEO system was unworkable (Perman 1988; U.S. Congress. House. Committee on Government Operations, Subcommittee of the Committee on Government Affairs 1986). His explanation for EEOC inaction at this hearing and at previous ones had been that the agency lacked resources, staff, or clout to ensure agency resolution of a complaint within the 180 days required by Title VII and EEOC regulations. In 1985, it took EEOC an average of 411 days to reach closure for all reasons on complaints from its own employees (Perman 1988; U.S. Congress. House. Committee on Government Operations 1986). The average time for closure of all cases in 1985, government-wide, was 349 days (Perman 1988; U.S. Congress. House. Committee on Government Operations 1987).

Perman concludes from her extensive study that in the area of federal enforcement of equal employment opportunity, the rule of law was replaced in the 1980s by the "rule of men" for whom ideology was the criterion for action. That is, when the Reagan administration could not persuade Congress or the U.S. Supreme Court that affirmative action,

goals, and timetables were unconstitutional, the administration ignored their failure and let ideology drive their public policy actions.
The net result was that between 1981 and 1987, enforcement of the
national policy on EEO came to a standstill (Perman 1988). In other
studies, data from EEOC reports show that over a five-year period,
agencies rejected an average of 45.6 percent of the findings of discrimination recommended by Hearing Examiners at the EEOC while
accepting an average of 92.3 percent of the recommended findings of
no discrimination. (This information was compiled from various re-
cords and reports from the U.S. Departments of Agriculture, Health
and Human Services, Veterans Affairs, and the U.S. Postal Service, as
cited in Perman 1988.)

The Office of Federal Contract Compliance Programs has not established a much better record. The agency has been described as one "in
substantial disarray" between 1981 and 1987 by the Majority Staff of
the Committee on Education and Labor of the U.S. House of Representatives (U.S. Congress. House. Committee on Education and Labor
1987). In addition to disarray, the committee staff found that OFCCP
had suffered political and ideological turmoil at its national office, and,
as a result, the field offices were often in a state of confusion as to the
official policies and practices of the agency (U.S. Congress. House.
Committee on Education and Labor 1987).

Thus, one can readily conclude that the current state of affirmative
action programs at the federal level is plagued with many problems.
These problems range from lack of funding and personnel to perhaps
the most serious of all—the leadership provided by the eight-year
Reagan administration which sent a negative message about these programs to the Congress, the U.S. Supreme Court, and the public at
large.

Although the passage of the Civil Rights Act of 1991 brought a
glimmer of light, this bill brings only a grudging accession to women's
employment concerns. On November 21, 1991, President George Bush
signed the Civil Rights Act of 1991. But he accompanied his signing
with a statement that declared only weak support for affirmative action
and for procedures that level the playing field. His signing statement
emphasized that the bill included caps on the amounts of damages that
injuries may award and stated that the bill ensures "that employers can
hire on the basis of merit and ability without the fear of unwarranted
litigation" (U.S. Code. 1992).

Affirmative Action and Equal Employment Opportunity

As one further examines the paradox of more women in the work force and yet the apparent absence of significant gains in many areas, it becomes evident that key attempts to eliminate discriminatory personnel practices have failed. One very important piece of legislation was the Equal Opportunity Act of 1972. It extended federal prohibitions against discrimination in hiring, firing, promotion, compensation, and other conditions of employment to state and local governments. The act further required systematic data collection and reporting on the employment of minorities and women. The previous year, the U.S. Department of Labor had issued Revised Order No. 4, which specified implementation of affirmative action programs as outlined by Executive Order Number 11246 as amended.

At about this same time, the U.S. Supreme Court handed down the *Griggs* v. *Duke Power Company* decision. This decision upheld the congressional requirement that applicant tests measure bona fide job requirements (Bremer and Howe 1988; Samuels 1975). Prior to the passage of the 1964 Civil Rights Act, it had been alleged that Duke Power Company had routinely discriminated against blacks by denying them employment in all classes of jobs except as laborers. After 1964, it was argued, the company continued to discriminate against blacks by requiring those employees wishing to transfer to non-laborer positions to pass a mathematical and verbal aptitude test. The Court ruled that an employer could not use a selection technique having an adverse impact on minorities unless that technique had been shown to measure job-related skills (Hays and Kearney 1983).

Bremer and Howe (1988) conducted a study sponsored by the Oregon Chapter of the American Society for Public Administration to determine the most successful strategies used by government agencies in Oregon to increase representation of women in management. Although seven agencies representing local, state, and federal levels of government were selected, the results were quite similar. The most successful agencies in advancing women's careers were those with a positive focus on action to bring about change, a strong commitment from key managers, and a high value placed on employee excellence. The two researchers concluded that there must be commitment from the top and a pledge to hire the most qualified person available, regardless of gender, before agencywide change can be expected. They also found that the more successful agencies used recruiting strategies to maintain a pool of qualified women. They achieved this by building networks with other agencies and with universities and colleges (Bremer and Howe 1988).

Yet another study concluded that immediately following 1972, women, particularly white women, made significant gains in state and local government (Daley 1984). However, there are indications that the progress slowed considerably through the 1980s. Dennis Daley (1984) found in a five-state survey that more legislators, executives, and administrators opposed affirmative action than supported it. And Hendricks (1984) found in a study of affirmative action implementation in sixteen state agencies in Delaware that the future of affirmative action was in jeopardy. From her research, she concluded that: (1) support from the top for policy is of utmost importance for successful state implementation; that is, the support of the chief executive and top-level managers is crucial; (2) pressure from interest groups was another important element for change. In other words, environmental pressure is an important motive for implementation. And (3) federal initiatives are a positive influence and are most effective when accompanied by technical assistance and monitoring that carries probable sanctions for noncompliance. Cayer and Sigelman (1980) used data gathered by the Equal Employment Opportunity Commission to determine the status of women and minorities in state and local governments as of 1973 and 1975, shortly after the 1972 amendment of Title VII of the 1964 Civil Rights Act. Their study analyzed two specific issues: (1) Where did minorities and women stand with respect to both the quantity and quality of the jobs they held in state and local government agencies? and (2) To what extent could changes in the status of minorities and women be observed over the course of the 1973–1975 period? They found that the percentage of white males decreased in the state and local government work force. And they also found that the percentage of employees in every other racial/ethnic and sexual category increased. However, in 1975, white males still comprised more than half of the state and local government work force. Their work also revealed that female and minority employees had made little headway in terms of the quality of the positions they held.

An update of the Cayer and Sigelman study included an analysis of the years 1973, 1975, 1978, and 1980. It concluded that in quantitative terms, women and minorities had made progress in gaining jobs in state and local government. However, in terms of the qualitative dimension during the 1973–1980 period, women in every racial/ethnic category began the period at a substantial salary disadvantage to men in the same racial/ethnic category, and ended the period in the very same position (Sigelman and Cayer 1986).

What Does the Future Hold for These Programs?

With these dispiriting findings in hand, one wonders whether affirmative action and equal employment opportunity programs can effectively survive at the state and local levels. Several scholars have argued that the former Reagan administration's opposition to affirmative action set a negative agenda that has had the effect of encouraging state and local opposition to it. For example, numerous officials appointed during the Reagan years, including Clarence Pendleton, the Chair of the Commission on Civil Rights, have made blatant negative statements about affirmative action. Pendleton is reported to have commented, "Affirmative action with its goals and preferences is a bankrupt policy because it often leads to an emphasis on statistical parity rather than equal opportunity" (Hendricks 1984; Moore and Mazey 1986; Pear 1982)

In fact, shortly after Reagan's election in 1980, many prognosticators predicted affirmative action gains made in the past would have to be shielded in the future. For example, the Heritage Foundation, a conservative think tank, quickly urged the newly elected president to challenge court-ordered affirmative action policy. The foundation argued that affirmative action imposes an unjust burden on "innocent students, workers, and firms who through no fault of their own must now suffer" because groups of past victims rather than individual victims are given preference (Preston 1986).

Concern has also been voiced over the numbers of commissioners President Reagan was able to appoint to the Civil Rights Commission and the former president's attacks on affirmative action policy regarding employment. According to some civil rights groups, a new set of regulations would have exempted 80 percent of colleges and universities from having to write affirmative action plans. The opposition to these new regulations by civil rights groups, some business leaders, and others caused the Reagan administration to delay publication of these procedures (Preston 1986).

Several Supreme Court decisions also posed threats to affirmative action and equal employment opportunity programs. These include *Firefighters Local Union No. 1784* v. *Statts*, in which the Court held invalid a layoff plan that circumvented various seniority privileges in order to preserve the goals of Memphis's affirmative action plan, and *Grove City College* v. *Bell*, a 1984 case that limited the federal government's role in Title IX sex discrimination suits. In this case the Court interpreted Title IX of the 1972 Education Amendments to forbid sexual discrimination *only* in the program or activity actually receiving federal aid. Thus, programs or activities of the college or university not receiving federal assistance were free to discriminate sexually if no other provision of federal law was violated.

Still another concern is related to the Justice Department's opposition to changes in the last-hired, first-fired system. Women tend to be penalized more by this system than their male counterparts because they generally lack seniority. Following the 1984 Supreme Court decision that rejected a layoff plan based on the affirmative action consent decree involving Memphis firemen, civil rights and labor attorney Douglas Seaver observed that, as soon as the Supreme Court's decision had been issued, William Bradford Reynolds, then head of the Justice Department's Civil Rights Division, announced that he would order a review and assess the validity of hundreds of court-ordered affirmative action programs where the courts had employed racial quotas and goals in hiring to effectuate appropriate relief (Preston 1986).

In addition, federal agencies involved in monitoring affirmative action experienced losses of authority and resources, both in budgetary terms and in number of personnel. Travel budgets were also cut for federal monitoring agencies that were supposed to exercise oversight over state and local governments (Hendricks 1984). Cabinet officials have asked for and received congressional and presidential approval to retreat to an earlier position with regard to agency rules and regulations. Recent retrenchments have been twofold. They involve the loss of the Office of Personnel Management's presence in the enforcement of merit guidelines. They also involve the Justice Department's movement away from punitive measures applied when discriminatory circumstances are found, and a simultaneous movement toward punitive sanctions to be awarded only when intent to discriminate has been proven (Hendricks 1984).

Women in the Corporation

How have female managers advanced in the private sector during this period? Generally, studies document that, despite the great advance into the corporate world made over the past twenty years, women are still having an increasingly difficult time making it beyond the mid-level management plateau. Top-level management and key decision-making positions are still predominantly reserved for men (Hymnowitz and Schellhardt 1986; Maital 1989; Nicholson and West 1988).

In 1985, of 1,362 senior corporate executives surveyed by Korn/Ferry International, only 2 percent (29) were women (Hardesty and Jacobs 1986; *Wall Street Journal* 1986). Studies show that women make up just 10 percent of senior managers and just 6 percent of company directors (Coyle 1989; Rytina and Bianchi 1984). Research also indicates that very few women make it to and remain in "mainstream" line management in industry. Instead, women dominate the staff and personnel management functions while the top management positions remain male-dominated.

Hardesty and Jacobs (1986) identified myths associated with the process or life cycle of integrating women managers into corporations. They maintain that these myths almost always lead simultaneously to success and betrayal. Corporations maintain that they provide avenues in which women can be successful by offering women the same opportunities to advance through the corporate ranks as are available for men. However, women are betrayed in that they are stalled before reaching the top levels. Thus, even though executive ranks look attainable, women in the middle-range corporate levels are finding that they just cannot make it to the top. Women managers realize that they are trapped in a corporate home of glass walls (and ceilings) through which they can see the top, but cannot penetrate to move upward within the organization. After interviewing 100 women managers, 25 male managers, and several former CEOs, Hardesty and Jacobs found other myths to include the misconception that there are "ideal" industries that are more receptive to women.

Findings also reveal that many women who do move into middle management positions find themselves to be particularly vulnerable to corporate restructuring or downsizing (Coyle 1989; Hardesty and Jacobs 1986). This is partially attributable to the large numbers of women who are clustered in the staff jobs (heading legal, financial, and human resources departments) as contrasted with the large numbers of men in line jobs (production, marketing, or sales). Cuts are traditionally made first in staff areas because they are deemed to be less essential. Also, women as a group in the corporate world have traditionally had less seniority and have become the victims of "last-hired, first-fired."

Even though studies show women go into management for the same reasons as men, females encounter sex discrimination and problems associated with stereotyping of women once they get there (Fisher 1990; Harlan and Weiss 1981; Rosen, Templeton, and Kirchline 1981). There appears to be little significant change over time in this negative corporate attitude toward women as managers. For example, in 1973, Virginia Schein asked male managers at nine insurance companies across the country to characterize either "women in general," "men in general," or "successful middle managers." Using a 92-item attribute inventory, she found a strong concurrence between the ratings of men and the ratings of successful managers, and only a weak concurrence between the ratings of women and the ratings of successful managers. Also, successful managers were viewed as more similar to men than to women on attributes considered critical to effective work performance such as leadership ability, self-confidence, objectivity, forcefulness, and ambition (Heilman, Block, Martell, and Simon 1989; Schein 1973). These findings appeared to indicate that women are not believed to possess the qualities essential for success in management positions. The results of this study were consistent with those reported earlier by others (Basil 1972; Bowman, Worthy, and Greyser 1965).

In order to uncover more current perceptions of women as managers, a similar study in 1989 revealed findings that closely parallel those of the earlier work. Two hundred and sixty-eight male managers from a variety of departments (sales, personnel, productions, purchasing, accounting, marketing, etc.) used an attribute inventory to rate target groups. Men in general were described as more similar to successful managers than were women in general. Results also indicated that although the correspondence between descriptions of women and successful managers increased dramatically when women were depicted as managers, they continued to be seen as more different from successful managers than were men (Heilman et al. 1989).

However, this difference in perceptions of women and men corporate managers does not appear to result in different behavioral patterns on the job. For example, Humphreys and Shrode (1978) studied decision-making profiles of female and male commercial bank managers. They found more similarities than differences in their profiles. Some differences were found in perceptions of difficulty, importance, and preference for decision-making styles. For example, the female managers experienced the most difficulty with budgetary decisions, which they least preferred. The male managers experienced the most difficulty with conceptual decisions, which they most preferred. Perhaps female managers do not relish challenging or unpleasant decisions as much as do their male counterparts. It was also found that the female managers considered task decisions most important, while male managers considered personnel decisions most important. This is in contradiction to the generally accepted notion that women are relationship-oriented and men are task-oriented. The study concluded that similar qualities are required from both sexes to be successful in managerial positions.

How Does the Future Look?

The past serves as prelude to the future. If the years prior to the 1970s were thesis, then the 1970s were antithesis. The 1980s and 1990s are synthesis, that creation of a middle ground between extremes. The changing characteristics of the work force, with more women entering and remaining in it throughout their childbearing years, contributes to the tension and the unsettled nature of women's place in the work force. Despite the indications that women now have an easier path for entering the right fields of study and even into the right management track, the statistics hold plenty of evidence that there are still many problems in moving women into the top management ranks. This holds true for women in government as well as women in business.

Various studies have compared the experiences of successful and derailed women and studied how they differed from their male counterparts, and how their male supervisors perceived them. These studies have identified the following barriers that women experience: (1) there is a lack of acceptance of women as part of senior management; (2) the myriad roles women must play are conflicting and exhausting; (3) the infrastructure tends not to support women through the system; and (4) women experience burnout and become demoralized because their advancement is blocked and they are hemmed in and isolated (Morrison, White, and Van Velsor 1987; Solomon 1990). As these studies point out, getting women into organizations is not the same as moving them up. The top management ranks of large corporations still seem to be nearly as forbidden to women as ever. One prediction foresees that senior management will be off-limits to women who are now in the corporate management pipeline—women in their twenties—to about the same extent as it is to executive women in the 1990s. Expectations exist that no more than a handful of women will reach the senior management level of Fortune 100–sized corporations within the next couple of decades (Morrison, White, and Van Velsor 1987).

Even in the midst of these obstacles, it is clear that perceptions are changing. For example, a 1985 *Harvard Business Review* study of about 800 male and female executives revealed some substantial differences over a twenty-year period in terms of readers' perceptions of the female manager. In 1965, 54 percent of the men and 50 percent of the women had thought that women rarely expect or desire positions of authority. Twenty years later, the same survey was sent to another sample of executives. In 1985, only 9 percent of the men and 4 percent of the women surveyed thought that women do not want top jobs. However, almost half of the respondents surveyed still believed women will never be completely accepted as executives in America's organizations (Sutton and Moore 1985).

If statistics from the past can be used to predict the future, female managers in the public sector will not increase at the significant rates one might expect, given the fact that more and more women are employed by the federal and state governments. In fact, with the low priority given affirmative action and equal employment opportunity programs by both the Reagan and Bush administrations, the projected budgetary constraints in the public sector, and overall economic downturn, one has to conclude that the picture is most gloomy. Women in the immediate future will continue to face obstacles for advancement to top management positions as well as entry into more "male" enterprises. And there are no real indications that women will be more equitably compensated in salary levels.

The role of women in management-level positions will also continue to be influenced by the demands placed on them by their family situations. In addition to caring for their own families and children, more and more women will also have to care for their own aging parents or elderly relatives. Men's and women's careers presently tend to be affected differently by their family situations. That is, women perform more of the household activities than men, and this leaves them less time and energy to pursue work careers. When one member of a couple takes time off from the work force or leaves it altogether to care for children or other family members, it is usually the woman (Berk 1985; Powell 1988). In order for this burden to be removed from female shoulders, there will have to be sweeping changes made in public policy (subsidization of child and parent care), revision of procedures and policies by government and industry to provide flexible working schedules as well as on-site child care, and the more equitable allocation of household responsibilities between couples.

It is likely that women will continue to face organizational barriers that are systemically and structurally built into the work environment. These barriers cross social, cultural, political, and economic dimensions. It would appear that before these obstacles can be dismantled, the organizational culture will have to undergo a major redefinition. The research reported in this series of surveys of managers in state government generally confirm prior findings over the past couple of decades. Unfortunately, the higher you look in the ranks of management, the fewer women managers you see. A masculine management style, in which people in power (who are mostly men) mentor, encourage, and advance people who are most like themselves, seems to remain the norm (Grant 1988; Powell 1988).

Conclusion

The data from surveys of women and men managers in the states show that women tend to move into management at a younger age than their male counterparts. Women do not appear to leapfrog over equally qualified men, but they do appear to be fast-tracked. That is, they are promoted from one position to another in less time than men are. Women receive lower pay and do not supervise as many employees as men. Women also continue to be under-represented in traditionally "male" occupations. Women tend to be clustered in public welfare, health care, and employment security, and are under-represented in highways, transportation, and corrections. However, both men and women viewed their career advancement and their behavioral patterns on the job more similarly than differently.

Gender differences between women and men are also evident in federal employment. Despite the fact that women represented 31 percent of all federal managerial workers in 1980, the median salary for female managers was only 60 percent of the median salary for males. Women were three times as likely as men to be placed into federal clerical positions while men were much more likely than women to shift from clerical work into professional, administrative, or technical occupations.

Women are still having an increasingly difficult time making it beyond the mid-level management plateau. Top-level management and key decision-making positions are still predominantly reserved for men. Some studies show that women make up just 10 percent of senior managers and just 6 percent of company directors. Very few women make it to and remain in "mainstream" line management in industry. Instead, women dominate the staff and personnel management functions while the top management positions remain male-dominated. Even though women go into corporate management for the same reasons as men, females encounter sex discrimination and problems associated with stereotyping of women once they get there. Despite this stereotyping, however, there are few differences in the behavioral patterns on the job between women and men managers.

Thus, one can conclude that female managers are more likely to experience structural barriers (whether employed in the state, federal, or private sector) than are men. These barriers include sex-segregated jobs, sex bias, and stereotyping of women, as is evident by the fact that opportunity channels for advancement are more often closed to women than to men, and women are paid less than men. Responses in the surveys of women and men managers in state government also reveal that women attribute greater interference from domestic responsibilities of housework, family commitments, childbearing, and child care than men do. In addition, more women than men are unmarried. This indicates that only when women do not have family obligations are they more likely to advance.

Based on the research reported here, one can conclude that while women are experiencing organizational barriers that stymie their career advancement to the upper levels of management, they are concurrently coping with domestic responsibilities of child care, housework, and other family responsibilities. This clearly distinguishes the female manager from the male. The male manager not only experiences fewer organizational barriers in his career progression, but he has a wife who takes care of family commitments.

What are the implications for women, and what can be done in order that more significant progress may be made in moving women into higher management levels in greater numbers in the future? It would appear that only through a process of significant change and reform could we expect to see a better balance between the numbers of women and men in management in public sector jobs. For example, Hale and Kelly (1989a) identified organizational reforms that would help to catapult women into top managerial positions. Within agencies, supervisors and department directors can (1) provide a working environment that prohibits sexual harassment; (2) maintain high employee morale; (3) "look out for" their employees, including seeing that collegial networks and mentoring experiences for junior and mid-level employees are available; (4) advocate affirmative action programs; (5) offer intra/interdepartmental job rotation experiences; (6) designate and create top decision-making positions for women; (7) restructure jobs and re-evaluate classifications; and (8) facilitate child care and parental leave. Only when such measures are taken can an unfair system be altered so that women are treated as equals when they compete for management positions.

3

Personal and Social Background as Determinants of Position

Mary E. Guy and Lois Lovelace Duke

The positions that public managers achieve are influenced by their backgrounds. Women and men who have attained equal position in state government differ in terms of their educational achievement, socioeconomic status, and, to a lesser extent, political activism. This chapter provides an analysis of the effects of these factors on managers in the public sector.   — Editor's Note

This chapter looks at the social context from which public managers emerge. It compares the backgrounds of women and men to show how education, socioeconomic status, and political activism play a differential role in men's and women's career advancement. Although a variety of single-dimension perspectives could be used to frame this discussion, including gender stereotyping, career development, or educational achievement, a more all-encompassing perspective is afforded by the concept of networks. The following discussion explains why.

Managers and Networks

Relations with colleagues, friends, neighbors, and relatives form patterned networks. Patterns vary according to the nature and purpose of the affiliation, but the concept is equally germane to a discussion of work groups, neighborhoods, families, or any other set of connections or acquaintances (Kadushin 1983). Networks contain within them opinion leaders who have a significant influence on those with whom they come into contact. In fact, most people do not rely directly on formal channels of communication for guidance in their decision-making on most issues; rather, they turn to someone in their own circle of friends and acquaintances—that is, their network—who is an "opinion leader." This was confirmed when researchers studied the relationship between voting behavior, individual decision-making, and reliance on mass media as a primary information channel (Berelson, Lazarsfeld, and McPhee 1954; Katz and Lazarsfeld 1955; Lazarsfeld, Berelson, and Gaudet 1944). Researchers have found that the connection between the mass media and individual voting behavior is really a chain linking people to one another. Even though a message will appear in a formal communication, such as a newspaper, it will not spread far until an opinion leader picks it up and passes it on to another person, who passes it on to still a third, and so on. Among the population at large, as well as in work settings, it is people-to-people contact that makes the difference in how individuals behave, the jobs they seek, and the subordinates they promote.

The relationship between the notion of networks and career development lies in the social support systems and natural referral circles that networks afford. Individuals receive assistance from acquaintances in their network of friends, neighbors, relatives, and co-workers. Just as mentoring is an advantage to those who are mentored, being among a network of acquaintances is an advantage to those who are in it. Networks of relations rather than bonds of kinship characterize life within organizations. They provide a means for individuals who seek the support of similarly minded people. They also provide opportunities for social and professional support, sharing information and skills, learning about new job opportunities, and pursuing new paths for personal or occupational development.

Through networking, women and men not only gain information for themselves, but pass along information to others. They offer their personal expertise to one another. Within the network, people communicate through channels as formal as newsletters, but more often through person-to-person, informal connections, passing on information and pooling expertise. Men have used networks for the purpose of furthering their careers for generations. Strong network ties have traditionally been perceived as a means of developing the connections that are critical to a manager's success (Bacharach and Lauer 1988). As a result, frequent reference is made to the "Good Old Boys," and much research has examined these organizational networks that result from informal as well as formal connections (Smeltzer and Fann 1989).

Women have long been excluded from the "Old Boys' Club." These all-male, informal relationships seem to control the power and the resources of the organization, sharing vital information and reaching prior consensus on important decisions, all the while excluding all of the women and most of the men from full participation in organizational activities (Harriman 1985; Richbell 1976). Dubbed "the locker room syndrome," men conduct transactions in these networks that are carried out on exclusively male territory (Marshall 1984). This occurs in outdoor outings, such as golfing and fishing weekends, and membership in traditionally male settings such as civic clubs, athletic clubs, and country clubs.

Faced with exclusion, women have formed their own organizations, or networks. These take various forms, such as occupational groups, social groups, and breakfast clubs. Their stated purpose is usually to replicate the advantages that men enjoy from their wide range of contacts. What little evaluation has been done on these groups suggests that they are useful in teaching women the importance of building contacts and the fine art of doing so (Harriman 1985). Powell (1988) maintains, however, that until recently, there have not been enough women managers to constitute separate "Old Girl" networks. But as more women enter management ranks, mixed-sex and "Old Girl" networks are becoming more prevalent. It is for this same reason that women now have more opportunities to have mentors (Powell 1980, 1988).

Research that compares women's networks to men's indicates that women establish different methods for facilitating contacts than do men. For example, DeWine and Casbolt (1983) explain that men's networks are generally informal while women have formalized this activity. Women's networks are the result of a deliberate strategy of linking women with other women to expand contacts, provide successful role models for each other, generate solutions to problems, and disseminate information. These networks are largely women communicating with other women. Still other research has found that many female-dominated networks exist because women may not be allowed to break away from the all-female network. For example, several researchers found that women were less central to mixed male/female

networks, especially the network of the dominant coalition in an organization (Brass 1985; Rosen, Templeton, and Kirchline 1981).

Adding credibility to this finding is prior research conducted in the
1970s which indicated that men did not perceive women to be compat-
ible with high-achieving business positions. These studies show that
women have not broken into the formal male-dominated network, possibly because they are perceived as tokens and as being less competent
(Schein 1973, 1975). Added to this is research that reveals that both
men and women prefer interacting with members of the same sex
(Larwood and Blackmore 1978).

There is little question that successful managers develop and use
networks. Strong network ties have traditionally been perceived as a
means of obtaining power that is critical to a manager's success (Bacharach and Lauer 1988; Smeltzer and Fann 1989). Kaplan (1984) calls
networks "trade routes" and defines them as reciprocal sets of relationships that stabilize the managerial world and give it predictability.
These networks include people both higher and lower in the organizational chart, as well as people at the same level in other units or
functions. They also include people outside of the organization.

The relationships are lateral and reciprocal—hence the name "trade
routes." Managers enter these trade relationships for one compelling
reason: they depend on these people and literally cannot get their jobs
done without them (Harriman 1985; Kaplan 1984). Instead of trading
goods, however, they trade services, information, technical expertise,
advice, political backing, and moral support. They obtain these services by setting up reciprocal relationships. Every promotion or job
change in position requires rebuilding the network (Harriman 1985).
Cultivating networks is a continuous process that occurs as a natural
process of getting acquainted with those with whom there is regular
contact and it is also a deliberate process in which people purposefully
develop acquaintances with those who may be of help in their own
career advancement.

Women's networks differ from men's "trade routes" in that the
number of women wanting support is usually far greater than the number available to give it. For example, a case study of a women's network in a large midwestern city found that the majority of the
participants were at the supervisory or middle management level: very
few had executive level positions. While middle and upper-level managers could increase their contacts at their own level, there were few

opportunities to find career links and role models among executive-level women (DeWine and Casbolt 1983).

Opportunities develop through the informal system as well as through the formal system. Hennig and Jardim (1977) argue that individuals, by becoming members of key informal groups, enter a world of ties of loyalties and of dependence, favors granted and owed, mutual benefit, protection, and promises that must be kept if one wants to be a player in the future, and connections with people who already have influence. Powell (1988) maintains that these actions represent a more active stance toward one's career than simply relying on one's own competence. Networks are not necessarily unisex. But women, more so than men, need to develop skill in building their trade routes, including their network of pals, from a wide range of sources, both male and female. There is a shortage of upper-level women in the nation's agencies and corporations. Because of this, many women receive minimal to no support from women above them in their organizations, because there are likely to be none.

Networks That Boost Careers
for Public Managers

Just as the literature shows that there are differences in the general networks available to women and to men, surveys of managers in the states show that these differences persist in public administration. Managers were asked to register, on a scale ranging from 1 to 5, their assessment of how much they thought family and friends, political connections, and professional contacts contributed to career success for their male colleagues, their female colleagues, and for themselves. A score of 1 indicated the connection was not important, while a score of 5 indicated it was very important. Table 3.1 shows the results for respondents in Alabama. It shows that women managers, to a significantly greater degree than men, think that their own political connections contribute to their career success. They also credit the professional contacts of their male peers with being responsible for men's career success.

The table shows that women and men place about equal importance on networks of family and friends for male colleagues, female colleagues, and for themselves. This also holds true for their assessment of the degree of career success attributed to political connections of

Table 3.1

Contribution of Networks to Career Success: Alabama

Nature of network	Level of attribution for:		
	Male colleague	Female colleague	Self
Family and friends			
Women	3.04	2.91	2.56
Men	2.93	3.01	2.53
Political connections			
Women	2.87	2.88	2.20*
Men	2.67	2.76	1.87*
Professional contacts			
Women	3.91**	3.58	3.47
Men	3.51**	3.45	3.25

* $p < 0.05$
** $p < 0.01$

male and female colleagues. However, women respondents attribute a significantly higher influence to their own political connections than men do in terms of their career success. Women also attribute a significantly greater effect of professional contacts on their male colleagues' career success than the men in the sample do. In other words, while women believe that men are more advantaged than they are by their professional contacts, the men evaluate the benefit of their contacts less positively. Perhaps this reflects the fact that women believe that "the grass is greener on the other side of the fence." Or perhaps it means that men take for granted connections that are denied to women. And perhaps men are largely unaware of the positive influence of networks on their own and their friends' careers.

These findings from the State of Alabama are consistent with those reported by Texas respondents, who also report that women credit their career success to their political connections, whereas their male colleagues are more likely to feel hurt rather than helped by political activism. In fact, over 40 percent of the males in Texas characterized their political involvement as hindering their careers while women were significantly more likely to consider campaign involvement and political aide experience as important to their careers (Stanley 1987,

1989). Likewise, in Arizona, a slightly larger proportion of women than men rated working on a political campaign as being important to their career success (Hale, Kelly, and Burgess 1989). The relationship between political partisanship and career success will be discussed below. Now, we turn to a discussion of socioeconomic status and how it differs for the women and men surveyed.

Network Membership as a Function of Social Class

One's identification with social class affects the kinds of people with whom one associates and the expectations that are set for one's own career success. For these reasons, another vantage from which to view networks is by looking at the socioeconomic strata from which managers emerge. The neighborhoods in which future managers grow up, the level of education of their parents, and their own level of educational attainment combine to influence the types of people they associate with as a youth as well as an adult, the colleges they attend, and the careers they select. For this reason, respondents were asked to describe the socioeconomic status of the household in which they grew up (Jacobs and Powell 1985).

Socialization promotes sex role behaviors that ultimately constitute powerful individual barriers to career advancement for women. The barriers result from women's attitudes about their appropriate roles in the workplace and from men's attitudes about women's appropriate roles (Beckman 1976; Col 1985; Gutek and Larwood 1987; Hale and Kelly 1989a; Stewart 1976). To some degree, this is related to social class. For example, variations within social class have been found in child-rearing practices, in family structure, and in achievement. These variations produce higher expectations for achievement and less differentiation between the sexes in middle-class and upper-middle-class homes as opposed to working-class homes (Basow 1980; Lott 1973).

Surveys of female and male managers in Alabama, Arizona, Texas, and Utah found that men and women differed in terms of the social standing of their parental families (Bayes 1989; Hale, Kelly, and Burgess 1989; Kawar 1989; Stanley 1989). Table 3.2 displays these findings. The table shows that women recruited into management positions grew up in families that were more advantaged than those from which their male peers emerged. In other words, surveys of managers in these states reveal that top administrative women are more likely than their

Table 3.2

**Relationship between Manager's Sex and Self-Reported
Social Class while Growing Up (%)**

	Women managers	Men managers
Upper/upper-middle		
Alabama	24	11
Arizona	29	3
California	14	2
Texas	13	7
Utah	27	11
Wisconsin	16	9
Lower/lower-middle		
Alabama	25	44
Arizona	29	46
California	18	59
Texas	No data	No data
Utah	20	38
Wisconsin	32	45

male peers to have come from upper- and upper-middle-class families. Conversely, the top administrative men are more likely than their female peers to have come from lower- and lower-middle-class families. This is true in states as geographically and politically diverse as Alabama, Arizona, California, Texas, and Utah. This difference can be interpreted several ways. Two possible explanations follow: First, it may be that women must have the extra boost that comes from growing up in more affluent families in order for them to have the connections necessary to break into the management ranks, while men do not require this extra boost. Or it may be that women who grow up in middle- and lower-middle-class homes are more likely to adopt the traditional role of mother and wife and thus may not be able to free themselves of domestic obligations sufficiently to devote the energy to their careers that is important for the upwardly mobile career women.

Occupation of Parents

Useful measures that corroborate respondents' self-report of their childhood socioeconomic status are their occupations and educational

Table 3.3

**Percentage of Managers Whose Parents
Held Professional/Managerial Jobs**

	Women managers	Men managers
Mother		
Alabama	28	13
California	11	12
Texas	16	9
Father		
Alabama	44	29
California	43	22
Texas	43	32

levels. These are surrogate indicators of social class that serve to sub-
stantiate managers' self-reports of their backgrounds. Such data help to
rule out semantic differences in subjective descriptions of class. Thus,
respondents were asked about their parents' occupations and about
their education and their parents' education. These responses support
the self-report of social class. They show that the women who were
surveyed grew up in more advantaged circumstances than did the men.
In other words, the women's parents were more likely to have held
professional or managerial positions and were more likely to have had
more education than the men's parents. Table 3.3 reports the findings
of the three states from which this information is available: Alabama,
California, and Texas.

This table shows that women managers have mothers and fathers
who have achieved higher ranks in organizations. Parents serve as role
models for their daughters. Those who are career-minded socialize
their daughters into a similar frame of reference. The networks that
children experience through their parents also affect the networks
within which they, entering the work force, expect themselves to circu-
late. It is notable that men who had reached managerial levels were
less likely than women to have had either a father or a mother who
worked in a professional or managerial capacity.

Education

Networks and education are closely linked since friendships that are
developed in college often serve as important links to jobs in the fu-

Table 3.4

Relationship between Manager's Sex
and Educational Achievement (%)

Master's, doctorate, or professional degree	Sex of manager	
	Women	Men
Alabama	76	50
Arizona	64	56
California	26	35
Utah	63	58
Wisconsin	50	44

ture. And even if the person-to-person links are lost through geographic relocation, the aspirations that are developed through advanced education, along with the skills necessary to handle top-level posts, translate into a greater likelihood for women that they will achieve higher positions. Table 3.4 documents the educational levels for women and men in Alabama, Arizona, California, Utah, and Wisconsin.

Women who achieve managerial ranks in state agencies typically hold higher degrees than men who hold similar ranks. Only in California did a higher proportion of men than women hold advanced degrees. Generally speaking, women who have advanced to managerial positions are more likely than men to hold advanced degrees. While slightly over half the men in the states listed in Table 3.4 hold advanced degrees (other than in California), about two-thirds of the women hold advanced degrees. Although not displayed in the table, Stanley (1989) found a similar circumstance among Texas public administrators. She found that slightly more women than men completed bachelor's and master's degrees. Apparently, women must have more education to achieve upper-management ranks than men.

In addition to the findings reported in Table 3.4, it is instructive to look at the parents' education to see what relationship this has with the career levels of women and men. Table 3.5 shows the differences between the levels of education of managers' parents. The parents of female administrators are generally better educated and employed in higher-status occupations than male administrators' parents (Kelly and Boutilier 1978; Presley, Weaver, and Weaver 1986; Sigel 1975; Stanley 1989).

Table 3.5 shows that the parents of women managers are much more likely to have reached higher educational levels than the parents of male

Table 3.5

Educational Achievement of Managers' Parents

	Women managers	Men managers
Mother holds bachelor's degree or higher		
Alabama	24	9
Arizona	38	16
California	31	23
Texas	43	24
Wisconsin	23	20
Father holds bachelor's degree or higher		
Alabama	22	10
Arizona	32	18
California	40	34
Texas	No data	No data
Wisconsin	27	21

managers. Once again, this supports the self-report of socioeconomic status of managers' parental backgrounds and demonstrates the difference between women who reach high levels and men who reach the same levels.

The difference in educational level, and the concomitant levels of sophistication that accompany such achievement, pose barriers in terms of social distance between women and men. This is especially true when women enter traditionally male careers. For instance, when the Grievance Director for the Alabama Department of Corrections was interviewed and asked to tell about her job, she credited having been mentored by those in the "Old Boy" network. She said she was advised not to tell of her education and to play dumb when she was around the older prison wardens, many of whom had far less education than she. She said "it worked beautifully." While she had to have more education to gain her position, once gained, she had to diminish the differences between her and her male colleagues. While education is a surrogate for years of experience, it also brings with it a frame of reference somewhat different from that gained by years of on-the-job training. Thus, what starts out as merely a difference in background between men and women grows into a difference in frames of reference, beliefs about appropriate sex role behavior, differences in the kinds of people with whom one associates during off-work hours, differences in the neighborhoods in which one lives, differences in the schools to which one sends one's children, and so forth. In other words, demographic differences stand for much more than differences: they stand for cleavages between work colleagues that create barriers to communication and close interpersonal understandings.

Political Activism

At both the federal and state levels, political activism sets the stage for women to be seen and heard by elected officials who control appointments. For example, at the federal level, a surge of female presidential appointments occurred during the presidency of Franklin Roosevelt. His wife Eleanor successfully exerted pressure on the president and his political advisors to reward women with patronage appointments (Hartmann 1989). Many of those so rewarded were partisan activists who were veterans of suffrage and social welfare campaigns. They included the appointments of Frances Perkins as Secretary of Labor, Ruth Bryan Owen as Minister to Denmark, Florence Allen to the U.S. Court of Appeals, and Mary McLeod Bethune as Director of Negro Affairs in the National Youth Administration (Hartmann 1989). After President Roosevelt had set the precedent for appointing women to visible positions, President Truman appointed Georgia Neese Clark as Treasurer of the United States, Anna Rosenberg as Assistant Secretary of Defense, and Freida Hennock to the Federal Communications Commission. (Truman refused, however, to appoint a woman for the Supreme Court on the grounds that the male judges would not be able to relax around a woman [Hartmann 1989].) When President Eisenhower named Oveta Culp Hobby as Secretary of Health, Education, and Welfare, Hobby became the second woman in the history of the United States to hold a cabinet-level position. Eisenhower's record on appointing women surpassed Truman's, just as Truman's had exceeded that of Roosevelt. In Hartmann's assessment, these appointments were accompanied by much fanfare but little substantive effect. Few of the appointees identified with issues of concern to women, and even when they did, their numbers were too few to influence policy. But even though they functioned in the shadow of substantive decision-makers, they gave women a toehold for gaining further ground in the federal bureaucracy and showed the payoff for political activism.

Women have not fared much better in the U.S. Civil Service. In 1960, women filled 24 of the 2,050 supergrade positions in the federal bureaucracy, and they held 3 of the 425 federal judgeships (Hartmann 1989). Lewis (1988b) reports that women's share of federal white-collar jobs rose from 45 percent in 1980 to 49 percent in 1986. Of the managerial-level jobs in the federal service, those ranked as GS–13 and above, 13 percent were held by women in 1986. In 1976, women held only 5.4 percent of the GS–13 and above jobs (Lewis 1988). At the state level, the number of women in state legislatures was 351 in 1961, 293 in 1971, and 906 in 1981 (Hartmann 1989). By 1980 women held about 15 percent of elective offices at the state and local levels, and by 1987 women held 15.5 percent of seats in state legislatures (Hartmann 1989). At the local level women fared somewhat better although they were still vastly under-represented. In 1960 women held 10 percent of school board seats, while more than half of the nation's school boards had no women at all. Women's percentage of school board seats remained constant at around 10 percent from 1920 to 1970. But by 1981 it had jumped to almost 33 percent (Hartmann 1989). In 1982, women held about 16 percent of the city council seats in the United States. But of the 317 cities surveyed, 26 percent had no female council members and only 1 percent had a majority of women (Sinkkonen 1985). The survey also revealed that women were more likely to hold council seats when the status of the seat was lower. For example, in those cities whose councils had no legislative responsibilities and whose council members received no pay, 80 percent were held by women. In councils that have legislative responsibility and for which the council members are paid, 83 percent of the seats are held by men (Sinkkonen 1985). Bullock and MacManus (1991) report that by 1986, 18 percent of councilors in cities with populations of at least 25,000 were women. They also refute the so-called desirability hypothesis, providing evidence that desirability is not the deciding factor in women being elected to city council seats. Finding that structural factors do not influence the likelihood of women earning seats, they conclude that sexual stereotypes may be greater influences on election outcomes, or even on women being willing to serve as candidates.

Women have typically utilized informal networks cultivated through volunteer organizations to make advances in gaining elective office. Activity in volunteer groups is strongly associated with the political success of women candidates. At the state level, women moved into state politics from civic activism in women's organizations such as the League of

Women Voters (Hartmann 1989). Activity in religious, civic, charitable, or political groups can be functionally equivalent for women to men's prestige occupations. Like prestige occupations, voluntary groups form the base for developing leadership skills and experience, community visibility, and widespread contacts (Darcy, Welch, and Clark 1987).

Women at all levels of government have often served apprentice-ships in party work, but a majority have also developed political knowledge and skills through leadership in women's organizations. For example, Margaret Chase Smith, who represented Maine in the U.S. House of Representatives from 1940 to 1948 and in the U.S. Senate from 1948 to 1972, had been president of her state Federation of Business and Professional Women and a member of its national board. Before her election to two terms in the Oregon legislature and one in the U.S. Senate, Maurine Neuberger had been active in the American Association of University Women (AAUW) as well as in the League of Women Voters (LWV). Eleanor Roosevelt developed her leadership capabilities, a network of political friends, and her unique commitment to public affairs through involvement in the League of Women Voters, the Women's Trade Union League, and the New York City Club (Hartmann 1989; Roosevelt and Hickok 1954).

Community activism is by far the most common avenue to active involvement in politics for both sexes (Diamond 1977). The differences for women and men occur in the types of activism that serve as the most effective launching pads for successfully seeking political office. There are sex differences in the kinds of party activities in which individuals engaged. As might be expected, women are more active in the routine aspects of campaign work, men in the nonroutine aspects. Women usually distribute literature and contact voters, while men make policy decisions (Diamond 1977). Despite numerous studies that document how women have used networks and volunteer organizations to gain elective office at all levels, little has been done in the way of research that links networking and volunteering as a means of obtaining public sector employment at the state level. Yet Table 3.1 shows that women credit political networks as important contributors to their career success.

After surveying 281 cities from across the United States, Warner, Steel, and Lovrich (1989) conclude that women are clearly under-represented on municipal police forces around the nation. They con-clude that cities that elect women to city council positions constitute a favorable environment for female utilization in policing. They believe

Table 3.6

Relationship between Manager's Sex and Political Partisanship (%)

	Women managers	Men managers
Democrat		
Alabama	47	35
Arizona	72	34
California	42	32
Utah	62	31
Wisconsin	46	32
Republican		
Alabama	29	24
Arizona	8	43
California	29	38
Utah	19	39
Wisconsin	11	11
Independent		
Alabama	18	38
Arizona	21	21
California	6	18
Utah	19	30
Wisconsin	32	52

that for women to make substantial headway into traditionally male bastions, such as policing, it may take strong action by decision-makers who have similar interests and stakes in seeing women integrate where they have been previously excluded.

Political party identification appears to be sex-linked for top-level managers. Table 3.6 shows that women are far more likely to identify themselves as Democrats, while men are more likely to be spread rather evenly across partisan loyalties. In addition to the data in the table, Hale and Kelly (1989, p. 143) report that in Texas women are predominantly Democratic while men are more evenly divided across party lines, with the plurality being Republican. This is the case in Alabama, Arkansas, California, Utah, and Wisconsin as well.

Another measure of the influence of political activity on the career success of men and women is reflected in Table 3.7, which shows that in both Alabama and Wisconsin, women rate their political activism as being substantially more important to their careers than men do. Respondents were asked to use a rating scale from 1 to 5, with 1 meaning that political activity hindered their careers and 5 meaning that it

Table 3.7

**Contribution of Political Activity to Managers'
Careers: Alabama and Wisconsin**

	Women			Men	
	mean	s.d.		mean	s.d.
Alabama					
Working on political campaigns	3.65	1.06	*	2.71	1.31
Wisconsin					
Working as aide to legislator	4.90	.26	*	4.20	1.13

$* p < 0.05$

helped their careers. Ratings 2, 3, and 4 indicated the degree to which their political activity leaned toward being a hindrance or a help.

Managers were asked to rate the degree to which working on political campaigns or being an aide to an elected official contributed to their career success. Working on political campaigns was seen as being significantly more helpful for women than for men in Alabama, and having worked as an aide to legislators was seen as significantly more helpful for women than for men in Wisconsin (Johnson and Duerst-Lahti 1990).

In surveys conducted in Arizona and Texas, Hale, Kelly, and Burgess (1989) and Stanley (1989) found that women reported using the political process as a means for gaining access to upper levels of public administration. A survey of female and male managers in these two states revealed that women continued to enhance the probability of more women being hired at higher administrative levels by participating in politics. For example, Texas women were significantly more likely to consider campaign involvement and political aide experience as important to their careers than were men. Conversely, over 40 percent of the males characterized their political involvement as hindering their careers (Stanley 1989).

Conclusion

The similarity of the effects of sex across the states cannot be overstated. Regardless of political traditions, economic differences, systemic differences, and geographic differences, the same patterns prevail. Women who make it to the top managerial ranks in state agencies come from more advantaged backgrounds than do the men who make it into those ranks. The women have more education than their male management peers and they grew up in families where their parents had more "successful" careers and were more educated. And women are more likely to have achieved their position through political connections than are men. What this means is that the women who make it to the top are different from the men, not as much because of their sex, but because of a social distance that creates an even deeper chasm across which they must struggle to communicate with men. When women and men perceive a lack of homogeneity between themselves, it results from not only a sex difference, but also a social and often political difference.

Markham, South, Bonjean, and Corder (1985/1986) surveyed 897 employees of a federal agency and found that the opportunity to reach the top is strongly linked to being male. Any differences between men's and women's priorities disappeared when GS level, age, and education were controlled for. But as these data show, by the time education has been controlled for, an important source of "differentness" has been excluded, including parental influences on career aspirations, socioeconomic status of the household in which one grew up, and networks within which one circulates and by which one is influenced, helped, and/or hindered.

The discussion in this chapter highlights demographic differences between women and men who reach the managerial ranks in state government. What structural elements help to explain this? One is that, as shown in the previous chapter, women are promoted into their current positions at a younger age than men. Education serves as a vehicle for meeting job requirements in lieu of on-the-job experience. Another is that, given the institutionalized bias against women in management, women who make it there are already outside the norm. Thus, while the average man is able to climb the bureaucratic ladder, the average woman is shut out. She must be above average to make it. Third, the networks provided by one's socioeconomic status, family connections, and education apparently help women to crack the barriers that they meet and gain a foothold where those without such networks would fail.

What does it take for a woman to get her foot in the door? It takes some things that are different from what it takes for men. Working on political campaigns of winning candidates helps. Holding visible positions in voluntary organizations helps. Being born to parents who have above-average educational achievement helps.

There is a downside to the fact that women in management are more highly educated than men and come from higher socioeconomic backgrounds than men. The downside is that their differentness of being female is exaggerated by their differentness in terms of social background. This differentness is responsible for a social distance that is attributed to gender when, in fact, it is produced by socioeconomic differences. If men are more likely than women to have come from blue-collar backgrounds, and women are more likely than men to have come from professional backgrounds, then differences in values between the sexes are bound to emerge. Each sex expects the other to behave in ways to which they are accustomed, and each sex is disappointed. Women will view the old boys as "rednecks" and "yahoos" and men will view the women as being "above their posts." The term "perceived homophyly" means that people like to associate with those whom they perceive to be like themselves. These men and women are likely not to perceive one another like this. There is a social distance that gets translated into a gender difference, or perhaps exaggerated as a gender difference.

If the women are from a more advantaged background, where are the men from the more advantaged background? In business, in elected positions, in the professions? What do we learn by knowing that public employment is a vehicle for women after they accrue advantage in terms of education, family background, or parents' occupations? What do we learn by knowing that the distance between men and women in management is complicated by the social distance factor? We learn that women in managerial ranks introduce more diversity than is assumed by the effect of sex considered by itself.

The information in this chapter points out how, when women are promoted into management posts, they bring with them diversity. In this case, at the least, diversity is manifested in differing backgrounds and levels of educational achievement. As a consequence, the traditional homogeneity of the managerial roundtable is disturbed. Women have to work doubly hard to "fit in" because they are different not only by gender but by life-style habits. And this is where the subject of networks enters. The point is that women must create networks of influence while men walk into already established networks. Thus, the world view of women and men differs. Men see an empowering environment while women see a fragmented and contradictory one.

4

Public Work, Private Lives

Cathy Marie Johnson and
Georgia Duerst-Lahti

All working women and men struggle at one time or another to balance
their private lives with their careers. Family and job obligations
frequently conflict and are compounded by gender stereotypes
characteristic of our culture. Traditionally we think of the female
executive wrestling with this problem; it is important to remember,
however, that many men are also juggling competing responsibilities.
This chapter examines the relationship between the private and public
lives of working women and men and offers suggestions for policy
changes that would ease those pressures. — Editor's Note

In the 1970s feminists declared that the personal is political. This statement challenges the supposed dichotomy between the public and the private. The terms "private" and "public" usually refer to the notion of private business contrasted with governmental services. We rely on women's vantage point and differentiate the terms so that the term "private" refers to home and personal life—those activities thought of as women's roles—and the term "public" refers to paid employment, politics, and other social institutions whose control is assigned to men (Elshtain 1981).

Because men and women have been associated with, respectively, the public and private spheres, men's conventions, norms, and assumptions have come to dominate the world of work and politics. Because

61

of this tradition, a bridge has connected men to professional careers in state public service and paid work more generally. But women who pursue careers encounter something more akin to a breach. As larger numbers of women entered the work force and embarked on professional careers, numerous questions were raised. How would society handle their entrance into the labor force? What would happen to traditional gender roles? Who would care for house, spouse, and children? How would employers treat pregnancy, maternity, and the other demands women might make?

While some change has occurred, we continue to grapple with these questions. Too often women—not men and not employers—carry the responsibility of fitting into the conventions of the workplace. Women are expected to accommodate their traditional gender roles as wife and mother to career with little recognition that male roles of husband and father have been constructed to better suit work conventions. As much feminist writing has detailed, women's ties to the home front meant that their entrance into public work was accompanied by political maneuvering at home, negotiating with co-workers, and battling with employers. The personal, then, is political for career women because questions about meshing a private life with public work could—and still can—be posed of women with little critical scrutiny of the system itself.

Even though the focus has been on women, the personal is political for career men too. Although they benefit from their association with the valued world of work, men are not supposed to be known for their private life roles. Instead, men are expected to devote themselves to careers and to function as breadwinners even though men too have private lives. As a result, men tend to be stigmatized should they be more devoted to family than to career, and many may suffer personal conflicts if they devote themselves to careers rather than family. The personal is political when gender ideology denies the private lives of men, conflating career success with manly success.

Because of the association between gender and the public and private spheres, the political reality of women and men who want careers differs considerably. The problem rests in the way careers are structured, and in the ways deviation from conventions are interpreted and explained. Consider societal responses to common reasons for work interruptions: veterans get preference points; mothers fight for unpaid maternity leave. Because conventional career patterns assume a particular relationship between family and private life obligations—a pattern

that might be thought of as "organization man with family woman"—
the conventions of careers tend to rest on assumptions about men's
roles and responsibilities rather than women's. The politics of gender
dictate that things men do are valued more than things done by women.

In this chapter, we examine aspects of the private lives of professional women and men in state public service, the relationship between
those personal lives and their careers, and the patterns of those careers.
We conclude with a discussion of the changes needed to allow individuals to integrate an enriching personal life with a demanding professional career. To set the context for this discussion, we first review the
development of ideologies surrounding careers.

The Modern Context of Professional Careers

Careers today suffer from an ideological residue of career patterns of
the 1950s. Successful careers are embedded in an ideology that includes both the public world of work and the private world of personal
life. These beliefs led organizations to construct "deceptive distinctions," sex and gender differences within the social order more imag-
ined than real (Epstein 1988). These constructions continue to
advantage men in careers despite the empirical evidence of a multiplicity of career patterns that fly in the face of simple gender dualisms.

Conventional ideology of the 1950s assigned distinct gender roles
and spheres of activity to men and women. Women took care of private life concerns in the sphere of home and family. Like Whyte's
"organization man" (1956), men devoted themselves to the role of
breadwinner in the public sphere of work. A product of this conventional ideology was the "two person, single career" household
(Papanek 1973). One career required two people to succeed, a husband
and a wife, but the husband and wife were positioned quite differently.
As noted author Warren Bennis (1969, p. 154) explained, a "good
wife" was to "undertake the profession of providing stability and continuity" for her aspiring husband. Because his career was the family's
career, it was "rational" for family members to contribute to his ability
to succeed. And, as Joseph Pleck reviews (1985), it was rational for a
man to fit this mold by forgoing home responsibilities very willingly.
As a result, professional men could balance the demands of work and
private life, thus meeting the organization "ideal" of keeping work
separate from the rest of life (Whyte 1956). Because ideology limited

men's family obligation to being breadwinner, organizations could treat professional men as though their career were their *only* pursuit. Organizations also benefited from the unpaid "professional" services of the wife.

As the 1960s gave way to the 1970s, the women's movement opened doors to higher education and pushed laws for equal treatment. The economy restructured away from heavy industry and manufacturing to service enterprises. Women had fewer children later in life. While women have always worked (Kessler-Harris 1981), more and more women left the home to enter the paid work force as economic opportunities expanded and social expectations changed (Rix 1989). In 1950, for example, 86.4 percent of men compared to 33.9 percent of women participated in the labor force; only 22 percent of married women worked outside the home (U.S. Department of Labor 1983, p. 11). By 1986, 57 percent of married women with children under age three were in the labor force (Blank 1988). With these changes, women's employment was no longer dictated largely by family roles of stable nuclear families (Bancroft 1958; National Manpower Council 1957). Breaking the pattern of secondary workers, women acquired the training and demonstrated a desire for career positions (New York Conference Board 1985). By March 1986, a majority of U.S. professionals were women (*Christian Science Monitor* 1986).

A "neo-conventional" ideology began to develop in the late 1960s. If women were equal to men, they could enter male professions—but on male terms. Women could adjust to meet the demands of the organization, not the other way around. The career structure remained rooted in the pattern of conventional ideology (Diamond 1987; Wallace 1982). Career women could follow the conventional path and be as much like men as possible by sacrificing personal life roles of wife and mother. Women who wanted to have children could "sequence" by working at a professional job, then take several years off to bear and raise children, and later re-enter the labor force when children were of school age (Cardozo 1986). Alternatively, they could become superwomen: the family woman of old who also worked outside the home.

Unfortunately, these options confronted women with unpleasant choices that often limited their careers as well as constrained their private lives. Some women regretted their decision not to have children. Women who "sequenced" lost momentum in careers, experienced underemployment, and fell behind their male counterparts (Bergmann 1986). Superwoman was exhausted and lost opportunities in her career due to personal life demands; in the early 1980s, she began bailing out (Loden 1986; Taylor 1986). Neo-conventional ideology did not suffice.

By the late 1970s, we saw the first glimmerings of post-conventional ideology as policy began to address both women's equality and their special needs (Costain 1988). Examples in employment policy include maternity leave, flex-time, part-time employment, and most recently, the mommy track (e.g., Kamerman and Kahn 1987; Schwartz 1989; Stewart 1976; Stoper 1988). To their credit, these policies recognize that work and family are not entirely separate institutions—a rather new admission although one long pursued in feminist and family research (Bielby and Bielby 1988; Gutek, Nakamura, and Nieva 1981; Mortimer and London 1984; Nieva 1985; Rapoport and Rapoport 1971; Walsh and Kelleher 1987). Special treatment policies also acknowledge that because women bear children and also shoulder responsibility for the care of children, house, and spouse, organizations must begin to accommodate employees with family obligations.

These special treatment policies "both reflect and influence ideology, often helping to perpetuate norms that lag behind social reality" (Lewis and Cooper 1988, p. 159). Special treatment policies focus on the private life needs of women but not of men. As such, they entail the risk of further promoting conventional roles of family woman and organization man. They do not challenge the propensity to use men's activities as the norm and view women's behavior as deviant, that is, special. They do not provide a sufficiently strong challenge to the conventional ideology and its assumptions about a successful career.

Although we have seen glimmerings of post-conventional ideology, the specter of William Whyte's "organization man" haunts us because the basic assumptions about the relative value of work and private lives have not altered much, and neither has organization practice. If the structure of a successful career remains based upon the organization man whose personal life presumably does not affect his work, neither career-and-family woman nor the emerging family-and-career man will find professional success. Post-conventional policy must recognize that men as well as women have responsibilities in their private lives.

The Conventional Family Arrangement

Clearly, conventional family arrangements of a working husband, with a wife at home to take care of the children, advantages a man in his

Table 4.1

Marital Status of Women and Men (%)

	Women	Men
Never married		
Alabama	11	3
Arizona	17	3
California	21	2
Texas	18	2
Utah	No data	No data
Wisconsin	18	8
Married		
Alabama	53	88
Arizona	45	84
California	50	88
Texas	55	87
Utah	52	92
Wisconsin	63	81
Once married		
Alabama	36	9
Arizona	38	14
California	29	10
Texas	26	7
Utah	No data	No data
Wisconsin	19	11

attempts to build a career. With a wife to attend to meals, laundry, and other family commitments, this arrangement surpasses even a single life-style. If, as we contend, conventional career structures assume the organization man with family woman, then those who come closest to approximating this pattern should find the strongest bridge to a successful career. Obviously, it is more difficult for women to approximate the conventional pattern than it is for men.

One of the ways that women can reduce the stress between career and family life is to abandon traditional sex roles of wife and mother. Much research on women and careers has documented this tendency (e.g., Carroll 1989). Our data confirm this finding. Women are more likely to live in family arrangements that minimize their roles as wife and mother, freeing them to focus on careers. Table 4.1 shows that women are less likely to be wives than men are to be husbands. In all states displayed, a larger percentage of women than men have never

Table 4.2

Percentage of Women and Men Living With and Without Dependents

	Women	Men
Alabama		
No Dependents	51	40
Living alone	28	9
Living with other adult	23	31
Dependents	48	59
Other adults and dependents	36	56
Sole adult with dependents	12	3
Arizona		
No Dependents	71	48
Living alone	31	9
Living with other adult	40	39
Dependents	29	52
Other adults and dependents	19	51
Sole adult with dependents	10	1
Texas		
No Dependents	59	37
Living alone	25	9
Utah		
No Dependents		
Living alone	20	5
Dependents	44	72
Sole adult with dependents	9	2
Wisconsin		
No Dependents	56	42
Living alone	18	11
Living with other adult	38	31
Dependents	44	58
Other adults and dependents	40	56
Sole adult with dependents	4	2

been married, and a smaller percentage of women are currently married. Women are also more likely than men to be once-married—divorced, separated, or widowed.

In addition to not being wives, women are less likely than men to be living with dependents. Table 4.2 shows that in the three states a majority of men live with dependents while a majority of women do not. These women have eschewed their gender's traditional roles of wife and mother. While these data show that women are more likely than men to have family arrangements that minimize the stress between family and career, they also show that when women have dependents, they are more likely than men to have a family arrangement that could make managing both a career and a family difficult. Among our respondents, women living with dependents are more likely than men to be the sole adult in the family. As the sole caregiver of dependents, these women may find that family interferes more with their career than is the case for married women. Consistent with conventional patterns, men with dependents are more likely than women to have a helping hand around the house.

While traditional sex roles give women the responsibility of caring for the family, they assign men the role of breadwinner. In fact, these traditional sex roles are tied inextricably with careers. Men meet their family obligation as breadwinner by devoting themselves to employment. Because the man's career is also the family's career, a "good wife" provides stability and continuity for her aspiring husband through her homemaking and helpmate functions.

Table 4.3 presents the percentage of men and women who contribute at least a majority of household income from their salary. This breadwinner's role is shared by both men and women. While a larger percentage of men than women contribute a majority of household income from their salary as conventional arrangements would dictate, substantial numbers of women also act as breadwinners. Despite small variations by marital status and living situation, women in all life circumstances contribute a majority of household income from their salary. For only one group, married women in Wisconsin, is the percentage who contribute a majority of household income less than 50.

The conventional family arrangement can be found among these respondents, but it has been challenged, particularly by these professional women. These women are less likely than men to be married and less likely to have dependents, although once they have dependents, they are more likely to be their primary caregiver. In addition, these women share with men considerable responsibility for providing for their families. The role of breadwinner belongs not only to men.

Private Life Obstacles to Careers

Since the 1950s, when wives and mothers entered the labor market in significant numbers, the United States has experienced a remarkable

Table 4.3

Percentage of Women and Men in Alabama, Arizona, and Wisconsin Contributing a Majority of Household Income from Salary

	Women	Men
Alabama		
Marital status		
Never married	77.8	100.0
Married	77.3	94.6
Once married	93.3	95.0
Living situation		
No dependents	61.9	96.7
Dependents	79.5	72.2
Age (years)		
22–34	66.7	100.0
35–44	84.2	97.8
45–68	85.7	91.5
All	83.1	94.4
Arizona		
Marital status		
Never married	92.3	100.0
Married	55.3	94.1
Once married	91.4	88.2
Living situation		
No dependents	75.0	88.4
Dependents	72.7	95.8
Age (years)		
22–34	70.8	93.9
35–44	78.7	96.4
45–68	61.9	92.0
All	73.7	93.8
Wisconsin		
Marital status		
Never Married	87.8	87.9
Married	44.4	89.4
Once Married	91.0	85.8
Living situation		
No Dependents	68.8	84.1
Dependents	53.4	90.8
Age (years)		
22–34	52.6	91.6
35–44	63.4	84.8
45–68	69.4	92.2
All	62.6	88.9

Table 4.4

Mean Level of Career Hindrances for Women and Men

Hindrance	Women	Men	Difference
Military service			
Alabama	1.13	1.39	−0.26*
Arizona	1.00	1.36	−0.36*
Wisconsin	1.10	1.70	−0.60**
Spouse's health			
Alabama	1.38	1.25	0.13
Arizona	1.00	1.29	−0.29*
Wisconsin	1.10	1.30	−0.20**
Housework tasks			
Alabama	1.61	1.22	0.39**
Arizona	1.45	1.17	0.28**
Wisconsin	1.80	1.50	0.30**
Childbearing			
Alabama	1.42	1.19	0.23*
Arizona	1.38	1.12	0.26**
Wisconsin	1.80	1.50	0.30**
Child care			
Alabama	1.69	1.27	0.42**
Arizona	1.75	1.29	0.46**
Wisconsin	1.90	1.60	0.30*
Other family commitments			
Alabama	1.76	1.47	0.29*
Arizona	1.73	1.61	0.12
Wisconsin	2.00	1.90	0.10
Children's health			
Alabama	1.45	1.20	0.25**
Arizona	1.05	1.24	−0.19
Wisconsin	1.30	1.30	0.0
Spouse's career			
Alabama	1.43	1.27	0.16
Arizona	1.58	1.32	0.26*
Wisconsin	1.80	1.70	0.10
Personal health			
Alabama	1.38	1.46	−0.08
Arizona	1.38	1.33	0.05
Wisconsin	1.40	1.60	−0.20

(continued)

Table 4.4 *(continued)*

Hindrance	Women	Men	Difference
Family's attitude toward work			
Alabama	1.39	1.37	0.02
Arizona	1.38	1.43	−0.05
Wisconsin	1.60	1.60	0.00
Age: too young			
Alabama	1.38	1.43	−0.05
Arizona	1.76	1.54	0.22
Wisconsin	1.60	1.50	0.10
Age: too old			
Alabama	1.23	1.32	−0.09
Arizona	1.26	1.45	−0.19
Wisconsin	1.50	1.60	−0.10
Parent(s)' health			
Alabama	1.27	1.29	−0.02
Arizona	1.21	1.16	0.05
Wisconsin	1.30	1.30	0.00
Parent care			
Alabama	1.41	1.24	0.17
Arizona	1.26	1.16	0.10
Wisconsin	1.30	1.30	0.00

$* p < 0.05$
$** p < 0.01$
Source: Adapted from Rita Mae Kelly, Mary E. Guy, et al. (1991), Public managers in the states: A comparison of career advancement by sex. *Public Administration Review* 51(5): 408.

change in family arrangements. Two-parent families with a spouse at home now comprise a minority of all family types (Rix 1989). And women have assumed more responsibility for the financial support of their families. As these changes have occurred, what has happened to the relationship between private lives and careers? To examine this question, we asked respondents to tell how various circumstances interfered with their careers, with their responses ranging from 1 (meaning "strongly disagree"—the item did not interfere with the career) to 5 (meaning "strongly agree"—the item interfered with the career). The mean values for these responses are presented in Table 4.4 for administrators in Alabama, Arizona, and Wisconsin.

Not surprisingly, a number of items interfered with women's careers more than with men's. In all three states, childbearing, child care, and housework tasks hindered women's careers more than men's. In Alabama, women found other family commitments and children's health to be greater burdens than men found them, and in Arizona women believed their spouse's career to be a greater burden than did men. Women more than men believed that family responsibilities interfered with their professional careers.

Table 4.4 also illustrates that men do not completely avoid interference with their careers from their private lives. Some of these items interfered with men's careers more than women's. In all three states men found military service to be a greater hindrance than did women. In Arizona and Wisconsin the health of one's spouse proved to be a greater concern to men's working lives than to women. Interestingly, most public organizations have extant policies related to military service and health, while care for house, spouse, and children are deemed private.

In order to understand the relationship between personal lives and careers, it is essential to consider the differences between men and women. One way of doing this is to compare how women and men rank career hindrances. Figure 4.1 lists the top interferences for women and men in the three states ranked by their means. More than five items are listed when there was a tie among the means.

Men as well as women believed that family responsibilities hindered their careers. "Other family commitments" was the top-ranked item for men in all three states and the top-ranked item for women in two states. Among women in Arizona, other family commitments was edged out of a first-place position by age (too young) and child care responsibilities. In addition, while the men's ranking does not include the specific family tasks identified by women (child care, housework, childbearing), "family's attitude toward work" made the top ranking for men in all three states. While family responsibilities weigh more heavily on women's careers than on men's, these rank orderings show that, when compared with other personal life factors that can hinder one's career, family responsibilities burden men's careers too. While private life responsibilities impinge on women more, organizations err in assuming that men face few if any private life obstacles.

These rank orderings show that women have a stronger *other*-orientation than men, but that men are also concerned about their responsibilities toward others. In light of research that shows women to have

Figure 4.1. **Rank Ordering of Top Career Hindrances by State for Women and Men**

State	Women	Men
Alabama		
	1) other family commitments	1) other family commitments
	2) child care	2) personal health
	3) housework tasks	3) age: too young
	4) health: children's	4) military service
	5) spouse's career	5) family's attitude toward work
	6) childbearing	
Arizona		
	1) age: too young	1) other family commitments
	2) child care	2) age: too young
	3) other family commitments	3) age: too old
	4) spouse's career	4) family's attitude toward work
	5) housework tasks	5) military service
Wisconsin		
	1) other family commitments	1) other family commitments
	2) child care	2) military service
	3) housework tasks	3) spouse's career
	4) childbearing	4) personal health
	5) spouse's career	5) child care
		6a) family's attitude toward work
		6b) age: too old

an other-orientation and men to have a self-orientation (Chodorow 1978; Gilligan 1982), we might not have expected these findings. Of the seven items on the top list for women, five are concerned with *other* (child care, housework tasks, children's health, other family commitments, and spouse's career); childbearing bridges self and other. Only one item—age (too young)—centers on self. Of the eight top-ranked items for men, three are focused on self (age: too young; age: too old; and personal health). Military service, like childbearing, bridges self and other. An "other" orientation among men, while not as prevalent as that among women, is supported by the fact that four of these top-ranked items focus on others. These are "family's attitude toward work," "other family commitments," "spouse's career," and "child care."

Perhaps we do not yet have a vocabulary to ask about men's family involvements, or perhaps men interpret family involvements in ways different from women. Some have suggested that men think about family care while women do it. Both types of family involvement can hinder a concentrated focus on career. In any case, ideology that denies men's private lives misconstrues reality. We have much to learn about men as gendered beings. We also must be careful not to attribute to gender something that emanates elsewhere.

A Closer Look: Gender or What?

A simple gender comparison yields some insights into the relationship between personal life and career among men and women, but it may well mask as much as it reveals. The interaction between personal life and career is bound to vary according to circumstances—whether or not one is married, whether or not one has dependents, whether one is just starting a professional career or whether one is well established in a career. While a straightforward comparison of women and men is informative, a more complex analysis is also needed. Perhaps life circumstances have as much to do with the interaction between personal life and career as gender has.

In this section we examine the effect of marital status, living situation, and age on the interaction between personal life and career. To do this, we created two indices from the fourteen items in Table 4.4. The first index, "family health," captures the need to care for family members who are ill. It includes personal health, spouse's health, children's health, parent(s)' health, and parent care. The second index, "family care," captures the need to care for house, spouse, and children. This index includes childbearing, child care, spouse's career, housework tasks, and other family commitments. The variables included in these indices were determined by a factor analysis of the Wisconsin data. The first factor accounted for 32.3 percent of the variance in these measures, and the second factor accounted for 13.7 percent of the variance. The first factor was labeled family care, and the second was labeled family health.

Table 4.5 compares the mean values of the family health index for men and women in different life circumstances. Only three of the differences between men and women are statistically significant. In Wisconsin, men with dependents believed that family health responsibilities hindered their careers more than women with dependents. In Alabama, once-married women faced greater burdens from family

Table 4.5

Family Health Index in Alabama, Arizona, and Wisconsin

	Women	Men	Difference
Alabama			
Marital status			
Never married	1.00	1.30	−0.03
Married	1.38	1.29	0.09
Once married	1.46	1.17	0.29*
Living situation			
No dependents	1.44	1.27	0.17
Dependents	1.34	1.30	0.04
Age (years)			
22–34	1.10	1.27	−0.17
35–44	1.41	1.25	0.16
45–68	1.43	1.30	0.12
All	1.38	1.28	0.10
Arizona			
Marital status			
Never married	1.25	1.10	0.15
Married	1.11	1.24	−0.13
Once married	1.55	1.29	0.26
Living situation			
No dependents	1.27	1.22	0.05
Dependents	1.31	1.24	0.07
Age (years)			
22–34	1.14	1.07	0.07
35–44	1.29	1.34	−0.05
45–68	1.43	1.20	0.23*
All	1.29	1.24	0.05
Wisconsin			
Marital status			
Never married	1.40	1.40	0.00
Married	1.30	1.30	0.00
Once married	1.20	1.30	−0.10
Living situation			
No dependents	1.30	1.20	0.10
Dependents	1.20	1.40	−0.20*
Age (years)			
22–34	1.30	1.50	−0.20
35–44	1.30	1.30	0.00
45–68	1.20	1.30	−0.10
All	1.30	1.30	0.00

*$p < 0.05$

health responsibilities than once-married men. Older women in Arizona found family health burdens to be more troubling than older men.

For all of the groups, the mean values of the index are fairly low, indicating that, on average, family health problems do not interfere much with the careers of these professionals. Life circumstances have little effect on the interaction between family health and career. Family health, getting married, getting divorced, and having children or other dependents are events that have little impact on the burden to one's career for either sex. One might expect to see an effect for age, as the likelihood of illness for oneself, one's spouse, and one's parents increases. No indications of age and family health interferences are evident in Wisconsin. In fact, the highest mean is for young men, the opposite of what one would expect. There is some evidence that family health concerns interfere more with career as one ages among the women in Alabama and the men and women in Arizona. In Alabama the mean value of the family health index for young women is 1.1, increasing to 1.43 for mature women ($p < 0.10$). In Arizona the mean value for young women is 1.14, increasing to 1.43 for mature women ($p < 0.10$). In Arizona middle-aged men and mature men have larger means for the family health index—1.34 and 1.20, respectively—than young men, with a mean of 1.07 ($p < 0.05$ and $p < 0.10$, respectively).

Table 4.6 compares the mean values of the family care index for men and women by marital status, living situation, and age. Marital status affects the interaction between family care responsibilities and career for women more than men. Staying single is a way for women to reduce the burden of family care tasks on their careers. In all three states, the differences between the means for never-married women and their male counterparts are not statistically significant, like the career-only pattern suggested by conventional ideology. This scenario changes, however, when women marry and when their marriages end. Married women and once-married women believed that family care tasks hindered their careers more than their male counterparts did. These differences result primarily from *intra*gender differences: married women and once-married women experienced greater career problems because of family care tasks than never-married women, while marital status made no difference in the way men viewed the relationship between family care and career. Again, the tension between careers and gender expectations in private life reveals conventional ideology: stay single or get a wife.

Table 4.6

Family Care Index in Alabama, Arizona, and Wisconsin

	Women	Men	Difference
Alabama			
Marital status			
Never married	1.04	1.20	−0.16
Married	1.75	1.30	0.45*
Once married	1.53	1.12	0.41*
Living situation			
No dependents	1.46	1.20	0.26*
Dependents	1.78	1.35	0.43*
Age (years)			
22–34	1.28	1.83	−0.55*
35–44	1.81	1.29	0.52*
45–68	1.53	1.24	0.28*
All	1.62	1.28	0.34*
Arizona			
Marital status			
Never married	1.18	1.14	0.04
Married	1.99	1.33	0.66*
Once married	2.04	1.34	0.70*
Living situation			
No dependents	1.64	1.21	0.43*
Dependents	2.08	1.36	0.72*
Age (years)			
22–34	1.57	1.36	0.21
35–44	1.92	1.50	0.42*
45–68	2.16	1.19	0.97'
All	1.90	1.32	0.58*
Wisconsin			
Marital status			
Never married	1.20	1.40	−0.20
Married	1.90	1.50	0.40*
Once married	2.40	1.50	0.90*
Living situation			
No dependents	1.60	1.30	0.30*
Dependents	2.20	1.70	0.50*
Age (years)			
22–34	1.80	1.90	−0.10
35–44	1.90	1.60	0.30*
45–68	2.00	1.40	−0.60*
All	1.90	1.50	0.40*

* $p < 0.05$

We see more evidence of conventional expectations when we look at whether or not these men and women live with dependents. In all three states, women—regardless of whether or not they have dependents—believed that family care tasks interfered with their careers more than men did. And again, not having dependents is a way for women to lessen the impact of their private lives on their careers. In all three states, women with dependents believed that family care responsibilities interfered with their careers more than women without dependents (for Wisconsin and Arizona, $p < 0.05$; for Alabama $p < 0.10$).

Unlike marital status, however, living situation affects the careers of men as well as women. Men, too, face greater strains between their personal lives and careers when they have dependents. The mean values for men with dependents are higher than men without dependents in all three states ($p < 0.05$), ranging from increases of 1.2 to 1.4 in Alabama and Arizona, to an increase of 1.3 to 1.7 in Wisconsin. The difficulties of juggling a career and a family, while greater for women, also appeared for men. The experiences of these men do not support the conventional belief that professional men can have a family with no disruptions to their careers.

While marital status and living situation are important factors, we also should consider age. The times have changed since mature professionals first embarked on their careers. While the organizational man–family woman might have been a useful description of professionals' work lives in the 1950s, few families now fit this stereotype. Even in 1980, only 29 percent of families fit this model, and the percentage drops to 10.7 for conventional marriages with children at home (Rix 1989). Young men and women starting their careers face different economic situations, different expectations about their career paths, and different views about future family configurations. These changes have inevitable impacts, and we have every reason to expect the intersection between career and private lives of young men and women to be very different from their older counterparts.

As one can see in Table 4.6, gender differences between men and women vary by age. Middle-aged and mature women found family care burdens to interfere with their careers more than men did. But this same finding does not hold true for young men and women. In no state did young women experience a greater family care burden than young men. In Arizona and Wisconsin the differences between young women and young men are not statistically significant. In Alabama the difference is statistically significant, but it is young men who experienced greater interference to their careers from family care burdens, not young women.

We find important gender differences in the interaction between personal life and career. We consistently find that women are more affected by the interaction between private life and career, but we also find that private lives affect the careers of men. In addition, life circumstances have a substantial effect on this relationship for both men and women. Intragender differences can be found for women according to marital status, men by age, and for both men and women according to living situation. A focus on gender is critical, yet we should not allow it to mask differences among men and among women.

Career Patterns: Ideology and Expectations

Conventional theories of careers assume that successful careers are built by full-time continuous employment from the time one enters the work force until one retires. This model is not only conventional, it is based on the male experience. As women enter the work force, with many starting their professional careers in their forties and fifties and others choosing to mesh work with family through part-time work and career interruptions, the shortcomings of this conventional, male model become apparent. Our task in this section is to examine the extent to which women—and men—fit the model of careers that stems from conventional ideology.

Table 4.7 presents the percentage of men and women who have worked part-time at some point in their careers by marital status, living situation, and age in Alabama and Wisconsin. (This information is not available from the other states surveyed.) While part-time work is not common in either state, it is not a rarity either. Twenty-four percent of women and 12 percent of men in Wisconsin worked part-time at some point in their careers, while in Alabama 22 percent of women and 23 percent of men have worked part-time. Associating part-time work only with women is erroneous. More women than men have worked part-time in Wisconsin; nearly equal percentages of men and women have worked part-time in Alabama. Clearly, the assumption that a successful career depends on full-time work is inapplicable to many men as well as to some women.

The conventional model of career development assumes that family

Table 4.7

Percentage of Women and Men Who Have Worked Part-Time in Alabama and Wisconsin

	Alabama		Wisconsin	
	Women	Men	Women	Men
Marital status				
Never married	61.0	3.7	16.4	6.3
Married	50.0	89.0	22.7	12.1
Once married	44.0	7.4	37.9	18.3
Living situation				
No dependents	38.0	31.0	16.7	11.2
Dependents	61.0	67.0	31.7	14.2
Age				
22–34	22.0	1.9	13.6	22.9
35–44	33.0	46.0	25.8	18.0
45–68	44.0	52.0	26.2	5.4
All	21.7	23.4	23.6	12.3

roles affect men's and women's careers differently. Once they become breadwinners, men are believed to come to work with renewed energy and commitment, knowing that their wives and children depend on them for their livelihood (Gilder 1981). Women, on the other hand, are believed to reduce their commitment to careers once they become wives and mothers. Because of conventional assumptions and gender-based interpretations of full-time work, part-time work by women is treated as evidence of their lack of attachment to the labor force (Duncan and Corcoran 1984).

As we can see in Table 4.7, marital status affects the likelihood of part-time work for men as well as women. In Wisconsin, more women than men, regardless of their marital status, worked part-time, yet the likelihood of part-time work varied with marital status for both women and men. Never-married men and women were least likely to have worked part-time while once-married men and women were most likely to have worked part-time. In Alabama, never-married women and once-married women were more likely to have worked part-time than were their male counterparts, yet married men were more likely to have worked part-time than married women. In fact, almost 90 percent of married men, compared to 50 percent of married women, worked part-time at some point in their careers. For Alabama's women, marriage actually decreased the likelihood of working part-time. Never-married women had the highest rate of part-time work (61 percent), and once-married women had the lowest rate (44 percent). Clearly, marital status along with factors within states shape part-time employment, not just gender.

Another presumption of conventional ideology, associating part-time work only with women with children, is not supported by these data. Men with children, not just mothers, worked part-time. True, having dependents increased the likelihood that women worked part-time, but it also increased the likelihood that men worked part-time, especially in Alabama. In fact, it is quite clear that in Alabama, having dependents is much more likely to predict part-time work than gender. Furthermore, men and women without dependents also worked part-time. In Alabama, about one-third of men and women without dependents worked part-time at some point during their careers. In Wisconsin, 11 percent of men and 17 percent of women without dependents worked part-time.

When we consider part-time work among different age groups, we see that part-time work is used by men and women of all ages. The assumption that only women work part-time is not supported by these data. In Alabama, middle-aged and mature men were more likely to have worked part-time than were their female counterparts. Young men in Alabama rarely worked part-time, but given the high rates of part-time work among older men, it is quite likely that many of these young men will work part-time at some point in the future, although it is possible that the high rates of part-time work among older men are due to generational effects and not age itself. In Wisconsin, more young men than young women worked part-time. We would expect the percentage of women working part-time to increase with age. After all, the older an individual, the more likely it is that she would encounter life circumstances in which it would be useful to work part-time. The higher rates of part-time work among young men suggest that in the future, a larger percentage of men in Wisconsin will have worked part-time at some point in their careers.

Like part-time work, a career interruption violates the assumptions of the conventional male model of careers. Data on career interruptions are available only for Wisconsin. The career interruptions of these men

Table 4.8

Career Interruptions among Women and Men in Wisconsin (%)

	Women	Men
Marital status		
Never married	15.5	37.9
Married	52.4	23.8
Once married	44.6	23.9
Living situation		
No dependents	30.3	25.8
Dependents	56.4	25.1
Age		
22–34	28.2	23.5
35–44	43.7	29.8
45–68	51.6	19.8
All	42.2	25.0

and women show patterns similar to those of part-time employment (see Table 4.8). More women have interrupted their careers than men; 42 percent of women and 25 percent of men stopped working at some time in their professional lives.

Marital status and living situation increased the likelihood of career interruptions for women, yet not for men. Fifty-two percent of married women and 45 percent of once-married women interrupted their careers while 56 percent of women with dependents quit working for a short period. Unlike part-time work, career interruptions declined for married and once-married men and remained stable for men with dependents. Twenty-four percent of married men and 24 percent of once-married men interrupted their careers while 25 percent of men with dependents did so.

Career interruptions, however, are not experienced only by married women and women with dependents. On the contrary, a substantial number of civil servants interrupted their careers. Career interruptions are higher among younger men (24 percent) and middle-aged men (30 percent) than mature men (20 percent). Sixteen percent of never-married women and 38 percent of never-married men interrupted their careers; 30 percent of women and 26 percent of men without dependents interrupted their careers. Although a larger proportion of married women and women with dependents have career interruptions, the phenomenon is not linked to gender so closely as to warrant the conclusion that career interruptions are the province of women.

Part-time work and career interruptions are two options individuals can choose when balancing career and personal lives. In fact, it is the combination of the two that is most inconsistent with the concept of organization man and that has led to the belief that women do not build careers. But the men and women in Wisconsin did not combine part-time work with career interruptions very often. Only 3 percent of the men and 15 percent of the women relied on both part-time work and a career interruption. The majority of men (65 percent) and a near majority of women (49 percent) experienced continuous full-time employment. Those who did not follow this pattern opted either to work part-time or to interrupt their careers for a short period.

Conventional ideology assumed that professionals worked full-time without interruptions and that this work pattern was necessary for a successful career. But it is clear that many men as well as women have careers that do not mesh with these assumptions. It is also clear that successful careers can be built even when professionals work part-time or interrupt their careers.

What Should Be Done?

While conventional ideology has been challenged in many respects, remnants of that ideology continue to shape our thinking about careers. Organization practices and career structures continue to stress the importance of full-time, continuous employment and the need to keep one's private life out of the office. As we have seen, however, these norms, practices, and career structures do not fit most lives of today's professional men and women.

Employment policies and career structures need to be fashioned so that all different kinds of people are allowed to meet their private life needs. Policies and career structures should be based on the assumption that employees' lives are complex and varied, not on the assumption that employees fit a norm based on the conventional (male) model of careers—a model that empirically suits neither men nor women very well. Simple dualism based on gender misses the complex and dynamic reality of people's lives, and models of careers should not be based upon such dualism.

Some may argue that employers should not be expected to consider the private lives of their employees when fashioning employment policies. But employers already recognize those lives. Sick days are a standard benefit for full-time workers. The federal government requires businesses to guarantee the jobs of military personnel called up for active duty, and all of the state governments provide some type of preference in the employment and/or promotion of veterans. Through such policies, employers recognize some aspects of the private lives of some of their workers. But these policies tend to accommodate the needs of men, especially men with little family involvement, much better than the needs of women. These policies need to be re-examined in order to accommodate the needs of all workers. They need to be further adjusted and expanded to allow women as well as men to have a personal life, and they need to take into account the variation in life circumstances people bring to organizations.

First, public policy should require employers to establish policies that provide for paid leave to cover the medical aspects of pregnancy. The Pregnancy Discrimination Act of 1978 forbids discrimination against women because of pregnancy and childbirth and requires employers to treat pregnancy and maternity as temporary disabilities under employers' sickness, accident, and medical plans. While this is an important act for working women, it falls short of requiring employers to establish health, disability, or maternity policies. Only five states, covering one-quarter of the female work force, have temporary disability insurance programs (Hyde and Essex 1991), and the percentage of women with paid maternity leaves has not increased since the act was passed. Indeed, there has been pressure to shorten the "disability" period after childbirth from the six to eight weeks considered acceptable by physicians to four to five weeks (Hyde and Essex 1991).

A specific policy establishing paid maternity leaves would extend a benefit to women yet not to men. Some oppose such policies with arguments of fairness, contending that, because men cannot take advantage of such policies, they should not exist. Such arguments ignore the extent to which children constitute a public good—the workers, citizens, and taxpayers of the future—and deny the energy, effort, and health threats women face to bear children who ultimately benefit all of society. Even some feminists oppose such policies because they provide special treatment to women, and special treatment policies have been used to discriminate against women. They fear that employers might opt not to hire women rather than provide this benefit. But opposing paid maternity leave on such grounds is like cutting off your nose to spite your face. An employment system that uses men as the norm, and then treats women equal to—the same as—men, ignores those things that women do but men do not do. Women get pregnant; men do not. We need to develop strategies for policy that can approach equity rather than hold rigidly to equality. The latter results in absurdities, such as men being eligible for pregnancy leave, and women taking time off for prostate problems.

Second, public policy should require employers to establish paid family and parental leave to cover the birth of a child, adoption of a child, and the illness of a family member. Parental leave should be extended to men as well as to women. Following Sweden's example (Hewlett 1986), the policies should allow parents to decide how they would like to split the leave period, and equally important, men should be encouraged to take advantage of such leaves in the same manner as women. Practices within organizations should not continue to perpetuate gender-biased norms that assume that women but not men have child-rearing responsibilities.

Although a family leave bill was debated in Congress when Richard Nixon was president, to date no act has been adopted at the national level. Many states have adopted such policies, but unfortunately, all too often the leaves are short, and the policies rarely provide for income continuation. While even an unpaid leave is an improvement over the status quo, paid leave is necessary to benefit all workers (Hyde and Essex 1991). In a time of scarce resources and stubborn budget deficits, it is difficult to think about financing new benefits. But workers' compensation, unemployment compensation, and social security illustrate the ability of the United States to discover creative financing. Paid parental leave could be funded through a combination of government revenues, and employer and employee contributions. Family leave is an issue critical to the future that is not as burdensome as it might first appear. For any one individual worker, the time off work would be short in the context of a thirty-five-year career, and the cost would be temporary.

In addition to parental leave, government should fund child care, and employers need to provide child care assistance of some form to their employees. Although the number of employers providing child care assistance increased substantially in the 1970s and 1980s, only one in 2,000 employers provides some type of assistance (Hyde and Essex 1991). Studies have found that employer-supported child care programs improve recruitment, reduce turnover and absenteeism, and increase positive recommendations from employees that the organization is a good place to work (Bergmann 1986). Child care assistance can take a number of forms, from referral and information services to the establishment of on-site day-care centers. As we end the false dichotomy between public and private spheres of life, the concerns of parents for their children must be taken seriously by employers.

Finally, we need to re-think the structure of careers and the nature of work in order to foster a career life view—a notion that places career fully within the context of one's entire life rather than pretending it is all of life (Johnson and Duerst-Lahti 1991). Policies such as maternity and parental leave would improve the lives of working men and women significantly. Yet they ignore the assumption that successful careers are based on full-time continuous employment with little or no interference from one's personal life. Thus, they do not accommodate fully those who want to integrate a rich personal life with a successful career. They also ignore those workers who do not have children.

Employers need to consider the nature of work as well as the career structures within their organizations. They need to develop a range of flexible work options, including flex-time, job sharing, working at home, prorated benefits for part-time work, reasonable work loads, and more personal days. They also need to build career structures within organizations that recognize many different paths to a successful career. Too many organizations depend on a linear career model in which advancement depends on full-time continuous employment (Crompton and Sanderson 1986; Kelly 1991).

More flexibility should be built into the rigid career tracks of academia, law, and civil service systems. One need not achieve early in a career to be considered top material later. The apprenticeship model can pose great problems for women, whose reproductive work often clashes with the time clock of career success. Civil service examinations that award points according to years of experience should be changed to test for skills. Higher-level civil service positions should not be open only to those individuals who already work in state government. There is no reason to limit the promotion and reward of those individuals who want to take a personal leave, work part-time, or work reasonable hours. As millions of displaced homemakers have proven, one can be a productive professional despite not following the conventional model. Employers need to think about what really matters for their professional workers in order to reap their productive energy.

Conclusion

The personal is political and the private is public where careers in state service are concerned. In this chapter we explored the nexus between private lives and public work by examining empirically the family arrangements of professional men and women, the effect of their personal lives on their careers, and the patterns of careers.

Although we found residues of conventional ideology in the lives of these professionals, we also saw that conventional ideology does not accurately describe the lives of many women and men. Family arrangements, particularly those of women, did not fit the stereotype of organization man and family woman. These professional women were more likely than men not to be married and not to live with dependents, and most women have considerable responsibility for breadwinning. Despite these changes in the family, women more than men believed that their private lives interfered with their careers. Women's other orientation—their concern for family—continued to constrain their public work. Yet we also found that men, too, are concerned with others and that their responsibilities, especially for dependents, limited their careers. Life circumstances—marital status, living with dependents, and age—shape the interaction between private lives and careers. Finally, we found that professionals had work histories that deviated from the norms of full-time, continuous employment. Many professionals worked part-time at some point in their careers, and career interruptions were not uncommon. Again, this demonstrates the preeminence of life circumstances on career paths.

The structure of careers was based on a conventional ideology predicated upon male assumptions. The system was built by men with male needs in mind. As a result, career structures fit a particular kind of man, a man whose family responsibilities other than breadwinning are handled by a wife. While the system is changing slowly, the career structure remains, and it is a structure that limits women and suits many men poorly.

In order to meet the needs of today's professionals better, we need to alter employment policies and practices and revise our assumptions about careers. Because it does not completely overthrow conventional ideology, neo-conventional ideology does not provide a firm ground for the necessary changes in careers. The special treatment policies that flow from neo-conventional ideology make an important contribution in recognizing that private lives and public work are not separate institutions. But these special treatment policies do not go far enough in casting aside conventional ideology. They retain the emphasis on full-time continuous employment, and, more important, they continue to treat women's needs as "special." We need to get beyond conventional and neo-conventional ideology by altering our view of the relative importance of work and private lives. We need to acknowledge a variety of personal life needs and numerous career patterns, and we need to rest our career structures on assumptions that are not based on simplistic gender dualisms.

Governments, employers, and workers should move forward with these initiatives. Because of changes in work force demographics and in labor force participation rates, there will be so few white males in the work force that diversity will be a simple necessity. According to the *Work Force 2000* report (1987), white males will constitute only about 20 percent of new work force entrants in the coming decade. Declining birth rates and increasing female labor force participation rates make urgent the adjustment of organizations to workers' lives. Contemporary career structures and dynamics, and the assumptions behind them, must shift from a base that assumes organization man and family woman. A post-conventional model of professional careers, one that recognizes a multiplicity of private life needs in a public world, must evolve.

5

Mentoring

Mary M. Hale

For women and men interested in advancing their careers, having a mentor can be extremely helpful. A mentor not only offers friendship, support, and career advice but also provides help in promotion and in gaining access to influential organizational leaders. This chapter examines the benefits of mentoring in the public sector and highlights gender differences. — Editor's Note

Mentoring is known to influence strongly one's professional career development and upward mobility. It is a particularly important issue for those who pursue advancement into managerial careers. Being mentored means involving oneself in a relationship with the intention of being taught, guided, or coached by a higher-ranking and more influential individual in order to learn from his or her skills, knowledge, or expertise.

While mentoring in public management has not been rigorously evaluated, initial research findings from private business show that the influence of mentoring in executive development is double-edged. The "good news" is that being mentored assists individuals in five important areas: (1) learning organizational norms and values, (2) being socialized into the organization, (3) coping with structural barriers in organizations, (4) gaining information on career path experience, and (5) advancing in organizations. The "bad news" is that without access to a mentor and his or her collegial network, one's participation and achievement in organizations can be severely limited.

The issue of mentoring is growing both as a research topic and as a concern for organizations that wish to improve management development programs and increase retention of bright and talented individuals. Four questions are of primary interest to both contemporary researchers and human resource managers:

- What differences are found in the mentoring experiences between women and men?
- To what extent do peer and supervisory relationships support individual advancement at various career stages?
- How do same-sex and opposite-sex mentoring relationships differ?
- What are the implications of mentoring for management?

This chapter addresses these challenging questions by reviewing the literature on mentoring, using research to identify the differences in the mentoring experiences of women and men currently working in state governments, and recommending practical strategies to both individuals and organizations wanting to utilize the mentoring process.

Overview of Mentoring Research

In recent years, interest in mentoring has grown in both the private and the public sectors and research has provided considerable information about several aspects of the mentoring experience (Bolton 1980; Bowen 1985; Carr-Ruffino 1985; Collins 1983; Collins and Scott 1979; Farren, Gray, and Kaye 1984; Henderson 1985; Johnson 1980; Kram 1980, 1985; Noe 1988; Orth and Jacobs 1971; Plimpton 1984; Radin 1980; Ragins 1989; Reich 1986; Roche 1979; Schein 1971; Speizer 1981; Thompson 1976; Vertz 1985; Wigand and Boster 1991; Zey 1985).

Most of what has been learned can be categorized into the following areas: (1) the nature of mentor assistance and the functions of mentors, (2) the importance of mentoring, (3) the mentoring relationship, (4) the special nature of women's mentoring, and (5) mentoring programs.

The Nature and Functions of Mentoring Assistance

Descriptions of the nature of administrators' mentor–protégé relationships and the variety of functions they serve have been offered by previous investigators (Hunt and Michael 1983; Kram 1983,

1985; Zey 1984). The mentoring process is described by Kram (1980) as having, first, a "career function" (a combination of sponsoring, coaching, creating visibility and access, shielding from mistakes, and assignment to creative tasks), and second, a "psychosocial function" (offering personal friendship, advising, confidence building, and nurturing managerial skills). As articulated by Noe (1988, p. 66):

> The mentor may advance the protégé's career by nominating him or her for promotion (sponsorship), by providing opportunities for the protégé to demonstrate competence and special talents (exposure and visibility), by suggesting strategies for achieving work objectives (coaching), by minimizing the likelihood that the protégé will be involved in controversial situations (protection), and by assigning challenging work assignments. In the psychosocial area, the mentor may enhance the protégé's sense of competence and identity by serving as a role model and encouraging the protégé to experiment with new behaviors, and the mentor may provide performance feedback (acceptance and confirmation).

Mentors can be sympathetic listeners for protégés to discuss their personal concerns and fears. They may also "serve as a buffer between the organization and the individual by running interference for the protégé and providing special access to information, contacts, and resources" (Ragins 1989, p. 2). These mentoring functions are considered very important contributors to career development. Bowen (1985, p. 32), who has evaluated the types of mentoring functions performed, reports that "the functions provided by the mentor . . . accounted for almost twenty percent of the variance in perceptions of career progress" in terms of whether or not one sees one's career on the fast track to advancement.

The Importance of Mentoring

While the study of mentoring is still "in its infancy . . . [and] few rigorous quantitative studies of the antecedents or outcomes of mentoring have appeared in the organizational behavior literature" (Noe 1988, p. 66), it is widely acknowledged that mentoring provides multiple benefits. For protégés, the significance of mentoring lies primarily in its assistance in the following:

1. Coping successfully with organizational barriers (Bolton and Humphreys 1977; Hale and Kelly 1989a; Lunding, Clements, and Perkins 1978);
2. Developing useful contacts, connections to collegial networks, and the ability to join winning teams (Almquist and Angrist 1971; Bolton 1980; Burke 1984; Col 1985; Dalton, Thompson, and Price 1977; Douvan 1976; Hale and Kelly 1989a; Kanter 1977; Kemper 1968; Kram 1980, 1983, 1985; O'Connell and Russo 1988; Orth and Jacobs 1971; Plimpton 1984; Vertz 1985);
3. Disseminating information on career path experiences, career pay expectations, and facilitating career development and advancement (Bolton 1980; Henderson 1985; Kram 1983; Phillips-Jones 1982; Reich 1985, 1986);
4. Attaining job and career satisfaction (Riley and Wrench 1985; Roche 1979).

In addition, mentoring provides a "seal of approval" to others and indicates one's entrance as a new member of the professional "club."

Of particular importance to junior individuals in an organization is the contribution mentoring can make to facilitating their career advancement. In the mid-1980s, senior executives in large public organizations (those with over 100 employees) in municipal, state, and federal governments were examined in a study that linked mentoring with career advancement (Henderson 1985). The results showed that compared with those without mentors, public executives at all levels of government with mentors are more likely: (1) to be willing to relocate for their careers, (2) to be satisfied with their careers, (3) to have career plans, (4) to have feelings of career success, (5) to work longer hours and enjoy their work more, and (6) to reach executive levels at earlier ages. Henderson also found mentoring to have a positive impact on executive compensation and education. Public executives with a former mentor made an average of over 11 percent more than executives who had never had a mentor. In fact, every public executive in the study who attained a salary over $70,000 had had a mentor. The study also revealed that twice the percentage of executives in local and federal government with mentors had master's degrees; in state governments a slightly higher percentage of those without mentors had master's degrees.

Studies undertaken by Reich (1986) indicate that mentoring also assists protégés by stimulating their thinking and setting of job goals; increasing opportunity to develop abilities, skills, and creativity; gaining awareness of one's strengths and weaknesses; and facilitating the discovery and use of their talents. As in Henderson's research, mentoring was also found to contribute to more rapid promotions.

Mentors also receive benefits from the process. In addition to gaining work satisfaction from helping younger people, both women and men noted that mentoring improved their managerial talents and performance of their work group, and reported that keeping a top protégé on their work team contributed to their own careers (Reich 1986).

Benefits outside the mentoring relationship have been uncovered as well. Bowen (1985) studied 32 mentor–protégé pairs in which all protégés in the study were female, while 18 mentors were male and 14 were female. The results showed that mentoring increased protégé acceptance or stature among colleagues (this was particularly true of male-mentored women), and improved their ability to function more effectively at work. Mentors also noted salutary effects for themselves, in that it relieved their own stress and reinforced their image with peers.

The Mentoring Relationship

Mentoring relationships are characterized by substantial emotional commitment by both parties (Bowen 1985; Shapiro, Haseltine, and Rowe 1978) and a high level of personal interaction (Bolton 1980). These relationships may be initiated by either party and usually last an extended period of time—most often from two to ten years (Bolton 1980; Bowen 1985; Collins 1983; Hunt and Michael 1983; Kram 1985; Noe 1988; Ragins 1989; Roche 1979). While the length of term as a protégé is typically shorter for a woman than for a man (although still averaging over four years), women are much more likely to maintain a relationship with a former mentor than are men (Henderson 1985).

Particularly in public sector organizations, mentoring occurs primarily during the first five years of a career. It has been reported that many public executives develop mentor–protégé relationships with their college professors and that this is particularly true for women executives (Henderson 1985). These findings are important since women who advance in their careers often do so at an earlier age than men, that is, they are *fast-trackers*. [Editor's note: see chapter 2 for an elaboration of this point.]

The degree to which a mentor identifies with and considers the protégé as "a younger version" of him or herself (Ragins 1989, p. 8) has been found to be a key element in the selection process (Blackburn, Chapman, and Cameron 1981; Bowers 1984; Lunding et al. 1978). Bowen (1985) mentions several interesting findings regarding identification with one's mentor. First, identification tends to be highest at the beginning of the mentoring relationship. Second, while identification is important in bringing people together in a mentoring relationship, it does not appear to be essential to effective mentoring thereafter. Third, more intense psychosocial mentoring occurs where identification is lower and when the mentor is male (Bowen 1985).

Gender Differences and Problems for Women

There is some evidence that female managers may need and acquire different kinds of mentoring than their male counterparts (Burke 1984; Fitt and Newton 1981; Ragins 1989; Reich 1985, 1986). For example, Fitt and Newton's (1981) research found that female protégés were viewed by mentors as needing more encouragement than males. Additionally, the study supports the idea that gender differences in mentoring relationships "may change as a function of organizational rank; females at lower ranks needed role modeling and assistance with learning the ropes of the organization, while at higher ranks the focus shifted to career development and insuring legitimacy within the organization" (Ragins 1989, p. 5).

Researchers seem to disagree about whether female managers recognize the importance of having a mentor. While several researchers report this is not a problem (Collins 1983; Graddick 1984; Hennig and Jardim 1977; Keown and Keown 1982), others (Reich 1986) believe that women fail to recognize the importance of gaining a mentor and "may naively assume that competence is the only requisite for advancement in the organization" (Ragins 1989, p. 6). Regardless of the contradictory literature, researchers agree that women are less likely than men to develop mentoring relationships (Brown 1985; Burke 1984; Cook 1979; Farris and Ragan 1981; Nieva and Gutek 1981; Ragins 1989; Shapiro et al. 1978). Two possible explanations for this conclusion are that women may not seek mentors, or that mentors may not select female protégés. Whichever is the case, the fact remains that there is some sort of barrier between women and the mentoring process.

Two types of barriers occur that can prevent women from seeking mentors in organizations. The first potential hurdle women experience in finding a mentor is that they may not "know how." In other words, they may lack the necessary knowledge, skills, strategies, or comfort and familiarity to initiate a mentoring relationship (Ragins 1989). This lack of knowledge regarding how to develop informal mentoring networks may lead them to prefer interacting with their peers, since they are of similar status to themselves in the organization (Noe 1988). Fearful that attempts to initiate a relationship might be misconstrued as a sexual approach by either the mentor or others in the organization, women find it particularly difficult to approach potential mentors who are male (Clawson and Kram 1984; Ragins 1989; Reich 1986). A related obstacle is that fewer formal and informal opportunities to obtain mentors exist for women than for men, and women have fewer interactions with individuals in positions of power (Brass 1985; Noe 1988; Rosen, Templeton, and Kirchline 1981; Stewart and Gudykunst 1982). This access problem also prompts women to turn to peer relationships, hoping these can provide support for personal and professional growth that is at least similar to that which exists in the mentoring function (Kram and Isabella 1985). However, because peers do not have as much power and influence as higher-level mentors, they fail to promote advancement successfully, and instead provide little other than social support (Riley and Wrench 1985).

The second explanation for why women enjoy fewer mentoring relationships than men is that mentors may be unwilling to select female protégés. If this is so, then it is a crucial constraint on women's opportunity. Male mentors, because of their greater power, are often in an excellent position to "confer organizational legitimacy" on their protégés and provide them with the resources required for success and organizational advancement (Ragins 1989, p. 11); however they may intentionally exclude or not even consider female managers as candidates for protégé roles. This reluctance is primarily attributed to a number of factors, including:

1. Sex-role socialization (Cook 1979; Reich 1986; Shapiro et al. 1978);
2. Negative attitudes toward women in management (Bolton 1980; Bowman, Worthy, and Greyser 1965; Donnell and Hall 1980;

Dubno 1985; Harlan and Weiss 1982; Moore and Rickel 1980; Rosen and Jerdee 1978; Vertz 1985);
3. Greater comfort developing a professional and personal relationship with another male (Ragins 1989);
4. Fears/misgivings about potential sexual involvements (Bowen 1985).

Sexual involvements often have negative implications for the female protégé's career. Such relationships can interfere with work roles and may result in the loss of her mentoring relationship and possibly her job. For the mentor, sexual relationships can lead to problems with jealous spouses and resentful co-workers (Driscoll and Bova 1980; Gutek 1985; Ragins 1989; Spruell 1985).

Another factor may be loss of control (Bolton 1980; Bowen 1985; Clawson and Kram 1984; Collins 1983; Fitt and Newton 1981; Lean 1983; Schein 1971; Thompson 1976). Fears regarding loss of control involve an implicit challenge to one's security status; gender competition or challenge underlying the transfer of knowledge, skill, or experience; threat of change to a non-gender-based group identity; or fearing unwanted sexual overtures and possible harassment.

Because gender role behavior is a confounding variable when opposite sexes enter into a mentor–protégé relationship, there is much support for same-sex mentoring (Bolton 1980; Bowen 1985; Brown 1985; Col 1985; Orth and Jacobs 1971; Reich 1986). Female mentors are believed to offer several advantages to female protégés, including greater empathy, more comfort, less likelihood of encountering unwanted sexual overtures, increased self-confidence, and perceived fit between professional traits and self-image. However, some researchers believe that female executives may be less available or less willing to mentor than their male counterparts (Brown 1985; Ragins 1989; Warihay 1980).

Two factors most inhibit the use of female mentors. The first is the lack of women in management positions in general, and their particular shortage in male-dominated occupations (such as public administration). Because of this, the few females in upper levels of organizations may receive a disproportionate share of requests from the greater number of women at lower organizational levels and have less time available for mentoring. The second factor is that the positions most likely to give access to valuable information concerning job openings, pending projects, and managerial decisions are held by men ensconced in the "old boy network" (Noe 1988, p. 67; Barnier 1982; Smith and Grenier 1982). Because of this, a male mentor may have a wider base of power and access to more valuable resources, may be more able to set realistic career goals, and may provide greater visibility to important organization members than a female mentor (Noe 1988; Woodlands Group 1980).

Other barriers faced by female executives who are sought after as mentors include time pressures, nonsupportive environments, a sense of protégé dependency, high visibility, and the perception and negative reaction of others in the organization that "female coalitions" and "divisions along gender lines" are being built (Bowers 1984; Ragins 1989). Overall, the primary disadvantage of female mentors is the fact that they tend to be less powerful than male mentors and therefore may be less able to promote the careers of their female protégés (Hill 1980; Ragins and Sundstrom 1989; Wolf and Fligstein 1979).

Opposite-Sex Mentoring Relationships

Regrettably, substantial perceptual and situational barriers against establishing opposite-sex mentorships exist, particularly for women. The following barriers are mentioned most frequently:

1. Norms regarding opposite-sex relationships. These include the preference of both women and men to interact with members of the same sex in the work environment (Larwood and Blackmore 1978; Vertz 1985).
2. Misperceptions about, and more traditional attitudes toward, the role of women in employment held by men at higher levels in organizations (Vertz 1985). Such men may perceive women to be less motivated and less interested in career advancement than their male colleagues (Rynes and Rosen 1983; Siegfried, Macfarlane, Graham, Moore, and Young 1981). They may also believe that women have less potential than men and, therefore, they do not take women's career concerns seriously enough to want to help them in a mentoring relationship (Bolton 1980; Noe 1988).
3. Continuation of stereotyped beliefs that women do not possess specific traits necessary for managerial success. Traits considered crucial for success in management and administration include leadership,

assertiveness, competitiveness, self-confidence, aggressiveness, ambition, legitimate authority, and emotional control (for example, see Massengill and DiMarco 1979; Noe 1988; Nyquist and Spence 1986; O'Leary 1974; Schein 1973; Taylor and Ilgen 1981).

4. The perception that women's good performance "is viewed as an exception based on (temporary) effort, rather than a more stable cause such as ability" (Noe 1988, p. 69).

5. Lack of socialization practices. Without a mentor to provide psychological support, reinforcement for achievement-oriented behavior, and specific task feedback, women's motivation, aspiration levels, feelings of self-confidence and efficacy, and needs for achievement and power may stagnate (Barclay 1982; Hackett and Betz 1981; Noe 1988). They may also have more difficulty becoming recognized as legitimate candidates for managerial positions (Noe 1988).

Each of these biases constrains career advancement opportunities for women. On a brighter note, opposite-sex mentoring dyads have the advantage of providing a highly visible model of men and women working closely together in a constructive relationship (Ragins 1989). As these relationships become more common and accepted, the problems associated with women and men working closely together, such as unfounded suspicions from spouses and co-workers, unwillingness of male mentors to accept females as protégés, and reluctance of female protégés to seek male mentors, may decrease (Ragins 1989).

There are more similarities than there are differences between women and men, both as mentors and as protégés (Reich 1985). As noted earlier, male and female mentors report similar experiences regarding the benefits they receive from their mentoring relationships. Both emphasize the professional nature of mentoring and caring about the future of their protégés. It is important to note, however, that women generally consider this last function as more important than men (Reich 1985, p. 54). Women are more likely than men to emphasize the importance of "good chemistry" to the success of the relationship; to stress the caring, nurturing, and teaching aspects of the relationship; and to care about promotions for, and have stronger feelings toward, their protégés. Men more often say they have been helped by keeping a top protégé on their work team, while women attribute more importance to the satisfaction gained from helping younger people and from improving their own managerial talents as a result of the mentoring process. Fewer female than male mentors believe that the worth of mentoring is recognized by senior management (Reich 1985). Only a small percentage of mentors, either male or female, become disillusioned with protégés or report trouble in terminating the relationship.

As protégés, more women describe their mentors as role models who help them identify their strengths and weaknesses. While most women do not report a close attachment to either their mentor or their protégé, more women than men state that their relationships develop into close and continuing friendships with their mentors. In fact, very few men report developing close emotional ties with their mentors. Likewise, female protégés are more likely to believe that their mentors view their career development as important (Reich 1985).

Relatively few gender differences have been communicated regarding problems or drawbacks of the mentoring relationship. Female mentors have related difficulty "when they recommended their protégés for other positions and when their top people competed for the same job" (Reich 1985, p. 53). Female protégés noted fewer negative aspects of mentor relationships than did men; in fact, half of the women protégés reported few or no disadvantages. The major hindrance noted by both women and men was being too closely identified with one's mentor. Others mentioned less frequently included being kept from better jobs, being too protected, or perceptions or suspicions by co-workers or spouses that the relationship was sexual in nature. For some respondents, the association was said to have caused a moderate amount of stress and that "one or more of the above conditions truly hurt the relationship" (Reich 1985, p. 53).

Effectiveness of Mentoring Relationships

In examining the effectiveness of mentoring relationships, there are two issues of importance to researchers: the differences between how female and male protégés use mentors, and whether the mentor's gender influences the effectiveness of the relationship (Ragins 1988). With regard to the first topic, gender of protégé, some research suggests that mentors are used more effectively by men than by women (Collins 1983; Lunding et al. 1978). Ragins also notes that the relative effectiveness of opposite- and same-gender mentoring relationships is influenced by the protégé's career stage. At early career stages, "where support, identification, and role modeling functions are needed," same-gender mentoring relationships may be most effective for female protégés (Ragins 1989, p. 14). However, as women advance in the organization, the mentor's power and organizational influence may be more important than his or her gender.

Drawing upon the scant comparative research that exists on gender differences in mentor effectiveness, three findings are noteworthy. First, while males generally have more power than females in organizations, and may therefore be more effective than females in enhancing their protégés' advancement, female managers are perceived as having as much, if not more, power than their male counterparts when organizational rank is held constant (Ragins 1989; Ragins and Sundstrom 1989; Tannenbaum 1968). Second, friendship and personal bonds are reported as being closer between female mentors and female protégés than with male mentors and male protégés (Reich 1985, 1986). The third factor that can influence the relative effectiveness of male and female mentors is the gender-typing of the organization:

> [F]emale mentors may face fewer barriers to mentoring in organizations where women constitute the numerical majority. Female mentors in female-typed organizations may also be more likely to hold higher ranking positions than female mentors in male-typed organizations. Female mentors may therefore have more power, and may be more effective mentors in female-typed than in male-typed organizations. [Ragins 1989, p. 15]

The Special Nature of Women's Mentoring

While the number of women seeking management positions is expanding, the number of mentoring relationships available to women is not keeping pace with the increasing need (Berry 1983; Reich 1985; Shockley and Stanley 1980; Warihay 1980). This is important because mentoring research indicates that women who are included in mentoring relationships are more likely to succeed in organizations than those who are not (Ilgen and Youtz 1986; McIlhone 1984; Ragins 1989; Riley and Wrench 1985). The problem of mentoring not being as available to women as it is to men is explained by Jean Marie Col (1985, pp. 3–4):

Besides providing behavioral cues, the existence of role models serves to legitimate the choice of a woman to be active in professional and managerial work. . . . Finding plenty of examples of men at higher levels, each upwardly mobile man can easily identify with at least a few of them. On the other hand, women find few, if any, women who are already highly placed in most organizations. . . . The lack of female role models broadcasts a "no entrance" signal to the most qualified and interested women.

While mentoring has been related to the advancement of men (Barnier 1982; Orth and Jacobs 1971), its role in the career development of women is not as easily defined. This is, in part, because "later career selection, more frequent career interruptions, and fewer advancement opportunities complicate career development for women" (Bolton 1980; Noe 1988, p. 66; Shapiro et al. 1978). In addition, compared with their male counterparts, female managers face greater organizational, interpersonal, and cultural barriers to advancement. These barriers can take several forms: employer bias and discrimination; occupational segregation and its attendant problems of promotional and salary inequity, and sexual harassment; and lack of an appropriate mentor and attendant access to his or her collegial networks. Mentioned frequently in the literature, these barriers are particularly important for women pursuing advancement within organizations.

Mentors can help their female protégés by mitigating overt and covert forms of discrimination, and other structural and social barriers to advancement in the organization (Hale and Kelly 1989b; Ragins 1989). Four of the most important ways mentors promote their female protégés' advancement are: (1) to build their self-confidence; (2) to furnish insight, training, and counseling on organizational politics; (3) to enhance awareness of their management style, skills, and effectiveness; and (4) to advise how to balance career, family, and household duties (Brown 1985; Collins 1983; Ragins 1989; Reich 1986). The few studies investigating the impact of mentoring functions for women have found that mentors are necessary to overcome gender-related obstacles to advancement in organizations.

Mentors can also provide valuable concrete assistance such as assignment to special projects or difficult tasks, creation of new positions, early transfers to challenging jobs, and so forth. This last type of aid, early transfer to challenging jobs, has been found to be provided more to male than to female executives. Reich (1986) reported that 63 percent of men queried compared to 49 percent of women reported such assistance. In general, guidance has been found to be valued at least as much as concrete action by women. Perhaps this is because women are relatively new entrants to management and have much less experience in the politics of large organizations (Reich 1986).

Finally, mentors promote advancement of their female protégés by "conferring legitimacy and altering co-worker's stereotypic perceptions" (Ragins 1989, p. 3). In his research, Reich (1986, p. 52) found that "over half of both male and female mentors applied pressure on others to obtain promotions for their protégés." Studies focusing exclusively on women in mentoring relationships have found that greater job success and job satisfaction are reported by women who have one or more mentors compared to those who have no mentor (Riley and Wrench 1985). Mentors create opportunities for protégés to operate outside of organizational norms; they stimulate personal motivation by setting high performance standards; they publicize achievements; and they provide an environment conducive to experimenting with new behaviors and ideas (Missirian 1982).

Comparing gender differences in mentoring illustrates the experiences of both women and men, and provides insight into how mentoring is involved in advancing careers in organizations. The findings reported in the following section provide a window through which one can see how mentoring has affected the professional socialization and career development of top-level administrators in state governments.

Survey Findings: Differences in Mentoring for Women and Men and Their Implications for State Government

The research findings from the surveys of public administrators in the states show noticeable gender differences in the mentoring experiences of high-level administrators. These findings lend support to the notion that peer and supervisor support, collegial networks, and same-sex mentoring are all important for career advancement.

An interaction effect between sex and mentoring is apparent (see Table 5.1). When asked about their mentors, high-level female administrators more often identify their mentors as female than do male administrators. As far as same-sex versus opposite-sex mentoring is concerned, well over twice as many men report having been mentored by men rather than by women.

Table 5.1

Mentoring (%)

Respondent	Woman mentor	Man mentor
	Type of mentor: Peers	
Women		
Alabama	54.0	54.0
Arizona	45.0	38.0
Utah	55.0	52.5
Wisconsin	52.7	41.7
Men		
Alabama	35.0	73.0
Arizona	22.0	55.0
Utah	30.0	65.0
Wisconsin	31.5	69.2
	Type of mentor: Supervisors	
Women		
Alabama	42.0	58.0
Arizona	31.0	64.0
Utah	47.5	80.0
Wisconsin	45.1	57.9
Men		
Alabama	23.0	85.0
Arizona	13.0	73.0
Utah	17.5	79.0
Wisconsin	18.8	78.3
	Type of mentor: CEO/agency director	
Women		
Alabama	24.0	48.0
Arizona	17.0	60.0
Utah	35.0	52.5
Wisconsin	12.4	23.2
Men		
Alabama	12.0	57.0
Arizona	7.0	54.0
Utah	9.0	54.0
Wisconsin	8.6	41.3

Source: Rita Mae Kelly, Mary E. Guy, et al. (1991), Public managers in the states: A comparison of career advancement by sex. *Public Administration Review* 51(5): 408.

The percentage of women and men who have had access to same-sex and opposite-sex mentors at the level of supervisors and agency directors is shown in Table 5.1. The percentage of male administrators who have supervisors or chief executive officers (CEOs) as mentors tends to be larger than that for female administrators, and women are more likely than men to have opposite-sex mentors. Male supervisors are more often listed as mentors by men than by women. Most men (from 73 percent to 85 percent) and slightly fewer women (from 58 percent to 80 percent) report having male mentors who are supervisors. Less than a quarter of the men (from 13 percent to 23 percent) and less than half of the women (from 31 percent to 48 percent) report having a female mentor who is a supervisor. The proportional difference increases at the level of CEO or agency director; that is, women directors were much less likely to be reported as mentors for either men (from 9 percent to 12 percent) or women (from 12 percent to 35 percent). At this level, a broader proportion of women (from 23 percent to 60 percent) and almost half the men reported having had male mentors (from 41 percent to 57 percent).

As the table shows, women report having mentors with about the same frequency as men. The difference between women and men lies in the fact that women are more likely to have female mentors and men are more likely to have male mentors. The data appear to contradict studies that conclude that women under-rate mentor–protégé networks (Bartol 1974; Carr-Ruffino 1985; Dexter 1985; Melia and Lyttle 1986). The frequency of female mentors for women denotes the importance of same-sex support.

In a study of California public administrators, Jane Bayes uncovered differential perceptions of mentors who worked in various state agencies. Both women and men in California Social Services and the Finance departments said mentoring was important but differed over whether supervisors or peers were more important as mentors. In the Department of Finance, male peers in large numbers were mentioned as being important to one's career advancement; in the Department of Social Services, supervisors of both sexes were viewed as more important, but more so for the men. "Since women have moved into management positions in the Finance Department only within the last ten years in any significant numbers, and since most of them are young, it is not surprising that female mentors are not identified in great numbers" (Bayes 1989, p. 131). This also suggests peer networking is more important to advancement in the smaller Finance Department, whereas being noticed by supervisors or CEOs makes a difference in the larger Social Services Department (Bayes 1989).

Summary

The vast majority of state administrators in these surveys report having had multiple mentors and the findings reported in this book show that public administrators in the states are indeed willing to relocate, have career plans, report feelings of satisfaction and success with their careers, and, particularly for women, have been able to reach executive levels at earlier ages. While these findings cannot be said to be directly attributable to mentoring, such experience undoubtedly has a positive impact on one's abilities to increase managerial and administrative skills, effectively learn organizational norms and values, and advance in a chosen career. Although not fully answering the research questions mentioned at the beginning of this chapter, the findings from these surveys shed more light on these topics and have implications for future management development.

Prevailing patterns among the high-level administrators who participated in this research can be explained, at least partially, by the structure of the system. As can be seen from the survey data, organizational rank, type of department, organizational structure, and gender segregation by occupation account for many of the commonalities and differences between women and men.

Gender differences in mentoring relationships (for example, proportions of same- or opposite-sex mentors, sex and rank of mentors, and importance placed on mentoring) partially result from the smaller proportion of women in leadership positions in state governments and their disproportionate segregation in low-ranking positions (Blau and Ferber 1987; Dipboye 1987; Hale and Kelly 1989a; Lewis 1988a, 1988b; Peterson-Hardt and Perlman 1979). Since different kinds of departments offer more or less conducive environments for developing mentoring relationships, and women and men are often segregated in different departments (Blau and Ferber 1987), work units are also likely to confuse gender difference interpretations. Bayes's findings in California certainly underscore this point. Distinctions influence this (and future) mentoring research. It is important to know whether an organization is more humanistic, mechanistic, or concerned with social change; whether decisions are made by autocrats or through small groups or communication networks; whether the structure is more hierarchical or flat; whether job functions are shared or rotated; whether apprentice-type relationships or independent job functions are common; and whether or not intergenerational cohorts interact. Ferreting out the answer to these questions will help to learn which characteristics are unique and which ones are due to other factors.

The findings shown in Table 5.1 challenge some of what has previously been reported about the role of mentoring, particularly for women, in organizational life. The fact that these state government administrators report experience with mentoring, while it does not necessarily mean it is responsible for their reaching the highest organizational levels, does imply that the benefits derived from such relationships have contributed to their success.

The Future Research Agenda

Future longitudinal research is needed to examine and confirm mentoring theory in five key areas: (1) specific barriers preventing individuals from gaining access to mentors in organizations; (2) relationships between specific career stages, work/nonwork barriers to career advancement and development of effective mentoring relationships; (3) opportunities for developing mentoring relationships at specific career stages; (4) impact of organizational factors on mentoring relationships; and (5) effectiveness of specific mentoring relationships, including impact of same- and opposite-sex mentoring. Specific research questions offered by Noe (1988), Ragins (1989), and Reich (1985, 1986) are listed in Figure 5.1.

Earlier literature notes that mentoring provides potential benefits to all involved participants: mentors and protégés, as well as organizations. Both mentors and protégés experience decreased role conflict and feelings of isolation, increased productivity and achievement, well-being, and organizational commitment, and career development and advancement. Along with identification with role models, encouragement, and network development, protégés gain increased self-confidence, growth opportunities, familiarity with organizational politics, motivation to achieve career goals, support and cooperation of coworkers and peers, and visibility and promotion within organizations. These benefits, in turn, increase their probability of succeeding in organizations.

For organizations, mentoring is a good investment since it develops human capital, maximizes the contributions individual women and men can make to their agencies, and offers an opportunity to gain and

Figure 5.1. **Research Questions**

1. What types of functions do mentors provide protégés at each career stage and do the functions that protégés desire from mentors at each career stage differ by gender?

2. What are the characteristics of protégés who have benefited from mentoring relationships?

3. Are peers able to provide the same functions as mentors?

4. What support systems were available for women successful in traditionally male-dominated occupations?

5. What are the benefits and limitations of mentorships for mentors?

6. How effective are various strategies for obtaining a mentor?

7. What is the impact of mentors on career choice, career involvement, and career growth at each career stage?

8. What is the most important benefit protégés get from their mentor(s)?

9. Do the frequency and quality of mentorships for women in traditionally male-dominated jobs vary depending on the percentage of female job incumbents?

10. How does the organizational climate and culture influence the development of mentorships?

11. Are male managers who have had more experience with women as supervisors or colleagues in the workplace more willing than women to serve as mentors for women?

12. Do same-sex mentoring relationships have more congruence with the perception of needs of the protégé than opposite-sex mentoring relationships?

13. Are women mentors more sensitive to their protégés' needs than male mentors?

14. Do gender differences exist in the use of mentors by female and male protégés?

15. What gender differences exist in the use and effectiveness of mentors over the course of a career?

16. What are the number and length of mentoring relationships and how do they vary by gender and level of the mentors?

17. Are same-sex mentoring relationships more or less effective than opposite-sex relationships?

18. What differences exist within given gender combinations, i.e., do same-sex pairs (female mentors with female protégées and male mentors with male protégés) report closer friendship and personal bonds than opposite-sex pairs?

19. What is the impact of organizational factors on mentoring relationships?

retain valuable managerial talent of women and men. Given the apparent lack of mentoring of women by top executives in the public sector, the need for future leaders, and the strong competition between the private and public sectors for bright, competent, and energetic managers, government is advised to improve management development programs and motivate a greater proportion of the large numbers of professional women in the labor force to reach, alongside men, higher management and administrative positions.

6

Sexual Harassment in the States

Rita Mae Kelly and
Phoebe Morgan Stambaugh

Sexual harassment is a very real problem in the workplace. It is
experienced by women and men of all races, in all occupations, and
in all avenues of organizational life. Not only is the target of sexual
harassment victimized and humiliated, but the organization suffers
from productivity loss, training costs, and litigation fees. This chapter
provides a survey of sexual harassment and analyzes its effects and
policy implications. — Editor's Note

This chapter outlines the current discourse concerning sexual harassment. It compares and contrasts the experience of sexual harassment between genders, between occupations (traditional versus nontraditional occupations), and between sectors (private versus public), and finally focuses on sexual harassment at the state level. Data from the surveys of public administrators in the states are analyzed and policy implication areas are discussed. Analysis focuses on Kanter's thesis that structural and systemic characteristics play an important role in the experience of sexual harassment.

We wish to thank Robert Schwartz (Arizona), Mary Ellen Guy (Alabama), and Cathy Johnson and Georgia Duerst-Lahti (Wisconsin) for their assistance in completing the data analyses for their respective states.

What Is Sexual Harassment?

The term "sexual harassment," coined by activists in the mid-1970s, was first used in reference to the imposition of unwanted sexual attention endured by women at their place of work (Backhouse and Cohen 1981; Farley 1978). In 1976, the public's interest was sparked by a *Redbook* survey that reported an incidence rate of more than 80 percent among its readership (Safran 1976). While the emergence of sexual harassment as a concern may coincide with the sharp increase of middle- and upper-class women in the labor force, evidence indicates that since colonial times sexual harassment has been the working woman's nightmare (Bularzik 1978; MacKinnon 1987).

Many feel that efforts to remedy the problem have been thwarted by the lack of an agreed-upon definition. In terms of social science research, the lack of a narrow definition has resulted in a wide range of findings (Gruber 1989). Thus, the validity and reliability of scientific explanations and definitions are often suspect (Gillespie and Leffler 1987). The lack of a consensus among social scientists reflects the subjective nature of the experience of sexual harassment as well as the impact of sex role ideology in the identification of unwanted sexual attention.

In 1980, the Equal Employment Opportunity Commission (EEOC) issued guidelines for employers in the development of policies to forbid sexual harassment policies. These guidelines portray sexual harassment as a discriminatory action that is sexual in nature and that negatively affects an individual's experience of equality in his or her work environment. To put it another way, defined as a violation of Title VII, sexual harassment is an act of sex discrimination and violates a constitutional right to equality in the workplace. Thus, the EEOC definition is the one most commonly used by policy makers. For example, the Office of the Civil Rights Commission adopted the EEOC guidelines almost verbatim for application under Title IX. As a result, sexual harassment is also a violation of one's right to equal access to education. This is most important because the application of EEOC guidelines in the development, dissemination, and implementation of sexual harassment policies is the primary consideration in the assignment of liability once sexual harassment claims enter the judicial arena.

Who Gets Sexually Harassed?

Since the emergence of the concept in the late 1970s, sexual harassment has been considered a "woman's issue." Evidence indicates a disproportionate number of women report sexual harassment. As previously mentioned, in the *Redbook* survey more than 80 percent of the women reported having experienced sexual harassment. In a random survey of the working population at large, 21 percent of the women claimed they had been harassed (Gutek 1985). And in the largest and most comprehensive survey to date of governmental employees, the U.S. Merit Systems Protection Board found in 1981, and again in a 1987 replication, that 42 percent of all women employed by the federal government had experienced sexual harassment within two years of each study (U.S. Merit Systems Protection Board 1987).

Gender disparity in sexual harassment is very evident. Men do report sexual harassment, but the incidence—from 8 percent to 16 percent—is significantly lower than it is for women (Gutek 1985; U.S. Merit Systems Protection Board 1987). Interestingly, sexual harassment of most men is perpetrated by men (Gutek and Morasch 1982). Studies of sexual harassment in the private sector reveal comparable trends (Personnel Policies Forum 1987). In all fifty-seven companies surveyed by the Personnel Policies Forum, 96 percent of the complaints were filed by a female employee against a male offender (Personnel Policies Forum 1987, p. 17).

One explanation for the gender disparity is that men are more likely than women to find sexual behaviors to be positive (Powell 1986). Another explanation is said to rest with the disparity of organizational power between men and women. Women are more likely to be troubled by unwanted sexual attention and more likely to feel helpless to stop it because working women are outside the dominant power group (Kanter 1977). While women may have organizational status, they may still lack organizational power. Female teachers have reported harassment by male students (Herbert 1989), female supervisors by male employees (Clarke 1986), and female sales executives by their male customers (Nemec 1988). Female managers and administrators are no exceptions (Powell 1986).

This gender disparity in reactions to unwanted sexual attention has contributed to the 1991 judicial interpretation in *Ellison* v. *Brady* that the standard for assessing whether sexual harassment exists must be a reasonable woman's judgment, not a reasonable man's judgment. The decision in this case argues that women are disproportionately affected by sexual harassment and that women react differently than men to unwanted sexual advances. The decision also reaffirmed that an employer's failure to remove a perpetrator of sexual harassment from the workplace creates and perpetuates a hostile environment. The employer must be held accountable for this failure.

Evidence shows that sex segregation by occupation and workplace not only contributes to the prevalence of sexual harassment but also figures into how it is experienced (Gutek and Morasch 1982; Hemming 1985; Kanter 1977). For example, women working at jobs traditional for their sex role (such as secretary, clerk, receptionist, waitress) may experience sexual harassment as "sex role spillover" (Gutek and Morasch 1982). In other words, their traditional social roles as wife, girlfriend, mother, or daughter become inseparable from their work duties. When this happens, interactions with women in these occupations are more often sexual in nature than professional. And, as previously mentioned, this type of behavior in the workplace tends to be viewed positively by men but negatively by women.

Women working in nontraditional occupations often find themselves removed from women working in more traditional jobs in the organization and are assigned minority status in a culture dominated by men. In the role of "tokens" or "pioneers" (Kanter 1977), these women must often negotiate the resentment, anger, confusion, and frustration generated by their "invasion" of the masculine domain. When these negative responses to their entrance into nontraditional areas are manifested in sexual behavior, then they become sexual harassment.

What Is the Cost of Sexual Harassment?

The price paid by individuals, organizations, and society cannot be overestimated. "Sexual harassment syndrome" may manifest itself in the form of depression, chronic physical illness, and the deterioration of self-esteem and self-worth. Many victims of sexual harassment must take extended sick leave without pay (U.S. Merit Systems Protection Board 1987). A large portion are forced to quit their jobs (Coles 1986), forfeiting years of seniority, security, and benefits. Some even become suicidal (Gacioch 1987). Those few who risk filing a grievance rather than quit are stigmatized as "whistle-blowers" (Dandekar 1990) or malcontents (Branson and Branson 1988). Those who make it to a court of law and are awarded restitution, usually in the form of back pay, find that the award rarely compensates for the financial as well as emotional losses experienced.

At the organizational level, the cost in lost productivity, training, and support services and the cost of litigation are substantial. For example, the American Broadcasting Company paid $15 million to settle a claim made by one of its female executives (Garvey 1986). In 1987, it was estimated that sexual harassment cost taxpayers $189 million per year in employee turnover alone (U.S. Merit Systems Protection Board 1987). As one executive stated, "the cost [for employers] is high since many women just quit. There goes the kilobucks you just spent to train and market her" (Kiechel 1987, p. 20).

Sexual Harassment and the Public Sector

The public sector, especially the federal government, has taken the lead in addressing sexual harassment. At the federal level, the U.S. Postal Service and the civil service initiated the development and implementation of organizational responses at the agency level (Neugarten and Miller-Spellman 1983). Ironically, one of the first court cases involving claims of sexual harassment was filed against the EEOC (*Rogers* v. *EEOC 1972*).

At the state level, responses have been slow and diverse. In 1979, surveys of the employees of Illinois and Florida (McIntyre and Renick 1982) indicate the prevalence of sexual harassment of state employees to be near that experienced by federal workers. In Illinois, 59 percent of the women reported having been sexually harassed at their present job. In Florida, the rate was 42 percent. "Fear of deterioration in their working conditions, losing promotions or pay raises, poor references and loss of their jobs prevented resistance to unwanted sexual attention" (McIntyre and Renick 1982, pp. 284–85). At the time these surveys were in progress, Maryland was the only state with specific provisions for handling sexual harassment of state employees (McIntyre and Renick 1982).

By 1987, however, thirty-three states had published statewide sexual harassment policies (Ross and England 1987). About one-half of these policies were in the form of executive orders issued from the office of the governor. For example, in 1980, Utah's governor, Scott

M. Matheson, declared sexual harassment to "be prohibited in any and every workplace in which public employees are required to conduct business" (as cited in McIntyre and Renick 1982). In each case, state policy reflected the use of the EEOC employment guidelines and included the commission's definition (Ross and England 1987).

In 1981, California not only issued a statewide policy but also required each agency and department to develop sexual harassment guidelines within their own organizations. During that same year, Texas approved a proscriptive statute and Wisconsin's governor issued an executive order that included educational systems as well. Both Arizona and Alabama have executive orders prohibiting sexual harassment of all state employees. Given that the majority of states in the nation now have policies specific to sexual harassment, the question remains, how prevalent is sexual harassment at the state level? How is it experienced, and who reports it?

Patterns of Sexual Harassment

Table 6.1 presents the findings from our empirical assessment of the extent of sexual harassment in the five states of Alabama, Arizona, Texas, Utah, and Wisconsin. The data reveal several consistent patterns across these states as the following description explains.

Women in substantially higher proportions than men have experienced all forms of sexual harassment. Specifically, from 6 to 16 percent of high-level female public administrators have experienced unwelcome sexual advances, while almost none of their male counterparts have. While 11 to 24 percent of the females experienced requests for sexual favors, only 1 to 7 percent of males in any of these same states did. Whereas 14 to 36 percent of the women experienced offensive physical contact, only 1 to 5 percent of the men did. In addition, whereas 33 to 60 percent of the women experienced offensive verbal behavior, only 16 to 36 percent of the men did.

Similarly, women reported hearing about these types of sexual harassment at higher levels than men. Specifically, the percentage of women hearing about unwelcome sexual advances ranged from 29 percent in Texas to 67 percent in Arizona; for men the range went from 19 to 45 percent. In terms of requests for sexual favors, a low of 27 percent of the women in Texas heard about such requests and a high of 57 percent in Arizona did. Among the men, the range was a

Table 6.1

Type of Sexual Harassment Experienced and Heard About (%)

	Women		Men	
Type and state	Experienced	Heard about	Experienced	Heard about
Unwelcome sexual advances				
Alabama	11	46	1	45
Arizona	10	67	0	39
Texas	7	29	0	19
Utah	16	46	1	32
Wisconsin	6	39	1	22
Requests for sexual favors				
Alabama	12	42	1	46
Arizona	24	57	7	34
Texas	11	27	2	21
Utah	21	38	1	30
Wisconsin	12	36	4	18
Offensive physical contact				
Alabama	24	42	1	42
Arizona	14	62	3	42
Texas	16	28	2	15
Utah	36	38	2	37
Wisconsin	19	43	5	31
Offensive verbal behavior				
Alabama	57	54	36	49
Arizona	57	50	36	45
Texas	33	41	16	39
Utah	46	34	31	39
Wisconsin	60	53	36	50

low of 18 percent in Wisconsin to a high of 46 percent in Alabama. The range of women hearing about offensive physical contact was about the same: 28 percent in Texas to a high of 62 percent in Arizona. For the men, the range was 15 percent in Texas to 42 percent in Alabama and Arizona. The differences between the men and women in each state hearing about offensive verbal behavior was 34 percent in Utah to 54 percent in Alabama for the women; and 39 percent in Texas and Utah to 50 percent in Wisconsin for the men.

Background Characteristics and Harassment

It is evident from the variation in the data that not all women experience or hear about sexual harassment. To assess the extent to which background variables other than one's sex are related to sexual harassment, an index of the level of harassment experienced was created and compared to management rank for the women in the Arizona study. Data from Arizona and Wisconsin are used in this analysis because the sampling procedures in these two states make it possible to separate the respondents by managerial rank. This separation into middle and upper ranks allows comparisons between women and men at graduated ranks. Although it is not possible to generalize broadly from these two states, the insights obtained from this more microscopic view ought to be helpful. The general comparability of findings across the states reported in Table 6.1 indicate that the variations to be anticipated among the states are likely to be differences of degree rather than of kind.

The index was an additive one scored as follows: those respondents who had not experienced any form of either verbal or other harassment were assigned a score of 0; those who had experienced verbal harassment only in the form of jokes and snide remarks were assigned a score of 1; those who had experienced any or all of the other possible options (other offensive physical conduct of a sexual nature, requests for sexual favors from work colleagues, or unwelcome sexual advances in exchange for an employment opportunity by a superior) were assigned a score of 2. This scoring procedure creates an ordinal scale of gradations of the sexual harassment experienced.

Table 6.2 shows the severity of harassment experienced by the women in Arizona and Wisconsin by mid-level versus high-level ranks. About one-third of the women in each sample had experienced no harassment, one-third had experienced verbal harassment only, and another one-third had experienced more severe forms of harassment. Having risen in the administrative ranks provides no apparent protection against harassment. In fact, the pattern in Table 6.2 suggests that upper-level women might actually experience both more verbal and more severe forms of physical harassment than do the middle-level women.

For the State of Arizona, the harassment index was run against various background characteristics (age, race, religion, parental social

Table 6.2

Harassment Experienced by Sex and Management Level for Arizona and Wisconsin Administrators (%)

	Women		Men	
Arizona				
Grades:	18–22 (*n* = 53)	23–30 (*n* = 42)	18–22 (*n* = 118)	23–30 (*n* = 206)
None	35.8	26.2	60.2	61.2
Verbal only	28.3	33.3	33.9	29.6
Other forms	35.8	40.5	5.9	9.2
Wisconsin				
Grades:	13–17 (*n* = 104)	18–24 (*n* = 50)	13–17 (*n* = 135)	18–24 (*n* = 73)
None	38.5	30.0	60.7	64.4
Verbal only	37.5	46.0	33.3	24.7
Other forms	24.0	24.0	5.9	11.0

class, income, political party affiliation, years of service, and marital status) to assess whether any of these characteristics were associated with higher or lower levels of harassment. Only race and current marital status had any relationship with harassment levels.

Contrary to what might be expected, white women at all levels were more likely to experience harassment than nonwhite women. In the mid-level sample, whereas 30 percent of the forty-four white women did not experience any harassment, 67 percent of the nine non-white women did not. Among the upper-level group the key difference in sexual harassment experience by race/ethnicity was in terms of its severity. About one-fourth of each racial grouping did not experience any harassment, whereas 27 percent of the thirty-four white women but 63 percent of the eight black women experienced verbal harassment only; 43 percent of the white women but only 13 percent of the non-white women experienced the more severe forms of harassment.

The small sample size for both of these racial groups requires caution in extrapolating these percentages to other populations. Nonetheless, because the sample does include almost all of the women at the upper level in Arizona's state government, it does reflect the pattern of harassment in this state.

As one would expect, women not currently married were more subject to harassment than women who were. Among the mid-level women, about one-third of both the married and unmarried did not experience harassment, but 48 percent of the unmarried experienced the more severe forms of harassment whereas only 25 percent of the married women did. Apparently, marriage still connotes that a woman "belongs to" someone else and, therefore, has some additional protection from harassment by the men with whom she works.

Impact of Harassment on Job Performance and Effectiveness

J. L. Pereia (1988), a lawyer for the Securities and Exchange Commission in the 1980s, characterized sexual harassment as "psychological warfare with an old-boy network," stressing both the harm that can be done to women and the gender power differential undergirding such harassment. The argument that sexual harassment is a serious form of sexual discrimination derives from the assumption that it has a critical impact on a woman's ability to perform a job and to be an effective employee.

To examine the impact harassment has on job performance and effectiveness, analyses of variance were completed using twenty-two types of job functions and competencies. Given the probability that harassment is likely to have a greater impact on job performance of the mid-level than the higher-level women, we kept the two data sets separate for this analysis. Sexual harassment, or the possibility of it, is often a component of the invisible barriers that keep numerous mid-level women from "breaking through the glass ceiling" to the upper levels in both public and private sector management. These functions and/or competencies encompassed the following: communication abilities; organizational coalition formation/conflict management; specialized expertise (e.g., engineering, law); adaptability/flexibility, ability to balance short- and long-term considerations; the collection/assessment/analysis of information and making judgments; sensitivity to the environment; focusing on results/goal achievement; taking initiative/showing creativity; leadership; competency in interpersonal relations; personnel management; affirmative action/EEO management; budgetary resource management; keeping up with agency policies/priorities, external issues/trends; keeping subordinates informed regarding agency policies, issues, and trends; selling/defending work unit activities to supervisor and external groups; coordinating and integrating work activities with those of other organizations; identifying policy and program alternatives; managing programs (planning, coordinating, guiding staff); monitoring program compliance/program evaluation; and research and program development.

The results indicate that a substantial variation in the impact of sexual harassment on job performance and effectiveness exists by level within the hierarchy. The mean scores show that the importance of focusing on results and goal achievement is lower for mid-level women experiencing higher levels of harassment ($n = 53$; mean = 4.1; $F = 3.01$; $p < 0.10$) than it is for the mid-level women who experience lower levels of harassment ($n = 53$; mean = 4.1; $F = 4.32$; $p < 0.05$). At this same mid-level, the women experiencing higher levels of harassment also perceive "taking the initiative/showing creativity" as not being very important for their job effectiveness ($n = 53$; mean = 4.3; $F = 3.83$; $p < 0.05$).

At this mid-level in the Arizona public service it appears that sexual harassment sharply reduces a female employee's perception that focusing on results and goal achievement and taking the initiative on the job is important for her effectiveness as an employee. Over time it is obvious that such attitudes are likely to affect the quality of performance and to reduce the probability of promotion for these women. Managers typically must take the lead in setting goals, defining a unit's strategy, and launching new projects. Employees who do not show promise in engaging in these activities are unlikely to be considered managerial material. To the extent that sexual harassment contributes to deterring substantial numbers of women from being visible in these positive ways, sexual harassment is a concrete manifestation of institutional sexism and a major factor in enforcing the "glass ceiling" beyond which women find it hard to move.

At these same mid-level ranks, women who experienced the more severe forms of sexual harassment rated the importance of affirmative action and equal employment opportunity for both their job performance and effectiveness lower than did the women who experienced no or less severe harassment. The mean score on the importance of AA/EEO as it relates to job performance for women experiencing no verbal harassment was 2.53 (s.d. = 1.5); for the women experiencing verbal harassment only it was 3.27 (s.d. = 1.58); for the women experiencing the more severe forms of harassment the mean score was 2.00 (s.d. = 1.08). The means for the effectiveness data were comparable. It seems that the women experiencing less harassment sense a connection between the absence of harassment and the presence of AA/EEO policies. Perhaps the women who experience verbal harassment rate the importance of these policies higher than either the women experiencing no harassment or those who experience more severe forms because they think the harassment would be worse if no such policies existed.

Among these same mid-level women, those experiencing the most severe sexual harassment also rated "keeping subordinates informed regarding agency policies, issues, and trends" as less important for their job performance ($n = 53$; mean $= 3.3$; $F = 3.16$; $p < 0.05$) and effectiveness ($n = 53$; mean $= 2.84$; $F = 2.84$; $p < 0.10$). Women who experienced more severe harassment also indicated that identifying policy and program alternatives was less important for their job effectiveness than women at the same mid-levels who experienced less severe harassment ($n = 53$; mean $= 3.6$; $F = 2.6$; $p < 0.10$). The degree of sexual harassment that women experience appears to be related to the connection (or lack of it) a woman sees between her decision-making functions and her ability and effectiveness in performing her job.

Among the upper-level women administrators (GS 23–30), higher levels of sexual harassment had a different impact on their responses to the questions regarding job functions and competencies. These women seemed to have overcome some of the problems sexual harassment poses for attaining results and achieving goals.

The upper-level women administrators who had experienced more severe sexual harassment were more likely to indicate that coalition formation and conflict management were less important for their job performance than did those who experienced no harassment ($n = 42$; mean $= 3.6$; $F = 2.97$; $p < 0.10$). Although not reaching statistical significance, the upper-level women who experienced more severe levels of harassment also indicated that the functions of coordinating and integrating unit activities with other organizations were less important than did the women who experienced less harassment.

The findings on these two items suggest one of two things: either the majority of the upper-level women who experienced harassment had significantly less need to perform these functions, or harassment affected their perception of the importance of performing these functions. Because we have no reason to believe that the former situation is the case, we are inclined to think that sexual harassment does impact high-level female administrators negatively in the performance of inte-

Table 6.3

**Importance of Job Functions and Competencies
(Arizona Data, Grades 23–20)**

Job functions and competencies	Mean harassment scores				
	0	1	2	n	Tau C
Specialized expertise					
Importance for performance evaluation	3.18	3.46	4.00	39	0.25**
Importance for job effectiveness	3.50	3.90	4.30	40	0.24*
Ability to balance short- and long-term considerations					
Importance for job effectiveness	4.18	4.36	4.30	42	0.18†
Sensitivity to the environment					
Importance for performance evaluation	3.40	3.90	4.00	40	0.23**
Interpersonal relations/sensitivity					
Importance for performance evaluation	4.10	3.80	3.60	41	−0.19**
AA/EEO management					
Importance for performance evaluation	3.50	3.20	2.90	39	−0.16
Importance for job effectiveness	3.70	3.50	2.60	40	−0.35*

* $p < 0.05$
**$p < 0.01$
† $p < 0.10$

grating and coordinating functions. Given that conflict management and coalition formation are critical for managerial success at the upper levels, these data suggest, as the previous data have, that sexual harassment is indeed one of the barriers contributing to the creation of the "glass ceiling" in public organizations.

Table 6.3 details the relationship between job functions and competencies for higher-level women in Arizona. The results show a statistically significant increase or decrease in the average importance rating as the level of harassment increases (0 indicates no harassment experienced; 1 = verbal harassment; 2 = other more severe forms; importance was ranked from a low of 1 to a high of 5).

Table 6.3 shows the following: (a) that specified expertise, ability to balance short- and long-term considerations, and sensitivity to the environment were perceived as more important by those who experienced higher levels of sexual harassment; and (b) that AA/EEO declined in perceived importance as the level of sexual harassment increased. We also explored the relationship of the type of training desired to enhance job performance and sexual harassment. The women experiencing no harassment indicated that getting more training to improve their communication abilities would be helpful for their job performance (mean = 3.56; s.d. = 0.73); the women experiencing verbal harassment were least inclined to think training in communications abilities would be helpful (mean = 2.46; s.d. = 1.05); and the women experiencing the more severe forms of harassment were in between the other two groups (mean = 2.93; s.d. = 1.27).

These Arizona women administrators who experienced higher levels of harassment also indicated a desire for training to be sensitive to the environment, whereas the women experiencing lower levels indicated lower levels of interest in this type of training. No differences existed among mid-level women in terms of how sexual harassment experiences influenced their desire for training.

Impact of Harassment on Perception of Success

If sexual harassment is indeed some type of psychological warfare in the workplace, then the women experiencing its worst forms ought to react differently to it as a barrier to their career success than women not experiencing it so severely. To examine this possibility, the factors that have been important for their career success were correlated with the sexual harassment index. Given the status differential between the middle and upper levels, we explored each separately. Table 6.4 displays the relationship.

Among the mid-level women, those scoring higher on the harassment index indicated at significantly higher levels than the other women that their work style was the factor most important for their career success. Among the higher-level women, those scoring higher on the harassment index indicated at significantly higher levels than the other women that their personal attitude, self-concept, and motivation, and their mentors were most important for their career success. The mid-level women seem to rely on their behavior to protect themselves and their careers from the negative effects of harassment. The upper-level women, most of whom have advanced degrees, appear to rely on internal self-definition and supportive mentors to deal, apparently successfully, with more severe forms of harassment.

Harassment derives, in part, from a gender power differential and gives males an unfair advantage in the workplace. It is likely that women experiencing more severe harassment will view the factors

Table 6.4

**Tau C Correlations of Factors Contributing to Career Success
and Level of Sexual Harassment**

	Grade level	
	18–22 (n = 53)	23–30 (n = 42)
Attitude/self-concept/motivation	0.10	0.17*
Education	−0.34*	−0.08
Skills and abilities	−0.05	−0.09
Work style	0.44*	−0.10
Promotional opportunities offered	−0.10	0.03
Financial support from others	0.00	0.00
Training opportunities	−0.05	0.00
Mentor(s) or sponsorship	0.05	0.24*
Emotional support of others	0.00	−0.10
Having distinct career goals	−0.10	−0.08
Whom respondent knows	0.05	0.00

*$p < 0.05$

contributing to the success of males and females differently than women who experience less harassment. Indeed, we find that the mean scores for the women indicating they think male career success is related to ability and hard work declines as the harassment level rises. Among higher level women, the perception that male success is related to hard work also declines as harassment levels increase. Among the higher-level women, those who are more harassed also rate the importance of ability and hard work higher as a contributor to female success than those women who experience less harassment.

To determine if sexual harassment is related to individual perceptions of career success and satisfaction, the harassment index was correlated with items asking how successful and how satisfied each respondent felt. No significant differences were found for either the mid- or upper-level female administrators on these measures.

Conclusion

These data from the State of Arizona indicate that substantial percentages of both middle- and high-level female administrators in state government experience sexual harassment and that these experiences impact their job performance and behavior. Such harassment appears to affect work style, self-perception, and a woman's ability to perform particular job functions, such as managing conflict and organizing coalitions. Such harassment remains a contributor to the "glass ceiling effect," which keeps women both out of upper levels of management and from seeking entrance to those levels.

The fact that such harassment continues in the state civil service reflects quite negatively on the perception that state governments are dedicated to ending gender discrimination and gender power differentials. We recommend that all states re-examine the effectiveness of their sexual harassment policies so that progress can be made in ending this particular form of gender "psychological warfare."

7

Management Styles, Stereotypes, and Advantages

Georgia Duerst-Lahti and
Cathy Marie Johnson

Are women not attaining upper-level positions because of their
management style? Are certain gender-stereotyped traits exhibited in
management styles? Frequently, women stumble off the corporate
ladder when they do not fit the "normal" behavior style, the traditional
male model. This chapter uses summary data to explore management
styles and gender traits and offers the reader new insights into the
function of gender in organizations.   — Editor's Note

It is an old lament: We will not attain gender equity through mandated action programs if the assumptions that underpin organizations do not change. "Equal" treatment too often leads to enshrining what is conventionally done. And, because men have predominated, the conventional suits men well. Approaches that deviate from the norm are deemed lesser rather than different, so behaving in conventional (androcentric) ways can provide advantages. As we saw in chapter 4, employment policies and practices have been structured according to the private life assumptions of men. Hence, individuals who can fit those assumptions, usually single women and men in traditional marriages, find fewer interferences between their private lives and work.

Here we explore the management styles of women and men to understand better the ways in which gender operates in organizations.

The question of advantages will be explored in two ways. First, might the paucity of women in the upper levels be explained by differences in managerial style? If organizations whose top levels have been dominated by men develop androcentric expectations for "normal" behavioral styles, then men are far more likely to act managerially, and to rise. This implies, however, that behaving like men should provide advantages for women as well as for men. So the first question rests in the degree of difference between men's and women's styles: the greater the difference, the more style might explain the fact that women are under-represented at the top. Second, contemporary organizations confront an array of demands not faced by even those "modern" organizations of the recent past. Technology, work force demographics, changes in the problems the public sector addresses, all require new responses from organizations. To the extent that we find gender differences in style, those differences can be considered for the relative advantages they offer contemporary organizations. In other words, do some things stereotypically associated with women meet the needs of organizations today?

Polity, Organizations, and Gender

Too often the perception of both males and females is that gender, the culturally constructed differences between the sexes, relates to women, femaleness, and femininity. This practice implies that men and masculinity are not gendered. With male hegemonic advantage in the polity, culture, and society, maleness remains embedded throughout so it is not experienced as a problem. We must try consciously to see this. Male perspectives and norms become, well, normal.

The lack of serious theoretical consideration of gender is evident on a number of fronts. Wendy Brown (1987, 1988) has considered the place of sex and "manliness" in the writings of Hobbes, Machiavelli, Weber, and other forebears of modern organization theories. She persuasively shows how political thinking is infused with manliness; it is gendered. Nonetheless, male theorists may not see gender in society or its organizations because to do so would make explicit the ways current arrangements advantage men. Feminists conclude that this blindness toward male gender is rooted in power relations. To explore gender seriously is to explore the ways in which current structures and practices advantage men. Few male theorists find incentives to do so, even if they manage to see past "normal" male bias. Few female theorists were published in academic circles until recently, so even if they could see past "normal," they could not tell us about it. Nonetheless, gender implies a relationship: the masculine can only be known in relation to the feminine, and vice versa. Men and masculinity are gendered too.

Jeff Hearn and P. Wendy Parkin (1988) raise the question of gender in organizations. Both in an exhortation of concepts involved in "the sexuality of organization" and with empirical theory building, these authors unmask gender in organizations (Hearn, Sheppard, Tancred-Sheriff, and Burrell 1989). As Deborah Sheppard (1989, p. 142) aptly states,

> The notion of organizational structure as an objective, empirical and genderless reality is itself a gendered notion. In a structure where male dominance is taken for granted, the assumption of the invisibility of gender can be understood as an ideological position. It masks the extent to which organizational politics are premised on the dominance of one set of definitions and assumptions that are essentially gender based.

Based upon surveys of the treatment of gender within organization theory by Jeff Hearn and P. Wendy Parkin (1983, 1987, 1988), Burrell and Hearn (1989) argue that it is hard to avoid the conclusion that gender has either been ignored, treated implicitly as male, considered an organizational "variable," reduced to relative stereotypes, or analyzed in a blatantly sexist way. They go further to say that classics of organization theory such as Crozier's (1964) study of tobacco workers and power, and the Hawthorne experiments (Roethlisberger 1941) are implicit accounts of gender relations, yet they remain largely unexamined in organization theory.

Hearn, Parkin, and their colleagues have not been alone in seeing the gendered nature of organizations. In 1985, Kathy Ferguson offered a radical "feminist case against bureaucracy" using Michel Foucault's ideas on power and his approach to discourse analysis. More recently, sociologist Joan Acker (1990) explicitly worked to construct a theory of gendered organizations in which she illustrates the extent to which gender is an integral part of organizational processes, and that those processes cannot be properly understood without an analysis of gender. Though much of this work is based in private sector organizations,

Figure 7.1. **Exercise: On Seeing Gender**

Let's do a short exercise to help us "see" gender. The following clusters of factors represent behavioral styles of Arizona managers. The pattern in the left column is the most common; the pattern in the right column is the second most common behavioral pattern. They will be discussed later in the chapter. Your task is to come up with a one- or two-word descriptive label for each style.

Style I	Style II
managerial	attractive
competitive	affectionate
ambitious	opportunistic
assertive	
independent	
frank	
attractive	
interpersonal	

Style I:

What combinations stand out? A competitive, ambitious, independent male; one who is assertive, rather than aggressive, with a frank manner and good interpersonal skills; a manager who pays attention to his looks and who is attractive (and probably athletic). A touchy-feely, yuppie-type who belongs to the YMCA, and perhaps listens to self-help tapes. He tries hard to be the best manager he can be. He might accurately be labeled the "Consummate Manager" or the "Professional Manager."

Style II:

What stands out? The fact that this style has so few elements? A woman who uses her good looks to turn heads; one who freely expresses affection but perhaps does so instrumentally rather than genuinely? A woman who probably charms her way to the top, more like an interesting escort than a competent professional. The assistant a wife might worry about. She might be called a "Courtesan" but that has no place in public work. Her style might be labeled "Feminine Wiles."

After you have named each pattern of behavior, think about them again by switching the gender of the manager. Does the name you would give each also change? Do different impressions come to mind? How? Why? As you will read later, the above patterns describe women and men respectively, not men and women.

such patterns are likely no less true in state public agencies. In fact, given the "manliness" in Weber's thinking, and his influences on public organizations, public bureaucracies may actually be more gendered than others. Seeing the gender in state bureaucracies may prove difficult for many, however (see Figure 7.1).

The difficulty in analyzing gender in organizations rests largely in the overwhelming male advantage in the process of constructing orga-

Figure 7.2. **The Traits of Bureaucratic and Gender Stereotypes**

Gender Stereotypes	Bureaucratic stereotypes	
	Bureaucratic	Nonbureaucratic

Feminine	process-oriented
	do things "by the book"
		trusting
		attractive
		affectionate
		emotional
		skilled in
		    interpersonal
		    transactions

Masculine	predictable task-oriented loyal willing to use intimidation dominant managerial team-oriented	competitive creative independent ambitious assertive opportunistic risk-taking frank

(Reprinted from Georgia Duerst-Lahti and Cathy M. Johnson [1989], Gender, style and bureaucracy: must women go native to succeed? Paper presented at the Annual Meeting of the American Political Science Association, Atlanta, September, Figure 1. Used with permission of the authors.)

nizations. It is hard to see this, though, because masculine bias permeates organizations, and men have established what is "normal." Despite the shortcomings Burrell and Hearn critique, an overly simplistic analysis that relies on stereotypes can help us see this masculine bias. We used twenty-three behavioral traits drawn from a question on the survey to classify the traits according to gender and bureaucratic stereotypes. Bureaucratic stereotypes are derived from Anthony Downs's (1967, p. 99) "conservers." Due to the "Law of Increasing Conserverism," the vast majority of officials become conservers in the long run, and they are especially likely to be in the middle management ranks. Because gender stereotypes have been in flux, we relied upon pre–women's movement gender stereotypes in work settings. We then constructed a two-by-two overlay of them. Figure 7.2 shows the results.

Three things become clear from these stereotypes. First, most of the bureaucratic stereotypes are masculine, yet only about half of the male stereotypes overlapped with bureaucratic stereotypes. In fact, many of the masculine traits are nonbureaucratic *and* desirable to organizations, especially for their leaders; for example, being creative, independent, frank.

Second, few of these elements (seven of twenty-three) are stereo-typically feminine, and only two are consistent with bureaucratic ste-reotypes. This is not surprising inasmuch as "normal" characteristics required by adults have corresponded with male characteristics (Broverman, Broverman, Clarkson, Rosenkrantz, and Vogel 1970).

Third, traits may be associated with gender because of job segrega-tion rather than differences in behavior between men and women. The feminine traits of "process-oriented" and "do things by the book" cer-tainly are not exclusively female styles. Driven by concern for equity and accountability, all public bureaucracies include these elements; following rules—going by "the book"—is a major characteristic of Downs's "Conserver" behavior. As Kanter aptly demonstrated (1977), those in positions of limited power tend to rely heavily on rules regardless of gender. Because professional women have been clus-tered in positions lacking power resources, this trait has become associated with them, but the position, not gender, explains the stereo-type.

The view provided by Figure 7.2 illuminates a masculine bias in bureaucracies, at least as we commonly stereotype them. Yet an empir-ical analysis of the behavior of administrators in Wisconsin, one that included a gender-neutral category, revealed that stereotypically mas-culine traits did not prevail (Duerst-Lahti and Johnson 1990). These men and women used feminine traits as much as masculine ones. Gender-neutral traits were used most often by both women and men and were considered to be most important to the organization. This analysis demonstrates that bureaucratic stereotypes are ambiguous, and gender stereotypes require a context.

A closer look at the management literature reveals that interest in exploring gender in organizations coincides with the rise of the 1980s and 1990s wave of the women's movement, although explicit assump-tions of manliness clearly predate it. In any case, the increasing pres-ence of women in management positions disrupted and revealed social homogeneity or homosociality—"the seeking, enjoyment and/or pref-erence for the company of the same sex" (Lipman-Blumen 1984, p. 184). Homosociality does not imply sexual interaction, nor is it always con-scious or limited to men. In organizations, the critical dimension of the homosocial world of men and the homosocial world of women rests in the differential control of institutional resources and power. When men organize themselves homosocially, they have the resources to shape all relations whereas women's homosocial action largely affects other women only. The effects of such social homogeneity are especially pronounced in arenas of considerable uncertainty, where personal discretion is assumed and trust essential—as in management, for example (Kanter 1977). Thinkers began to question the relationship between gender and organizations.

Gender and Management Style

The gender of the manager has occasionally been part of management literature. Examples include the "organization man" (Whyte 1956), "bureaucratic man" (Kohn 1971), and "corporate man" (Jay 1972). Denhardt and Perkins even predicted the death of administrative man in 1976. Usually, however, managers were just assumed to be male and this assumption is telling for reasons detailed above. With a few early exceptions (Bowman et al. 1965; Cussler 1958; *Harvard Business Review* 1981), the serious contemplation of gender in organizations begins with Rosabeth Moss Kanter's work (1977), which focused on structural aspects of corporations, showing the ways homosocial processes operate within them. With men predominating, men were advantaged. A spate of books for women in management began with Harrigan (1977) and Hennig and Jardim (1977). The earliest of them advised women on how to learn the "games mother never taught you," or otherwise how to fit into extant organizational norms. Women learned how to present themselves as "promotable" (Carr-Ruffino 1985), but still confronted glass ceilings and began to bail out (Hymnowitz and Schellhardt 1986). As women explored gender in organizations, they began to realize that androgynous styles were insufficient (Arkkelin and Simmons 1985). Women could not simply emulate men's style and succeed, yet certain masculine traits seemed essential in organizations (e.g., Arnott 1988; Wiley and Eskilson 1982; Wong, Kettlewell, and Sproule 1985). The trick was to succeed in management without becoming one of the boys (Loden 1985). Jeff Hearn and others validly criticize early "sex-trait and variable" research. But because women entered the largely masculine domain of management, we needed at least some knowledge of sex traits in organizations. Thus, gender was used as a variable in organization studies. These studies serve as a vital first step both because they provide initial inquiries into the topic of organizations as gendered places and because the first women were subject to stereotypes.

Frequently, women entering management ranks pioneered alone, isolated and functioning as tokens. From research on token conditions (Kanter 1977, 1980; Ruble and Higgins 1976), we know that tokens face predictable dynamics: tokens operate in the limelight so all of their actions are highlighted. They are treated as symbols of their social category, which adds pressure because their success and failure reflects upon all (women) even though to have made it into an unusual spot likely means they are quite different from most (women) of their social category. Furthermore, stereotypical assumptions and mistaken attributions tend to force them into limited and caricatured roles. In addition, cultural boundaries tend to heighten in their presence. That is, nontokens (men) become more aware of their own commonalities, thereby further isolating tokens (women) and marginalizing their impact on important decisions. Being the single token (woman) proves most difficult. With a move to two tokens, dynamics dramatically alter again. As the spotlight is shared, divergent views make symbolically "speaking/acting on behalf of all" of the social category unrealistic, and having another like-person ameliorates isolation because it affords the possibility of "reality checks" with another to test one's perception. Kanter places 15 percent as a crucial threshold at which token conditions desist in the structurally rooted dynamics of organizational life and power. We will take this up further in the next chapter. Suffice it to say here that as more women enter male bastions, the bastions begin to budge, to change their gender ethos.

Nonetheless, progress for women occurs fastest in predictably gendered ways. Women are most likely to advance in those agencies and positions that are receptive to women because they are sex-appropriate (Falbo, Hazen, and Linimon 1982; Knight and Saal 1984; Larwood and Lockheed 1979), and women break few gender stereotypes by working on such issues as health, education, or welfare. Women are also likely to advance in positions that lack structural power resources (Bartol 1978; Smith and Grenier 1982). In Bartol's terms, they become "impotent tokens" who hold high-level positions, but their positions have a relatively small budget, few employees to supervise, and mainly routine decisions to make. Rarely do women lead major agencies, and even more rarely do a majority of women exist in top management. Be it a "glass ceiling" or a "bird cage," women seem not to make it out, in, or up—whatever is most valued—as well as men.

The numbers of women in management grow slowly, as the opening chapter reveals. Although the first women in positions generally had to adhere to the rules of conduct that spelled success for men, the second wave of women is moving up, and they are increasingly doing so by drawing on skills, attitudes, and experiences shared by women (Rosener 1990). The fact that some women are moving up *and* they are not fully mimicking men suggests that women who operate (more) on their own terms might indeed have something to offer organizations today. If women bring something new and useful to the workplace by drawing upon things associated with femaleness, then perhaps it is time to turn the question in *My Fair Lady* on its head and ask, "Why can't a man be more like a woman?" Notice that the well-known version of this phrase assumes women should be like men, thereby making men the norm.

Women and Style

Gender analysis implies comparison with other gender categories. However, it is also possible to think in terms of woman-centered analysis and man-centered analysis within the larger gendered context. The term "man-centered" reveals gender power. Many feminists contend that all of mainstream polity, society, and culture is man-centered, that is, "malestream." Suffice to say "man" has been used interchangeably with "human" for centuries, thereby erasing large portions of knowledge about "others." So, inevitably, to discuss women in organizations also means to discuss men as gendered beings. Here we focus explicitly and centrally on women—a case made necessary because they are (still) not advantaged and not "normally" found in top management. Nonetheless, we find claims that gender differences, and their complementarity, are beneficial to organizations. The gist of these writings can be captured in a few examples.

Sally Helgesen (1990), in a replication of Henry Mintzberg's work (1973), found a "female advantage" in management styles for contemporary organizations. Among Helgesen's findings is that women have a finely developed ability to communicate, to set priorities, and to see the broad picture. Their life experiences and socialization have forced them to integrate their lives and to shift roles easily. Both of these capacities result in an identity that is complex and multifaceted. In contrast, executive men's self-identities tend to be fused with, and dependent upon, their positions. Women executives also tend to see themselves as located in the center of a "web of inclusion" rather than on top of a hierarchy. By seeing oneself "in the middle of things," executive women can "reach out" to others in the organization, a vantage point more conducive to collaboration and the empowerment of others than that of a hierarchy where one must "reach down" to those below.

Patricia Lunneborg (1990) finds considerable evidence of "women's managerial potential." She makes a strong plea for a change in two spheres: in themes of "how-to-succeed" books that flourish in the popular press, and for those who dominate in the workplace—mostly men—to recognize and validate women's managerial potential. She suggests that the problem rests not in the inherent worth of the ways women work, because employers blatantly coopt women's capacity to manage and organize, but in men's unwillingness to promote or pay women for their contributions. In large part, the fact that men have structured organizations and defined management over time makes it possible to exploit but not reward women.

Lunneborg concludes that women's managerial potential stems from six elements of style. First, women's intuition about people means that they delight in discovering everyone's skills and they use this to match the right people to the right job. Second, they give people more praise than men typically do, and they do so publicly. Third, women are more likely to give orders "kindly," not because they are weak and indecisive but because asking politely involves others, helps to motivate them, and makes the workplace more supportive for all. As a wealth of literature reveals, women are expected to be more polite than men, and are punished for appearing to be too dominating (read "domineering"). In fact, women may be forced into this style because they are punished for acting "like a man." Some have argued that such approaches are also consistent with women's socialization and/or experiences as mothers. Fourth, as part of the "no 'us versus them'" philosophy, women are more sensitive to subordinates' needs. Dimensions include seeing problems from the staff's point of view, believing that if you take care of your people, they will take care of you, and in some instances changing the criteria for determining managers. Fifth, compromise and conciliation are more prevalent among women because they focus on problem solving more than on zero-sum game playing where someone must lose. They also prepare better for decision meetings, sense when the group is prepared to move, and try not to waste time (Duerst-Lahti 1990). Finally, teamwork, built upon a foundation of trust and openness is key. While men develop teams around the strengths of a single great talent with rules to govern the roles of each position (Loden 1985), women form teams as a natural result of acknowledging individual weaknesses, and recognizing the need to depend upon others to compensate for them. Talking, avoiding (artificial) structural barriers, and keeping everyone involved fosters loyalty and brings fulfillment.

Judy Rosener (1990) also looked at the ways women managers lead through a survey of all members of The International Women's Forum. Her findings support those of Lunneborg and Helgesen. Although she is careful to point out that the "interactive leadership" style is not biologically connected to women, the women she surveyed exhibit a pattern that differs from the command-and-control style commonly associated with men. Rosener identifies three major elements of these women's style. The first is that they encourage participation by trying to instill a group identity through shared decision making. Second, these women also share power and information rather than guarding it. Advantages to this approach are increased loyalty, enhanced communication, catching problems before they explode, and providing the wherewithal to reach conclusions, solve problems, and understand justifications for decisions. A related development is that employees come to expect bosses to be open and frank. The third element is simultaneously fostered by, and a consequence of, the prior elements: managers enhance the self-worth of others in large part by refraining from "asserting their own superiority, which asserts the inferiority of others" (Rosener 1990, p. 123). They also publicly praise good work, and take time "to celebrate ourselves." Finally, these women energize others by expressing their enthusiasm for work, and by developing credibility to do so through achieving easily measured results.

Rosener clearly calls for recognition of "another kind of diversity" because these women demonstrate that more than one kind of style can be successful. And, she echoes the above authors and other management thinkers such as Rosabeth Moss Kanter (1989a) and Peter Drucker (in Helgesen 1990) who suggest that "interactive leadership may emerge as the management style of choice for many organizations . . .

as the work force increasingly demands participation and the economic environment increasingly requires rapid change" (Rosener 1990, p. 125).

At the same time, Rosener cautions,

> For interactive leadership to take root more broadly, however, organizations must be willing to question the notion that the traditional command-and-control leadership style that has brought success in earlier decades is the only way to get results. This may be hard in some organizations, especially those with long histories of male-oriented, command-and-control leadership. Changing these organizations will not be easy. The fact that women are more likely than men to be interactive leaders raises the risk that these companies will perceive interactive leadership as "feminine" and automatically resist it. [Rosener 1990, p. 125]

This caution recognizes the predominance of men in organizations today, their advantage in determining the "right way," and as Lunneborg claims, men's unwillingness to share their power.

However, another caution may be in order as well. Ann Morrison, Randall White, and Ellen Van Velsor (1987) show that the obstacles women find result, at least in part, because such literature exaggerates the differences between women's and men's actual behavior. To discuss the female advantage is to risk (re)creation of stereotypes. Stereotypes have been, and too often still are, used to prove why women cannot work in certain units. While common observation suggests that the problem of stereotyping is lessening in general, and it probably is, the nature of problems for executive women may more accurately be thought of as transformed.

Morrison and her colleagues conclude that the "female managers had to contradict the stereotypes that their male bosses and co-workers had about women—they had to be seen as 'better than women' as a group" (Morrison et al. 1987, p. 20). Consistent with the analysis from the Wisconsin sample (Duerst-Lahti and Johnson 1990), anti-stereotypes seem to operate: women must avoid traits associated with women. And also consistent with our analysis, Morrison, White, and Van Velsor illustrate another layer of complexity. Women, they found, must constantly monitor their behavior to be neither too masculine nor too feminine—a situation that narrows the range of possibilities for women considerably. Even more distressingly, they found that women executives faced contradictory expectations as a result. For example, they must take risks, but be consistently outstanding. Frequently this meant both taking more risks than men, and being as competent as the best man (Morrison et al. 1987). Women were to be tough, but not macho. Often this was accomplished by being straightforward and frank, being very controlled, demanding results from subordinates, and taking the initiative. They also were to be ambitious, but were not to expect equal treatment. Family was definitely to come second, if at all. They should prove their abilities but not expect the same salary or titles. Finally, women were to accept full accountability for their own actions, yet they were praised for listening to and following the advice of men. In the end, despite the fact that women and men are remarkably similar,

> stereotypical perceptions have led to unrealistic expectations of executive women, and these expectations are part of the environment in which the women must work and live. This environment is qualitatively different from the environment executive men operate in, and this difference may be the crucial—and the only meaningful—one between male and female executives. [Morrison et al. 1987, p. 26]

The problem then follows from stereotypes, and the fact that men overwhelmingly dominate top positions in organizations, more so than anything women do or do not do. Under such conditions, the behaviors of women, and their utility for the organization, are less important than counteracting the stereotypes. These findings on women's style introduce important questions, especially given the evolution of state bureaucracies and the place of women in them. We face an interesting juncture: How important is style? Does women's style offer advantages? What kind of advantages does being male offer? What can be attributed to gender, and what to political context? To other factors?

Stereotypes and the States

The simplest way to explore gender is to see how the women and men of the states answered the same question. Respondents in three states were asked to think about the behavioral styles used within their organization and indicate the extent to which each characterized their style (1 = not characteristic; 5 = very characteristic).

Comparing the means by sex for all three states, the most striking fact is the degree of similarity. As Table 7.1 reveals, women and men can be distinguished on only three of twenty-two behaviors when the

Table 7.1

Behavioral Traits by Gender and State

	Alabama		Arizona		Wisconsin	
	Women	Men	Women	Men	Women	Men
Competitive	3.5 *	3.8	3.4 *	3.7	3.4	3.5
Creative	3.8	3.9	3.9	3.9	3.4 *	3.9
Processor	3.6	3.6	3.7 *	3.4	3.6	3.5
Predictable	3.5	3.5	3.3	3.5	3.4	3.4
Task-oriented	3.9	3.9	3.8	3.9	4.0 *	3.8
Loyal	4.5	4.5	4.4	4.3	4.1	4.2
Intimidating	2.0 *	2.3	2.2	2.1	2.1	2.1
Independent	4.5 *	4.0	4.3 *	3.5	4.2 *	4.0
Dominant	3.1	2.9	3.2	3.0	3.0	3.0
Managerial	4.0	4.0	3.5 *	3.7	3.6	3.5
Ambitious	3.8	3.9	3.8	3.7	3.8	3.6
Trusting	3.8	3.9	3.6	3.8	3.6	3.8
Assertive	4.1 *	3.7	4.0 *	3.8	3.8	3.7
Attractive	3.3 *	2.8	3.2 *	2.8	3.1 *	2.5
Affectionate	3.1 *	2.8	3.1 *	2.7	2.9 *	2.6
Opportunistic	2.7	3.0	2.9	2.9	2.5 *	2.9
Risk-taking	3.1	3.4	3.6	3.5	3.1 *	3.4
Interpersonal	4.0 *	3.7	3.9	3.8	3.8 *	3.5
Frank	4.1	4.2	4.2	4.1	4.0	4.0
Team-oriented	4.1	4.1	4.1	4.0	4.1 *	3.9
By-the-book	3.1	3.1	2.8	2.7	2.8	2.7
Emotional	na	na	na	na	2.7	2.7

* $p < 0.05$

results are studied across the states. We find only "independent," "attractive," and "affectionate" showing significant gender differences in all the states. Women gave higher rankings to these variables in each of the states. In contrast, on no single factor did men report higher ratings than women across the states. Overwhelmingly, women and men at the top of the states act the same.

Nonetheless, these three differences offer interesting insights into gender in organizations and society. For example, the fact that women report being more independent might simply reflect their token conditions: women cannot rely on a network as much as men because homosociality excludes them from central aspects of networks available to management men. Sex-segregated job structures exacerbate this isolation. Less obvious is the extent to which women who make it to upper management have to break the expectation (stereotype), and the ideology accompanying it, that women *should* be dependent. Hence, a woman at this level may be no more independent than her male counterparts, but she is considerably more independent than most women. Independence is itself engendered; its meaning shifts with the sex of the one to whom it is applied.

"Attractive" as a variable of style works similarly. As psychological studies show, attractive people are seen as more competent in general than unattractive people. However, being attractive is central for women in a way that is not so for men. Women have been classified as "body" and not mind at least since Aristotle's time (Jaggar and Bordo 1989). The problems of sexual harassment discussed by Rita Mae Kelly and Phoebe Morgan Stambaugh in chapter 6 have roots in women's sexual objectification. Yet women are also rewarded for being feminine, and working to make oneself attractive is part of femininity (Brownmiller 1984). So women are in the catch-22 of focusing on physical attractiveness in order to meet expectations and to reap the rewards; however, in the process, they risk being accused of "asking for" harassment or otherwise acting in a nonmanagerial fashion.

Masculinity bars men from public displays of affection, and the state agency workplace is public in more ways than one. So, we might readily expect women to score higher on being affectionate. Again though, one is left to ponder a pattern in which women are expected to do the emotional work of organizations, and then find that they are taken less seriously because organizations do not reward such displays.

In a more sensitive analysis, we considered differences in the styles of women and men in the upper and middle ranges of Arizona and Wisconsin. We wanted to explore the possibility that gender differences were hidden when we looked at the overall sample but became apparent when we compared men and women holding positions of similar rank. Thus, we divided the Arizona and Wisconsin samples into two groups: in the upper-level group are those at the very pinnacle of state service, while the middle-level group includes middle-level professionals (see Table 7.2). Because Alabama does not distinguish civil servants by range, the responses from that state could not be included in this analysis.

Again, we see few differences between women and men across the states. In the upper levels we found ten traits with significant gender differences in either state, yet only the traits "trusting" and "attractive" produced differences in both states. Men reported that they were more

Table 7.2

Comparison of Middle and Upper Levels

	Wisconsin		Arizona	
	Women	Men	Women	Men
Middle-level managers				
Competitive	3.4	3.3	3.2 *	3.6
Creative	3.4 *	3.9	3.9	3.9
Process-oriented	3.6	3.5	3.9 *	3.4
Task-oriented	4.0 *	3.7	3.7	3.9
Intimidating	2.1	2.0	1.9 *	2.3
Independent	4.2	4.0	4.3 *	4.0
Managerial	3.5	3.4	3.3 *	3.6
Ambitious	3.8 *	3.5	3.6	3.7
Attractive	3.1 *	2.6	3.2 *	2.8
Affectionate	2.9 *	2.6	3.2 *	2.7
Opportunistic	2.5 *	2.9	3.0	3.0
Risk-taking	3.0 *	3.3	3.4	3.2
Upper-level managers				
Competitive	3.6 *	4.0	3.7	3.8
Intimidating	1.9 *	2.3	2.3	2.2
Independent	4.2	4.0	4.3 *	4.0
Trusting	3.4 *	3.8	3.5 *	3.9
Assertive	4.1	4.0	4.1 *	3.8
Attractive	3.2 *	2.7	3.2 *	2.9
Opportunistic	2.6 *	3.1	2.7	2.9
Interpersonal skills	4.1 *	3.7	4.1	3.8
Frank	4.4 *	4.1	4.3	4.2
Emotional	2.1 *	2.5	na	na

$*p < 0.05$

trusting, and women gave greater weight to attractiveness. If the system is more comfortable for men at the top, it is not surprising that they are more trusting than women. In attractiveness, again, we see that women still must be concerned about their appearance even if it bears no relevance to the situation. At the middle level, only the traits "attractive" and "affectionate" had gender differences in both states, while twelve traits showed significant differences in either state.

Women and men of the state agencies are far more alike than different. In light of this information, it is difficult to claim that women do not hold top positions because they behave differently than men. Behavioral traits, often understood as gender stereotypes, provide little understanding of the dearth of women in top management. Why is it, then, that women and men are so disparately represented at the top?

Range, Hierarchy, Advantage

Perhaps women are not at the top because incumbent administrators prefer masculine traits, and they unconsciously (or otherwise) attribute feminine traits to women regardless of actual behavior. That is, women are not at the top because they are assumed to be feminine, and feminine behavior is not valued in administrators. However, advantage should accrue to whoever best fits the traits preferred in those at the top; understanding such preferences is therefore important if one wants to advance, especially if stereotypes cloud perceptions of actual behavior. And, given the dearth of women at the top, contrasting men's and women's views of preferred traits might help us understand if women are missing at the top because their notion of "good" administration differs from that of their male counterparts. Such analysis also may reveal the extent to which women are pressured to assume certain (masculine) behaviors if they are to share the advantages at the top. A comparison of those who have made it to the top with those who have not should help us untangle elements of gender from aspects of range or position, as well as show us the ways top positions might themselves be gendered. All of these approaches should reveal dynamics of range, hierarchy, and advantage.

In order to assess what women and men in public bureaucracies prefer in those whom they work with and under, we devised a list of twenty-six traits. Some traits are associated stereotypically with one or the other gender, and some are gender-neutral. The list of traits is a modified version of those studied by psychologists Arnie Cann and William Siegfried, Jr. (1987). They tested thirty-six traits, with twelve traits in each category. We eliminated traits with the lowest ranking (most of which were feminine; for example, submissive, gentle, mild, dependent), and recategorized "tactful," "helpful," and "sincere" as feminine traits based upon Loden's work (1985). This afforded more female traits relevant to the workplace and a sufficient number for comparison. Respondents were asked to indicate the extent to which each trait was important to "good" administrators and colleagues. Although this question was administered only in Wisconsin, it provides a

Figure 7.3. **Importance of Traits in Bureaucracies: Wisconsin**

Gender of trait	Unimportant	Somewhat important	Important	Very important
neutral				efficient
neutral				truthful
neutral				conscientious
neutral				adaptable
neutral				reliable
feminine				sincere
neutral			predictable	
feminine			appreciative	
feminine			tactful	
feminine			compassionate	
feminine			helpful	
feminine			understanding	
masculine			independent	
masculine			analytical	
masculine			ambitious	
masculine			assertive	
masculine			systematic	
masculine			competitive	
feminine		sensitive		
masculine		dominant		
masculine		tough		
masculine		forceful		
masculine		aggressive		
feminine	excitable			
feminine	sentimental			

(Adapted from Georgia Duerst-Lahti and Cathy M. Johnson [1990], Gender and style in bureaucracy, *Women & Politics,* 10[4]: 67–120, with permission from Haworth Press, Inc.)

solid empirical indication of traits preferred in a "good" public manager.

As shown in Figure 7.3, we established degrees of importance and categorized traits according to the importance that respondents attached to the trait in order for someone (regardless of his or her sex) to be judged a good administrator. Placement was fully consistent across respondents for all but six traits, suggesting that men and women generally agree on what traits are important. Traits in the "important" and "very important" categories are considered consequential in bureaucracies; traits in the unimportant and somewhat important categories are considered to be of limited utility. This approach provides the broadest possible measure of "good" administrators and colleagues, and it captures the perspective of both sexes.

The major finding of this analysis is that if those who manage bureaucracies ever preferred predominantly masculine traits, they no longer do, at least by this measure. Contrary to expectations, masculine traits do not dominate, and feminine traits are clearly valued. Six of ten masculine traits and six of nine feminine traits rate as consequential, in that they are rated as important or very important. Gender-neutral traits, rather than traits with a gender bias, are valued most in the consequential categories of "important" and "very important." Only one of the seven gender-neutral traits is not consequential; five fall in the "very important" category. The findings weaken theories purporting the masculinity of bureaucracies.

Two concomitant dynamics may explain these findings. First, more women now hold upper-level administrative positions and their presence has affected norms (Duerst-Lahti 1987). Some of that change is consciously brought about by feminists, some is due to the "new" perspectives women add, and some simply follow from mixed-sex groups rather than all male groups. Important thresholds in the structure of the work force, as delineated by Kanter (1977), have been crossed and the work environment has changed accordingly. Second, gender stereotypes themselves are changing. Expected norms for each gender seem to be broadening and loosening and more traits are deemed "gender-neutral." Technological, functional, and economic transformations may necessitate workplace changes more suited to feminine traits as well. While we cannot tell here if the organization rewards these particular traits, we do know that respondents value neutral traits most, and they value masculine and feminine traits about equally. From this we can make a case that few distinctions should be made on the basis of stereotypes in terms of utility for an organization. Some gender differences exist, however.

Table 7.3 reveals several insights about gender and beliefs about good administrators from the Wisconsin sample. Respondents were asked how important each trait was to good administrators. (Responses ranged from 1 = very unimportant to 10 = very important. The number of female respondents ranged from 159 to 161. The number of male respondents ranged from 223 to 225.) First, all of the stereotypical feminine traits of statistical interest are preferred more by men than by women. Men, more than women, want top-level administrators to be understanding, helpful, sentimental, and excitable. In fact, mean scores

Table 7.3

Traits Important for Good Administrators: Wisconsin

	Women	Men	Difference
Feminine			
Sincere	8.6	8.8	−0.2
Appreciative	8.2	8.3	−0.1
Tactful	8.4	8.3	0.1
Compassionate	7.3	7.4	−0.1
Excitable	2.8	3.4	−0.6*
Helpful	7.8	8.2	−0.4
Sensitive	7.5	7.7	−0.2
Understanding	7.9	8.4	−0.5*
Sentimental	2.6	3.8	−1.2*
Masculine			
Dominant	5.6	5.9	−0.3
Independent	7.7	7.5	0.2
Analytical	8.1	7.6	0.5*
Assertive	8.5	8.0	0.5*
Tough	6.3	6.2	0.1
Forceful	6.4	6.5	−0.1
Ambitious	7.0	7.3	−0.3
Aggressive	5.6	6.4	−0.8*
Competitive	6.5	7.0	−0.5
Systematic	7.1	6.9	0.2
Neutral			
Efficient	8.8	8.4	0.4*
Predictable	6.9	7.2	−0.3
Truthful	9.2	9.4	−0.2
Conscientious	9.1	9.1	0.0
Adaptable	8.6	8.7	−0.1
Reliable	9.1	9.2	−0.1
Conventional	4.2	4.7	−0.5*

*$p < 0.05$

Source: Adapted from Georgia Duerst-Lahti and Cathy Marie Johnson (1990), Gender and style in bureaucracy, *Women & Politics* 10(4): 67–120, with permission from Haworth Press, Inc.

indicate that men believe good administrators should exhibit more feminine traits than do women for eight of the nine traits. Second, for the ten masculine traits, those of statistical interest divide between the sexes. Women believe more than men that good administrators should be analytical and assertive. Men believe more than women that administrators should be aggressive. Third, for traits considered stereotypically neutral, women believe significantly more in efficiency and men in being conventional.

The pattern for gender as it relates to these traits reveals anti-stereotypes more than stereotypes. Men are more likely than women to want administrators to exhibit feminine traits. Women score only one of the feminine traits higher, and even then the difference is not significant. Men also prefer gender-neutral traits more than do women, and women prefer the same number of masculine traits as do men.

Two related explanations come to mind. Men have greater latitude in traits deemed "good" generally and confer that freedom to top administrators. And, women have been punished for being female/feminine, or at a minimum have been coached not to draw attention to their femaleness; hence their beliefs about good administrators now deny the feminine. Women appear to hold administrators more to a masculine standard than do men! In light of the findings of Morrison, White, and Van Velsor (1987) and their colleagues this finding is not surprising. Yet this also would seem to undermine others' arguments about a female advantage—that the way women executives approach their work actually offers special rewards for the organization. Or does it?

The choice of traits each sex prefers paints two different pictures of good administrators. For women, a good administrator is efficient, assertive, tactful, and analytical—all traits of consequence in bureaucracies. Men prefer the following traits more: understanding, competitive, aggressive, conventional, sentimental, and excitable—mostly traits that are of limited utility. Arguably, these significant differences show that women want administrators who think things through and then involve others in a way that does not offend but that accomplishes ends as quickly as possible. On the other hand, men prefer administrators who are sympathetic and tolerant of them as they enthusiastically, perhaps even belligerently, pursue a contest played by customary rules they view with some nostalgia. Paradoxically, this coupling of emotive feminine traits with combative masculine traits may manifest itself as "the machismo that drives women out" (Loden 1986) or the "games mother never taught you" (Harrigan 1977). The most meaningful insight from these findings is that women attend more to traits of consequence in organizations than men do. The female advantage may be just that: women focus on behaviors of consequence more than men.

Earlier we found anti-stereotypes causing women to hold administrators more to a masculine standard than do men. A crucial, and too

Table 7.4

What Separates the Men from the Boys and the Women from the Girls?

	Women				Men			
	Arizona		Wisconsin		Arizona		Wisconsin	
	Upper	Middle	Upper	Middle	Upper	Middle	Upper	Middle
Competitive	3.7 *	3.2	3.6	3.4	3.8	3.6	4.0 *	3.4
Creative	3.9	3.9	3.8 *	3.4	4.0	3.9	3.8	3.9
Process-oriented	3.5 *	3.9	3.6	3.6	3.4	3.4	3.4	3.5
Predictable	3.3	3.4	3.5	3.5	3.4 *	3.6	3.3	3.4
Intimidating	2.3	1.9	1.9	2.1	2.2	2.3	2.3 *	2.0
Dominant	3.4	3.1	3.4 *	3.0	3.1 *	2.8	3.3 *	2.9
Managerial	3.8 *	3.3	4.2 *	3.5	3.8 *	3.6	4.0 *	3.4
Ambitious	4.0	3.6	3.8	3.8	3.7	3.7	3.9 *	3.5
Assertive	4.1	3.8	4.1 *	3.7	3.8 *	3.6	4.0 *	3.6
Risk taking	3.8	3.4	3.9 *	3.0	3.7 *	3.2	3.7 *	3.3
Interpersonal skills	4.1	3.7	4.1 *	3.7	3.8	3.7	3.7	3.6
Frank	4.3	4.1	4.4 *	4.0	4.2	4.1	4.1	4.0
By-the-book	2.8	2.6	2.3 *	2.9	2.6 *	3.0	2.5 *	2.8
Emotional	na	na	2.1 *	2.8	na	na	2.5	2.7

*$p > 0.05$

often ignored, question becomes, "What might be attributed to gender, and what to range?" Through reports of self-behavior, we compared people in the middle and top ranges of Arizona and Wisconsin by sex. This analysis might be thought of as examining what separates the "men from the boys" and the "women from the girls." (The metaphor might strike your ear as odd for women, thereby illustrating the gendered quality of such concepts.) Because women operate in token or minority conditions and are relative newcomers to top jobs, it is impossible to know whether the same hierarchical behaviors would be true if women dominated organizations throughout society. These findings can show us how range interacts with gender, though.

Table 7.4 includes the fourteen traits that produced statistically significant differences between the sexes as shown in Table 7.1. Here comparisons are shown between those in middle- and upper-level positions. Note that no trait shows differences by management rank in both states for just men or just women. That is, when we look by range, we find no equivalent to the persistent gendered meaning of attractiveness for women, although women's greater use of interpersonal skills and frank discussion comes close. Rather, we find that several traits seem to distinguish those at the top from those at the middle regardless of sex. While only "managerial" proves statistically significant in separating men and women from boys and girls in both states, clearly "assertive," "dominant," "risk-taking," and "by-the-book" move in that direction. In other words, we can expect to find as many, if not more, traits that distinguish behavior at the top from the middle than we find to distinguish by sex of respondent. Note also that these traits have commonly been attributed to men, suggesting that the top is indeed gendered.

If women at the top find as much in common with men at the top as with women below them, then why are so few women in top positions? The answer lies in at least two arenas: power structures, and the advantages that accompany them, and in the tremendous diversity among women and among men, along with the various behaviors each of us employs situationally. Although the preceding discussion of the female advantage literature shows how power interacts with questions of gender, let us briefly consider intragender diversity first.

Beyond Traits and Stereotypes

The preceding analysis reveals the extent to which *beliefs* about differences between the genders—stereotypes—exaggerate differences where only a few exist. Women and men are not uniform and distinct groups. As Maccoby and Jacklin (1974) demonstrated nearly twenty years ago, males and females behave much more the same than differently. And, as Virginia Sapiro (1983) illuminated, "women are no more of like mind than are men." Rooted in life experiences that vary by race, class, family life, region, and so forth, individuals develop different standpoints and face differing vantages. And personalities permutate endlessly. Individuals are unique. Furthermore, the same person employs differing styles in various circumstances. Presumably, all of these influences result in unique and multifaceted management styles as well.

Still, the writings on women's style difference resonate as true even though simple trait analysis reveals few divergences at best. This may be because gender operates through patterns of behavior much more than through single traits. Rita Mae Kelly (1991) and her colleagues Mary Hale and Jayne Burgess (Kelly, Hale, and Burgess 1991) use

Table 7.5

Behavioral Patterns of Upper-Level Administrators in Arizona

Women		Men	
Label	Factors*	Label	Factors*
Attractive Manager		Boss	
24.0%	+managerial +independent +competitive +ambitious +assertive +frank +attractive +interpersonal	23.8%	+independent +assertive +creative +risk-taking +dominant +competitive +ambitious
Entrepreneur		Manipulative Opportunist	
38.2%	−by-the-book +risk-taking +creative −predictable	33.7%	+affectionate +attractive +opportunistic
Gentle One		Loyalist	
51.4%	+loyal −intimidating +affectionate +trusting	41.3%	+trusting +frank +loyal
Individualistic Opportunist		Coach	
59.6%	−team-oriented +opportunistic	48.8%	−team-oriented +managerial +interpersonal
Processor		Bureaucrat	
65.4%	+process-oriented −dominant	54.5%	+process-oriented +task-oriented +predictable +by-the-book
Task Master		Intimidator	
70.8%	+task-oriented	59.4%	+intimidating

*Factors indicate variables in the rotated factor matrix. Percentages indicate the amount of variance explained.

factor analysis to move beyond traits and stereotypes. They suggest that the ways various traits form patterns of overall style reveal greater gender difference than simple trait analysis. This approach also highlights the difficulty women face in trying to adopt or accommodate a masculine mode of behavior in order to fit expectations of those at the top.

Applying factor analysis to the behavior of upper-level men and women, Kelly, Hale, and Burgess uncovered six patterns of behavior for both genders. They gave each factor a descriptive label, shown in Table 7.5. The patterns for women are the *Attractive Manager, Entrepreneur, Gentle One, Individualistic Opportunist, Processor,* and *Task Master.* For men, the patterns emerge as the *Boss, Manipulative Opportunist, Loyalist, Coach, Bureaucrat,* and *Intimidator.*

Clearly, women and men exhibit a range of styles. Women's styles are more consistent and perhaps constrained than men's. These six patterns account for 71 percent of the variance among women and 60 percent among men. Of greater importance, given these labels and the behaviors they represent, both sexes have patterns that are more and less useful to organizations, and dimensions that suit some circumstances better than others.

The way we interpret behavior, however, continues to provide male advantage. Remember the exercise "on seeing gender" in Figure 7.1? You were asked to derive a descriptive label for two of these factors, the Attractive Manager and the Manipulative Opportunist, but we intentionally reversed the sex of the style pattern. We presented the cluster of traits for the Attractive Manager as though they derived from male managers. Because attractiveness seems less relevant for men, it is easy to label the very same cluster of traits "the Professional Manager" when applied to men. The Manipulative Opportunist, on the other hand, becomes Feminine Wiles when applied to women—a very unflattering combination of traits that suggests a woman who "sleeps her way to the top." It is striking that the second most common pattern for men clearly resembles the worst stereotype about women. And it is especially troublesome considering that these survey data exhibit no comparable behavior pattern for women.

Beliefs, rooted in gender systems, often prove more powerful than actual behavior. As Ann Morrison and her colleagues caution, discussing the female advantage solely in terms of style is reductionistic and can be very misleading. It is useful to understand patterns of behavior and the gender variation within them. It is also necessary to recognize the diversity of styles among women and among men. But it is critical to acknowledge the strength of gendered assumptions that shape our interpretation of the very same behavior.

The earlier chapters reveal just how dismally disproportionate the sex ratios are in top levels of administration. Can it be that an "Attractive Manager" is of so much less worth to an organization than "the Boss?" The explanation for differential representation in top levels must be rooted in something other than actual style. As Ortner (1974) pointed out, whatever women do, even if it is the same thing that men do elsewhere, is valued less than those things conventionally done by men. Power relations, and the access those with more power have to a multitude of resources found throughout the social system, best explain why women remain under-represented at the top.

Gender, Power, and Access to Structural Resources

A few authors have begun to investigate the intersection of gender, power, and access to structural resources. Critical here is the recognition of the systemic and institutionalized nature of men's power advantage. From an extensive review of literature, Belle Rose Ragins and Eric Sundstrom (1989) constructed a sophisticated conceptualization of the intersection of gender and power in organizations. They use four levels of analysis. Similar to Gary Powell (1988), they find that men are consistently favored in the accumulation of resources for power at critical junctures of career development. Women's paths to power, alternatively, resemble an obstacle course. If we are to make sense of men's apparent advantage in organizations, and the apparent inability for a critical mass of women to reach the top, we must broaden our focus beyond style. Structures of power—both inside and outside organizations—determine the value given to any particular style, not the style itself. Perhaps even, studies of style such as this one detract us from pursuing the critical facets of power that disadvantage women. Ragins and Sundstrom argue that the differences in the path to power for women and men reflect the many small influences of social systems, organizations, and interpersonal relationships. As such, "it is misleading to compare male and female managers without taking account of the development of their careers" (1989, p. 53). Their findings definitely point away from style as *the* explanation for gender power differentials in organizations.

Consider the advantage that might accrue to men in public organizations from elements of the social system such as sex-role socialization, training and education, economic pressures, gender roles and stereotypes, and role conflict. If organizations assume, reward, and even institutionalize socialization based upon men's participation in sports or the military (for example, veterans' preference points), then women must surmount obstacles. Role conflict is less for men if organizations assume private life and work can be separated.

Within organizations, where, when, and how one enters remains crucial for promotion. The recruitment, selection, and hiring practices become essential in sex-segregated workplaces. Opportunities for training, performance appraisal, and tracking also figure into promotion possibilities. Such activities inevitably take place through the lens of gender and the employer's interpretation of employees. Is assertiveness read as "appropriate" for men and annoying for women? More important, where did gender lead one to enter as a personnel officer or a budget analyst? How much power does the position have? Ragins and Sundstrom report on studies by Harlan and Weiss (1982), Kanter (1977), Strober (1982), and Wolf and Fligstein (1979), showing that women, compared to men, have less access to supplies, information, and support. Furthermore, the authors reiterate many of the arguments made above. Hiring policies are more likely to lead women into positions of limited structural power. And if women surmount pressures to take lesser-valued feminine jobs, they encounter the even more difficult contamination effect. A powerful position is likely to lose power once a woman enters it both because men are more likely to attain the power associated with a position, and because the perceived prestige of a job varies more when the incumbent is a woman.

At the interpersonal level, Ragins and Sundstrom point to the critical role of *perceptions* in fulfilling the hypothesis of "power begets power" for men. Through conflicts in expectations and roles, the prevalence of male prototypes (idealized mental images or cognitive categories that specify expectations of someone in a role) in organizations, and differential gender attributions of success, women are not expected to be as competent or as powerful as men. As a result, relationships relevant to power—those with supervisors, subordinates, and peers—become interdependent and mutually reinforcing. With men having structural power advantages, homosociality makes interpersonal relationships synergistic for men's increased power. In other words, male interpersonal relationships provide advantages.

At the individual level, Ragins and Sundstrom (1989) conclude that modest gender style differences exist, but that these are based more on situational differences than on gender. However, as we have illustrated throughout, gender makes the situation different as women and men are understood and advantaged according to gender. They conclude that "women who have succeeded in achieving powerful positions may differ from other populations, both male and female" (Ragins and Sundstrom 1989, p. 81). In other words, they constitute in large part a third gender in the workplace. Yet, at an individual level such women still face conventional feminine gender expectations and stereotypes.

Re-thinking Gender, Style, and Advantage

Organizations in general, and public bureaucracies specifically, are not neutral turf in regard to gender. Some styles are valued more than others, and women seem to attend more to the behaviors of consequence. Yet, differences as measured by trait analysis are minimal between women and men. Of greater interest are the many ways behaviors combine to make style. But, with few women in top positions and few "at the table" to interpret the worth of particular combinations, women's styles, whatever they may be, may not be judged as being valuable. Advantage may have less to do with one's style and more to do with one's gender.

As much of this analysis reveals, how women act is less important than who is doing the acting. We contend that gender power is the issue. For example, recent organizational studies suggest that intuition, flexibility, interpersonal communication—skills and behaviors commonly associated with women—now converge with the demands of postindustrial organizations. These circumstances should suit women well. Advantages should flow to whoever performs well, to whoever does what works best.

However, given the gender power arrangements of public bureaucracies, two things are likely to happen within the microcosm of style. First, women cannot validate a "feminine" style on their own; men must adopt it if it is to be recognized as worthwhile. So, one might think that if men do the same thing that women do, then women using that approach could also move into top positions. However, then we encounter the second problem. Style is defined by the gender of the actor more so than by the behavior itself. Women and men largely do the same things but are understood by their gender. What men do is perceived as more valuable and hence they have the advantage. So when men adopt a style, it becomes tHE way to proceed; and frequently a "new iron cage of rationality" is built around tHE style in a way that curtails women's full power. The move from tough, rational, command-and-control approaches to those based on intuition, communication, and flexibility suggests the dynamics of gender power.

We are playing with words here not to suggest an etymological root, but rather because we are attempting to illustrate gender tension in "tHE" and "tHEy" in public bureaucracies. As long as men have advantages in organization leadership and elsewhere in the polity, their homosocial choices provide differential resources to women and men. Women's style matters much less than men's perception of it. Unacknowledged gendered perceptions will cloud understandings and the ability to act in a fair manner. We must work toward a situation in which all participants in organization life understand that gender is integral to organization processes. If this magic moment occurs, women's style might actually help transform organizations.

From Gender-neutral to Transgendered

When we presented data in Table 7.3 according to gender stereotypes, we added a category for "gender-neutral," a term that denotes a condition in which either gender might use the trait or skill with equal facility. However, such a position decontextualizes the act itself (Steuernagel 1989). For example, assertiveness serves to illustrate the problem of gender-neutrality in traits. Women have long been discouraged from displays of aggression, and management women have been coached heavily in assertiveness (Carr-Ruffino 1985). In fact, studies reveal many negative consequences for women who display aggressive behavior. Hence, assertiveness, a male stereotype in 1970, has become increasingly associated with women, as Table 7.3 illustrates.

Yet, gender enters through interpretation in another important way as well. A woman who behaves assertively is likely to be labeled aggressive, that is, pushy, demanding, threatening, or just plain annoying—someone who does not know her place. The same assertive behavior by a man is likely to win him points for his tact and interpersonal skill (traits that are essential to women in professional roles). He will probably be rewarded for not acting aggressively when he could have.

Aggressive displays are perceived much differently for women than for men. Women might be seen as aggressive when they forcefully stand their ground, whereas the same behavior by a man would be interpreted as assertive. Precisely because women have not conventionally been thought of as standing up for themselves in the workplace, any strong behavior might be interpreted in accordance with conventional feminine expectations. This poses great problems for management women when other women in the workplace work largely in care functions due to job segregation.

So, women must behave differently than men in some ways in order to be as effective as men because culture has molded sex differences into gender differences. We must make the nonconscious conscious, and maintain constant vigilance if we are to avoid treating women and men according to gender expectations. Due to the predominance of gender in the polity, no act now is fully gender-neutral. Even when individuals try to surmount gender barriers, tHE legal, cultural, and thought structures impede tHEir efforts. We need to uncouple difference from dominance.

If we want to know more about how advantage works in organizations, then style is the wrong unit of analysis, especially when considered in the absence of other factors. Even with some modest differences in behavior patterns, women perform well by new standards; some men have noticed it and laud the behaviors. The trouble is that the behaviors are interpreted, in part, differently when done by women and by men. As a result, we should be dealing with thought structures, organizational structures, and other mechanisms of institutionalized sexism. As Florence Denmark (1977) declared in terms of women leaders, the problem rests not in what women do or do not do, but with the attitudes toward, and beliefs about, women and men in leadership roles. Fifteen years ago, Denmark suggested that workshops be conducted to adjust attitudes and correct perceptual bias rather than to provide more leadership training for women. The problem is not the women, nor is it simply a matter of attitudes. Rather, it rests in the structure and processes of organization which themselves are gendered.

In the short term at least, the best we can hope for is a "transgendered" status. Analysis of women's styles is helpful and worthwhile in this regard. Through such exploration we can hope to make behaviors and styles understood as acceptable and *valuable* for both women and men. We can also pursue the appropriate rewards for what women do, both the same as and differently from men. And in the process, perhaps we can shift our attention to behaviors of consequence for the organization. If that is done, women should fare well, especially if a critical mass of women hold positions with sufficient power to help determine what is consequential. To accomplish this, however, the assumptions, processes, and structures—formal and informal—of organizations must come under scrutiny.

Conclusion

We argued that organizations are gendered and that one way of exploring their gendered dimensions is through stereotypes and style. We found that bureaucratic stereotypes are largely masculine, yet respondents believe gender-neutral traits to be of greatest consequence in organizations, with feminine and masculine traits similarly valued in top administrators. Women honed in on traits of consequence to the organization to a greater extent than men. When we looked to see the consistency of gender differences across states, we found few consistent traits. Managerial level explains more than gender alone, even though we find some patterns that suggest somewhat different approaches. The best way to think about style is to make our concepts more sophisticated by granting any number of combinations of behaviors to both women and men. To consider gender an advantage, however, we clearly must move beyond style. Style explains far less than structures of power and the gendered processes that are integral to organizations. The critical task facing those who work in public bureaucracies is recognizing that we engender the behavior of managers. Toward that end, much work remains to be done on the topic of gender and organizations. We must explore structures of power coupled with an examination of the ways gender infuses organizational processes and shapes our interpretations of organization life. Knowledge of gender, styles, and advantages can help organizations to function optimally while simultaneously overcoming institutionalized, and largely invisible, male advantage.

Women and men use mostly the same style of management, even though we find different clusters of behaviors for each gender. The paucity of women in management then can hardly rest in approach. Men's and women's styles are far more similar than they are distinctive. The reason there are so few women in top-level administrative positions flows from the innumerable small influences that shape the way we organize, along with who decides how we do it. With so few women in top spots, it is hard to know whether organizations might benefit from a "female advantage" in style *if* more women were to enter top ranks. It seems more evident that we can say public organizations will benefit from more women managers, and only more women managers will make apparent the ways organizations are gendered. Such a change will also likely end organizations as we know them today.

We can say that we need more women managers for simple demographic reasons. We will have too few white males to "man"/staff all such positions as we have in the past. We can say too that if men who lead and study about organizations continue to ignore questions of gender, their inactivity fosters suspicion about the extent to which they consciously, rather than inadvertently, perpetuate male advantage. How sincere are policies for equal opportunity? The entire system of organizing must be considered for its genderedness—both manly and womanly. We can also say that public organizations have the greatest imperative to do so. The government establishes standards for other workplaces, so when it functions as an employer, the government ought to provide a model of the equal opportunities it mandates elsewhere. Public bureaucracies also enforce and create law. They are a powerful branch of government. The interpretation of law and the legitimacy of governmental action depends upon broadening the scope of vision in order to understand gender power advantages. Such change begins with "a turn of the heart" in thinking about gender and advantage in organizations. A good place to investigate the extent to which they become tHEy is in the structure and culture of agencies, which is discussed in chapter 8.

Agency Culture and Its Effect on Managers

Mary E. Guy and Georgia Duerst-Lahti

The discussion of styles in chapter 7 is closely related to the subject of agency culture. Styles that are effective in one culture may prove to be ineffective or unwanted in another. Similarly, what is considered appropriate behavior within an agency varies with the nature of the agency. This chapter uses the concept of agency culture to explain how agencies differ in the proportion of women they promote into managerial ranks. Because agency cultures sculpt and selectively reward behaviors, the authors speculate about the ways in which perception is mediated by culture, which in turn affects the proportion of women in leadership positions. — Editor's Note

No single work has shaped discussions of women in organizations as much as Rosabeth Moss Kanter's book, *Men and Women of the Corporation* (1977). In it, we learn the extent to which structural elements within organizations determine the behavior of individuals. Gender *per se* is less important than gender structure of the work force, or the relative proportion of women to men. The proportion of women in a work unit determines the dynamics women face in terms of whether or not they are spotlighted and stereotyped as tokens, or whether they are treated as comfortable members of the majority. Control over structural power resources—a large budget, decision-making discretion, supervising lots of employees—also shapes behavior, apparent confidence, and strategies of action. Kanter persuasively demonstrated that the behaviors often attributed to women's gender flow instead from overlapping structures in organizations. Gender explains very little; the location and position of women in various structures are the key.

Still, when we look across organizations, we quickly recognize that where and when women have entered top levels of state agencies is highly varied. Women fare much better in some places than in others. Structural explanations do not illuminate why such variation exists. Yoder (1991) details the shortcomings of overreliance on a structural approach for understanding the full range of gender dynamics. Influences such as the perceived gender-appropriateness of the position or work unit, and the extent to which women's entry is understood by co-workers as an intrusion also account for the variation. Yoder also questions the extent to which a structural explanation is applicable. Token men seem not to suffer consistently from similar dynamics, so gender mediates in some way. Furthermore, Kanter studied only professional women entering work units comprised of men, so her findings are not as instructive for librarians, nurses, or public school teachers, for example. Clearly, to understand the women and men of the states, we need also to know something more than the proportion of women in top jobs. An organizational culture approach might move us in the direction of better understanding gender at the top of state agencies.

Organizational Culture

The study of organizational culture is relatively new, although its roots go back at least to the work of Chester Barnard and Mary Parker Follett, and it certainly owes a large debt to Berger and Luckman (1966) for illuminating the "social construction of reality" (Ott 1989). The organizational culture approach has encountered resistance within the discipline in part because its analysis relies heavily on "subjective" qualitative methods. A larger concern, however, is that of control and manipulation: studying organizational culture may provide a tool too effective in controlling workers and their behavior precisely because culture goes unnoticed by most. It becomes normal and, hence, is not scrutinized. Manipulating culture offers the prospect of regulating workers whose control rests with other enculturated workers rather than with management, even though management explicitly works to shape that culture. On the other hand, managing organizational culture can lead to greater productivity and a richer utilization of employees when applied in a constructive fashion. Changing culture in an agency is necessary in order to bring about organizational change, so culture figures prominently in organization development efforts. Organization culture can be put to many uses, but first we must acknowledge it.

State agencies, just like other organizations, are human institutions that shape and are shaped by the people who work in them. Agencies define themselves by their mission statements, their work force, and the image they project. These attributes contribute to, and are affected by, the culture of the agency. Culture is that set of values, attitudes, and norms—along with accompanying artifacts—that guides the behavior, expectations, and evaluations of one's behavior. The culture transmits agency values and underlying assumptions. It provides the means for understanding how and why things get done and by whom.

Culture becomes obvious not so much in formal policy and procedure statements as in informal, often unstated messages such as the way people dress, the manner in which they address each other, and the types of behaviors and styles they emulate. Symbols and artifacts, such as rites of passage, jargon, awards, and legends are essential elements of the culture and serve to publicize and transmit it. The traditions, norms, rituals, policies, functions, and processes of an organization combine to create its culture and dictate the types of people, outlooks, and behaviors that are valued. Those who "fit"—who manifest favored behaviors or demonstrate valued perspectives—are rewarded. Certainly such fit is crucial for promotion to leadership positions. The leaders, in turn, perpetuate the desired tone through their style, norms, practices, and the reward system they use to reinforce desired behavior in others. Though leaders can shape an organization's culture, they do so within its traditions and conventions. Organization culture then is simultaneously dynamic and enduring. It is malleable and permeable, yet embedded within a given context.

An organization's culture is frequently difficult to see after one has become enculturated. Often it most becomes obvious through organizational "deviants" or "outlaws"—those members who do not match well with the organization culture. Their cultural deviance helps mark and define the boundaries of the culture. Such members can create a counterculture within an organization that disrupts the normal flow of events. Similarly, selected deviants can be used by leaders to foster change within the culture. In general, though, the better one fits an organization's culture, the more comfortable one feels, and the more likely one is to progress within the agency.

An agency's culture has enormous implications for women's ability to advance. If an agency's culture incorporates a masculine ethos, women are less likely to fit: they are deviants who threaten the extant culture and mark the dominant culture by their mere presence. Given the dearth of women in most agencies, and especially in top jobs, masculine dimensions of culture can be expected to dominate. If women have not been centrally involved in the creation of agency culture—if they have not held influential leadership posts over a prolonged time—they may find the cultural messages difficult to decipher and troublesome to emulate because those messages were fashioned by men.

The organizational culture perspective is important for understanding where and why women enter top ranks of state agencies. We will explore organization culture for its gendered dimensions in two of the states surveyed, Alabama and Wisconsin, but first present a brief review of some aspects of organizational culture.

Cultural Functions and Organizational Reality

Through organization culture we can discern an organization's reality for its members. Van Maanen and Barley (1985) conclude that culture emerges in four domains of organizations:

1. the ways in which activities are structured;
2. the formal and informal cleavages based on policy areas, tasks, and territorial segregation;
3. past organizational policies and structures;
4. the social demography, that is, the interests, expectations, and characteristics of the work force required by the organization's functions and the nature of its clientele.

One's work role influences the patterns of interaction that shape, and are shaped by, physical proximity, common tasks and/or shared status, and workflow dependencies. An earlier cultural study of four Wisconsin agencies helps illuminate the way these domains shape culture (Duerst-Lahti 1986, 1987). Duerst-Lahti explored the Wisconsin Departments of Administration (DOA), Natural Resources (DNR),

Health and Social Services (DHSS), and Industry, Labor, and Human Relations (DILHR) through in-depth interviews, observation, and reviews of documents. For the fourth domain, the social demography of the work force, differences among the agencies were striking.

In DOA, politics prevail. This agency houses the executive budget functions similar to those found in a combination of the U.S. Office of Management and Budget along with the comptroller's office. Because of this agency's control functions for other state agencies, a garrison mentality pervades daily operations and everything is weighed for its possible political ramifications. In contrast, DHSS members see themselves as advocates for the disadvantaged. They manage state care and treatment facilities, work on behalf of children and welfare, and distribute Medicaid and other social service monies. The enormous size of the department (over 10,000 employees) and its budget (over $6 billion) make it by far the most powerful agency if gauged by those structural measures. Yet the small DOA (with 600+ employees) is far more sensitive to power nuances. DILHR is an agency of competent implementors who distribute workers' compensation and unemployment checks, assure building safety, run the employment service, keep employment data, and enforce compliance with equal employment opportunity regulations. DILHR employees know that people depend on them for timely, accurate work, and these implementors are proud of their competence. DNR is responsible for environmental enforcement and wildlife, forestry, and park services. Few of these defenders of the outdoors transfer to other agencies. Turnover is low and members share a strong personal dedication to the work of the agency.

Clearly, we see cultural differences among these agencies, and can surmise the interaction between the nature of the work and the workers. The combination produces the cultural character of these agencies. Culture operates in the first domain—the ways activities are structured—and manifests itself in expected behaviors within agencies and their subunits. For example, although almost everyone has been involved in team sports, teams differ and the expectations of team members differ. In some teams, interaction and interdependence among players is critical, such as in football and basketball. In other sports, however, individual performance is most important, such as in swim teams and track and field events. If employees have been accustomed to being individual performers and find themselves on a basketball team, then drastically different behaviors and interpersonal skills are required and rewarded. In other words, if one expects a swim team member and gets a basketball player instead, the latter is judged negatively. On the other hand, if employees expect to perform in a closely knit department and have a lot of interaction with colleagues but find themselves working in isolation from others, they do not fare well.

Culture must be learned in organizations just as in other social institutions. Culture differs from one agency to another and, in a large agency, from one department or division to another. Since it is embodied more in unwritten than in written rules, the process of socialization is like a mysterious black box. New employees enter the organization and, at some indeterminate time later, emerge as socialized organizational members. Part of what is in the black box is an enculturation process whereby newcomers become aware of, and committed to, the shared interpretations and values of old-guard organization members.

Proper enculturation serves many functions. The assumptions and values that people share in the work setting tie the people together and give them common purpose. Shared values underpin a set of cultural codes that act as an informal control system. These codes tell people what is expected of them, how to behave, and how others are to behave (Siehl and Martin 1988). Because agency culture embodies the practices and procedures of an entire organization, including those characteristics that are formal and enforced, those merely espoused but not practiced, as well as those that are actually "in use," learning the culture is critical for long-term success. For example, a story about a fast-track employee who cuts corners to get the job done may reveal more about prized values than formalized statements found in the agency's policy and procedure guidelines.

Top-ranking officials in the same agency have similar work-related attitudes and habits, whether they are male or female. The organizational culture guarantees this because people who are subject to the same occupational experiences tend to converge in their work-related attitudes over time (Guy 1985). Occupational socialization reduces any attitudinal or behavioral gap between the sexes. In fact, there is more difference between women at the top and women at the bottom than there is between women and men at the top.

Work ceremonies integrate the informal with the formal (Dandridge 1988). Ceremonies let individuals transcend their work role and experience a sense of cooperativeness or community. In the face of retirements, group unity emphasizes the continuity of the organization.

When a ceremony or ritual provides a haven from a problem, it facilitates coping. Ceremonies open new lines of communication, leading to better integration of work units or vertical communication chains. And new members can be incorporated into the organization, with the ceremony serving as the rite of passage. Lessons are taught and status is changed, often in the context of fun.

Rituals serve as important vehicles for informal communication and mingling across groups. Some departments have a cordial, informal flavor that is manifested by brown-bag lunches and a lot of casual exchanges, such as after-hours get togethers, and departmental softball teams or bowling leagues. More formal cultures are marked by greater deference to rank, more formal styles of address, such as calling one another by "Mr." or "Ms.," and little informal socializing on the job or after hours. Cultural rites define power relations and send symbolic messages. Beyer and Trice (1988) detail several types of rites along with examples of where and how they operate in organizations. For example, rites of passage occur in managerial and occupational training programs. Rites of enhancement occur in performance awards and conferral of tenure. Rites of degradation occur in censure, firing, and demotions. Rites of conflict reduction occur in collective bargaining and the presence of ombudsmen. Rites of integration occur in departmental ball teams, picnics, and annual meetings.

All of these aspects of culture assume that "proper enculturation" is possible. However, like cultural accoutrements in the larger society, most cultural rituals and ceremonies are associated with, or prescribe, gendered roles. For example, in closing a bargaining session, the protocol for shaking hands in which women may sit but men must stand marks women as the cultural exception. While a woman certainly may stand, she must counter the gender association of women sitting in doing so. Some rituals carry explicit threats for a woman; she may hesitate to accompany "the boys" at a Friday night poker game (ritual) for fear of sexual innuendoes. On the other hand, she may never have learned to play poker, or she may know how to play but does not like it. When women's access to power-giving rites of passage is blocked because the rite has been associated with men, women can never become full-fledged players in the game. By the same token, women must be in a position to confer rites of passage and integration. When they act largely as passive recipients, they do not control the conferral of such symbolic acts, so they cannot shape rites—and in turn power relations—in ways consistent with women's perspectives. They also fall short on power.

Gender and Culture

Although Van Maanen and Barley claim that individual attributes of members have little relevance for the organization's culture, like Deborah Sheppard (1989) we contend that the attribute of sex has bearing on organization culture and the ways in which women and men experience work reality. Hearn et al. (1989) provide an impressive and provocative look at the "sexuality of organization." These authors explore the ways sexuality and gender infuse the process of organizing as well as the structures of organization. They ask readers to reflect upon the similarity of, and relationship between, masculine hierarchical orderings, dominance and subordination, gender patterns, and contemporary organizations. In the volume, Albert Mills (1989) is especially concerned with gender and culture, and he relies upon Clegg's (1981) conception of "rules of behavior" to organize his exploration of culture. Gender rules cannot be separated from organization rules. Simply put, an agency's culture cannot be totally separated from the societal culture.

Extraorganizational rules and understandings about the respective worth and function of males and females permeate the cultural arrangements of organizations even though many facets of organizations mediate culture (Mills 1989). Employers cannot take men and women out of organizations. Just as agencies hire workers and get human beings instead, employers talk of staff in sex-neutral terms but employ men and women instead. Their sexuality comes with them into the workplace. And, as time and numerous pieces of legislation reveal, rules such as the 1964 Civil Rights Act, the 1963 Equal Pay Act, or the 1978 Pregnancy Discrimination Act can only alter organization culture so far. Though equal opportunity, affirmative action, and other initiatives have worked their way into organizational culture, the guiding beliefs and root values of culture come from the top (Davis 1984). Unless those at the top of organizations choose to ameliorate bias against women, the more sexist aspects of societal culture will likely prevail.

Social-regulative rules, Clegg (1981) and Mills (1989) assert, mean that hegemonic forms of control are located within the social arrangements of production and organizational processes. Although any person might have the skill to perform a task, social regulation shapes the way one person is expected to relate to others in achieving that task. So even if women reach management ranks, they are expected to manage differently due to gender rules, which then may jeopardize a positive assessment of their management skill.

Outcomes of the process of socialization bring most women to management positions with different perspectives and values than men bring (Hennig and Jardim 1977). The development of an individual from child to adult in a culture that values being male means that, by the time they enter the work force, adults selectively emphasize certain behaviors and traits over others. Social regulation rules often filter women out of management jobs before they face this dilemma. Even today few women set forth clear career goals early in their careers, while most men assume this as a given. Thus, men have the advantage of having established career goals early. By the time that most women establish goals for upward mobility, they have already been in the work force for a decade (Hennig and Jardim 1977; Liscum and Guy 1991). All of these dynamics are confounded by the fact that how a person is viewed by decision makers—whether the person is seen as a *full* member, as someone who "fits in," as "committed"—filters through a male-dominant style of organization life.

Reproductive rules relate closely to women's and men's position in organizations. Eccles (1987) argues that sex differences in educational and vocational choices result from both differential expectations for success and differential values. Because of this, sex differences on both of these choices result from gender role socialization—roles usually predicated upon assumptions about biology and reproduction. Differential socialization experiences that girls and boys undergo result in the internalization of culturally defined and readily observable gender roles. These roles produce different choices for career preparation, work activities, and devotion to career over family for women and the converse for men (Eccles 1987). Such a set of assumptions is based on the single assumption that males and females have different goals for their lives. Yet we must recognize the ways organizational culture and management theory (e.g., Hofstede 1984; Ouchi 1981) *reproduce* and legitimize these assumptions rather than challenge them. By excluding gender from the recognized dynamics of organizational experience and from the construction of organizational culture, such theorists inhibit the potential for change (Mills 1989).

Technical rules shape culture as well. When an organizational understanding is that "there is a job to be done," the unspoken understanding is that there is a job to be done within specific behavioral parameters. And these behavioral guidelines often favor one gender over another. The culture develops gendered rules of control that guide decisions about what is and what is not appropriate behavior. To change the way things are done is to rock traditional habits that emerge from the culture. To expect change is to expect the culture to change. Thus, when women penetrate traditional male management ranks, the culture is forced to change, if even in the mere acknowledgment that a woman is now doing "a man's job." However, the effect on the culture once this acknowledgment occurs is less clear. Some Marxist feminists proffer the "contamination effect"—once a job becomes associated with women, it loses its status. In this case, the larger culture may not be noticeably altered, but the rules for the job shift, overlaying it with gender expectations for women rather than men. The job becomes less valued through its association with women, and men still predominate in positions to set cultural interpretations.

Thus far we have spoken of gender and organizational culture as though *only* men and masculinity establish and shape culture in state agencies. While we maintain that men have predominated in establishing cultural norms in organizations (and elsewhere), women are not merely passive and are not just victims. We might better understand the relationship between gender and organization culture through the concept of gender ethos.

Agencies, Gender Ethos, and Sex Segregation

Just as organizations have unique cultures, they may also have a particular gender ethos. Gender ethos is defined here as the distinctive characteristics of organizations and the attitudes of people within them that affect relations between the sexes and women's ability to gain and use power. The gender ethos of a department has as much to do with the nature of the work and traditions of the department as it has to do with the number of women in decision-making posts. Social and mission exigencies influence gender ethos. Some agencies deal with functions commonly associated with men, such as highways, natural resources, and agriculture. These are male bastions where very few, if any, women hold visible leadership positions and those who do are frequently singled out as exceptions. Other agencies have a greater mix of the sexes and, although men predominate, it is not considered unusual to have women in leadership positions. The latter usually have as their mission concerns that are stereotyped as "women's concerns," such as social services, or they are agencies with low controversy and little discretionary authority because policy is set elsewhere. The (gendered) nature of the work, along with the traditions of the agency and the relative proportion of women and men—especially in top jobs—determine the gender ethos of agencies. The factors interact, leaving tension among competing cultural and gender rules, and the outcome creates a gender ethos.

For example, in the earlier study of Wisconsin agencies, Duerst-Lahti (1986, 1987) found the Department of Natural Resources, the "defenders of the outdoors," to be a male bastion. In contrast, the Department of Industry, Labor, and Human Relations—the "competent implementors"—was conducive to women. In the Department of Administration, where "politics prevails," the gender ethos was mixed: tasks akin to those done by advanced clerical staff were in tension with the (masculine) power and control functions of executive budget review and the comptroller. Similarly mixed was the Department of Health and Social Services where the feminine work of caring and "advocating for the disadvantaged" competes with the consequences of tremendous size, budgetary, and structural resources.

Gender ethos is anything but simple, however, because all agencies operate within a larger context that privileges masculine orientations. How an agency's gender ethos plays out for women under such circumstances is indeed nuanced. McGlen and Sarkees (1990) examined the U.S. departments of Defense and State, two agencies known to be male-oriented, for their gender ethos. They found that, although the State Department's larger culture was generally more amenable to women than the Defense Department, women confronted informal practices and gender-rooted assumptions that formed barriers that were hard to crack. In contrast, the Defense Department was much more straightforward. Military experience, which most women lacked, was critical. However, because of the military hierarchy, if supervisors ordered co-workers to cooperate with women managers, compliance was likely. As a result, once women gained positions in the Defense Department, they actually confronted fewer barriers than in the State Department. Even within very masculine organizations, gender ethos plays out differently.

Cultures define the appropriateness of occupational and organizational segregation of the sexes. They define how women are to straddle the dual roles of being "feminine" and of being in a management position. That is, cultural expectations dictate how women are to choreograph their actions so as to gain acceptance by co-workers. Cultural codes also communicate the appropriateness of men as managers. One consequence is horizontal sex segregation (Kelly and Bayes 1988; Reskin 1984; Reskin and Hartmann 1986). This means that most men and women can be found in occupations in which members of the opposite sex are rare (Glass 1990). In fact, women tend to predominate in occupations that are task-oriented, less flexible, and have fewer possibilities of promotion (Glass 1990). Glass speculates that employers reserve certain privileges for "trusted" workers, and that these privileges are allocated and controlled through job segmentation and segregation. Yet even in nontraditional occupations, women report fewer benefits and less upward mobility than men in the same occupations—they are horizontally segregated, and apparently employers are less likely to see them as fully trustworthy.

Women usually find themselves limited to employment and significant management roles in female-dominated occupations, such as human service organizations, and organizations whose mission requires feelings of responsibility and caring. Alternatively, women will be found within structurally weak units of a larger agency. Often this means in administrative or management services, especially if policy and budgetary responsibility is delegated elsewhere (Duerst-Lahti 1987). In a study of barriers to women administrators in higher education in Alabama, Hart (1988) concluded that socialization practices interact with structural mechanisms to create an environment that effectively discriminates against women. Sex-linked expectations cause an initial under-representation of women in administration that, in turn, influences stereotypical reactions from both sexes and leads to a diminishing probability that women will attain top administrative posts. This interaction results in the perpetuation of the norms and values of a male-dominated hierarchy and the reinforcement of sociocultural stereotypes (Konrad 1990).

Rosabeth Moss Kanter (1977) theorized that once a critical number of women reached management ranks, then they would no longer face token conditions. They would constitute a large enough portion in the work force that the characteristic marking them as different from the majority, in this case sex, would fade from attention. According to this theory, when the tipping point is reached, culture changes to incorporate the differences that women bring to the work force, or in this case, to managerial ranks. As mentioned earlier, Yoder (1991) and Duerst-Lahti (1986, 1987) find that more than work force proportion is involved in such cultural shifts. Nonetheless, work force structures remain important indicators of gender ethos because they serve as both a cause and an effect of it.

An Empirical Look at Gender and Culture

The facts that are known about culture and its effect on an agency's selection of managers lead to four propositions, which relate to a connection between women gaining management positions and (1) stereotypical gender roles, (2) structural power resources, (3) agency history, and (4) the proportion of women already in management posts. By examining the proportion of women in management positions in the states, we can explore how gender operates within agencies and how its effects support the propositions.

1. The greater the congruence between conventional roles for women and the work of the agency, the greater the proportion of women in management

In "male" agencies at the local level, such as police and fire departments, women are accepted in their conventional positions of secretaries and dispatch clerks but are only rarely welcomed into the ranks of commissioned officers. Achieving representative numbers of men and women in male-dominated occupations is dependent upon a formal administrative structure established specifically to achieve this goal (Warner, Steel, and Lovrich 1989). When women police officers try to break out of the confines, male officers subject women to verbal harassment, commenting that women seeking such positions are "unwomanly," "emotionally unstable," and "unreliable" (Warner et al. 1989). Moving into management ranks proves difficult in the face of such perceptions. A number of authors report that the presence of a hiring quota imposed by the courts is one of the most important factors in explaining increased utilization of women in local governments (Hochstedler, Regoli, and Poole 1984; Riccucci 1986; Warner et al. 1989).

Two federal agencies, the U.S. Treasury Department and the Department of Health and Human Services, represent a contrast between a stereotypically "male" agency and one whose function is more consistent with stereotypical "women's" concerns. Jane Bayes (1987) reported that women held 5 percent of the highest ranks in the U.S. Treasury Department and 11 percent of the middle management ranks, while 15 percent of the highest ranks in the U.S. Department of Health and Human Services were held by women and 22 percent of the middle ranks were held by women. In both agencies, women in top posts were poorly represented, but their numbers were markedly fewer in Treasury than in HHS. Consistent with Kanter (1977), Bayes found that women in the U.S. Treasury Department and the U.S. Department of Health and Human Services exhibited behavior that could be described as simultaneously overachieving and limiting visibility. In Treasury, the women tended to dress in dark tailored suits, as did the men. They did not attempt to socialize within the department, but worked hard and in a competent manner to fulfill, or exceed, their responsibilities. This study may make it seem that tapping the gendered dimensions of organizations is rather straightforward. This is not the case, because perceptions of (and in) the agency are likely to shift when women assume top posts, as the following scenario suggests.

In 1977, to announce the appointment of Virginia Hart as the first female head of the Wisconsin Department of Industry, Labor, and Human Relations, a Madison newspaper's headline declared, "Woman to Head Housekeeping Department." Although one of Wisconsin's major agencies, with about 2,500 employees and a budget of over $83 million at the time, it was described in gendered and menial terms. Either "housekeeping" includes building and safety inspections (e.g., petroleum tank inspections), job services, worker's compensation, apprenticeships and training, and equal rights conciliation and compliance—all of which were the agency's functions in 1977—or gender assumptions of the newspaper writer shaped perception! It is hard to imagine that such a prominent agency would be described thus if a man had been named to the helm rather than a woman.

So the question arises: Is a gender ethos that reflects the proportion of women associated with departments? To answer this question, those agencies with either an exceptionally high or an exceptionally low number of women in administrative positions were reviewed. Approximately 26 percent of the administrative positions in California's thirty largest state agencies are occupied by women (Bayes 1989); approximately 15 percent of the administrative positions in Alabama's 30 largest state agencies are occupied by women; and approximately 21 percent of administrative positions in Wisconsin's twenty-nine largest or most prominent agencies are held by women. Those agencies with one-third more or one-third less than the average for each are listed in Table 8.1.

Without detailed knowledge of the workings of each agency, analysis of the gender association of functions is difficult. Yet a glance over the list in Table 8.1 reveals that most agencies seem gender-appropriate. For example, the "women's work" of health and social services appears exceptionally high in the proportions of women for all three states. Likewise, education appears in both Alabama and Wisconsin. Accounting functions, among the faster-growing professions for women, constitute the work of four of these twenty-three agencies that are "friendly" to women.

Well over half of these twenty-three agencies are readily associated with women's work. Only a few of these provoke serious explanation. Lotteries are new so they afford openings at a time when promoting women is an imperative. The transportation functions appearing for California and Wisconsin arouse curiosity. In the case of Wisconsin, the Office of the Commissioner of Transportation, with only twenty-four employees, serves a quasi-judiciary function for regulation and its regulatory functions were substantially reduced in 1982. In the case of California, the Department of Transportation was a high-growth department and had directors who pushed affirmative action programs aggressively (Bayes 1989). The Wisconsin Public Service Commission stands as an example of a powerful body, whose requirement for detailed technical knowledge makes it stand as an anomaly in the list of agencies having exceptionally high proportions of women. It does, however, fulfill a consumer protection role as well, a role commonly associated with women.

The agencies with exceptionally small proportions of women also elicit few surprises in gender association. One might ask why the Wisconsin Educational Communications Board has no women in top administrative posts, since little in its charge to license and oversee public television and radio seems overly masculine. Most of these agencies are readily associated with "male" activities, however. Although far from a perfect predictor, the more an agency's functions are

Table 8.1

Agencies That Are Exceptional in the Proportion of Women in Administrative Positions

One-third more women than the state's average

CA   Department of Transportation
CA   Department of Social Services
CA   Department of Consumer Affairs
CA   State Lottery

AL   Development Office
AL   Archives and History
AL   Department of Human Resources
AL   Department of Education
AL   Environmental Management
AL   Examiners of Public Accounts
AL   Medicaid
AL   Military
AL   Public Health
AL   Treasury

WI   Lottery Board
WI   Public Service Commission
WI   Department of Regulation and Licensing
WI   Office of the Commissioner of Transportation
WI   Office of the State Public Defender
WI   Elections Board
WI   Department of Employee Trust Funds
WI   Department of Health and Social Services
WI   Department of Public Instruction

One-third fewer women than the state's average

CA   Board of Equalization
CA   Department of Food and Agriculture
CA   Department of Veterans' Affairs

AL   Department of Agriculture and Industry
AL   Alcoholic Beverage Control Board
AL   Department of Banking
AL   Building Commission
AL   Department of Conservation and Natural Resources
AL   Department of Economic and Community Affairs
AL   Department of Emergency Management
AL   Department of Forensic Science
AL   Department of Forestry Commission
AL   Highway Department
AL   Pardon and Parole Board
AL   Department of Revenue
AL   State Docks

WI   Educational Communications Board
WI   Office of the Commissioner of Credit Unions
WI   Department of Development
WI   Racing Board
WI   Office of the Commissioner of Savings and Loan
WI   Board of Vocational, Technical, and Adult Education
WI   Department of Justice
WI   Department of Military Affairs
WI   Department of Revenue
WI   Department of Transportation

congruent with conventional female roles, the more likely it appears that we will find women in leadership posts (Duerst-Lahti 1986, 1987; Yoder 1991).

2. The fewer the structural power resources, the more likely we are to find women in top-level positions

Structures serve as determinants and mediators of an organization's culture. Structural dimensions include size, degree of centralization and discretion in decision making, division of labor, and the composition of the work force. Smith and Grenier (1982) conclude that structurally derived organizational power is greatest in larger and centralized departments, especially for line positions and positions that are unconstrained by rigid rules and regulations. Citing current employment statistics, they demonstrate that women usually do not hold such positions; hence, structural factors affect the distribution and use of power on the basis of gender.

Thus far, we have used the agency as our unit of analysis. But the power any individual within an agency has at her or his disposal clearly interacts with the position. Most agencies have clerical secretaries, after all, whose structural power is minuscule compared with that of their cabinet secretary bosses. We suspect that women are most likely to be found in the smaller, less prominent agencies and/or in those positions with fewer structural resources at their disposal. In other words, we expect to find more women at the top in less prominent agencies, and when found in prominent agencies, we assume they will be in weaker positions. These findings, however, are likely to be confounded by gender-appropriateness.

First, let us consider positions generically. Hanson (1991) reports that over 95 percent of all upper-level management positions in the United States are held by men. By considering the job titles of respondents, we might see a difference in the titles that women hold compared to those of men. The Alabama survey produces 69 different titles for 315 respondents, ranging from administrator to analyst, to accountant, engineer, warden, examiner, budget analyst, planner, inspector, officer, and so forth. By far, most respondents fall into one of the most commonly occurring "generic" titles shown in Table 8.2. Sixty-one percent of the women managers in Alabama hold such titles and 71 percent of the men hold such titles.

Table 8.2

Distribution of Titles between Women and Men (%)

	Alabama		Wisconsin	
	Women	Men	Women	Men
Administrator	31	69	26	74
Director	34	66	17	83
Chief	11	89	23	66
Supervisor	13	87	No data	No data
Commissioner	0	100	22	78
Manager	23	77	40	60
Coordinator	25	75	69	25

The Wisconsin titles are derived from the *Bluebook*, a source that indicates all positions in the State of Wisconsin deemed to be of sufficient prominence to be made available to the public. The fourteen largest and most prominent agencies produce 722 people holding 85 different positions. For Wisconsin, we consider six "generic" titles. These titles represent general administrative positions. Presumably, positions bearing these titles are linchpins of administrative hierarchy and therefore carry with them the structural resources of power. Titles may also reflect the "pipeline" to top positions. Table 8.2 shows the distribution of these titles between women and men in these two states. (Note: We have substituted comparability for precision in this table. Wisconsin and Alabama differ in the degree to which specific titles govern specific job functions. Because of the greater specificity of the Wisconsin system, some distinctions within the Wisconsin analysis have been collapsed, such as that for "Directors." The ability to compare titles across states makes this effort worthwhile despite its shortcomings.)

In Wisconsin, 67 percent of the women and 66 percent of the men hold one of these six titles. These titles constitute a critical mass within agencies. The gender distribution here provides some information about the gender ethos, and relative gender power, within a state's agencies. The positions in Table 8.2 are arranged roughly in hierarchical order. Beneath the cabinet secretary's office, the common pattern then proceeds with division administrators, bureau directors, section chiefs, and supervisors. Commissioners have varying amounts of authority in the two states, as do managers and coordinators.

A glance at the titles reveals a few quick facts. First, men predominate in these positions. Across all the titles in both states, men constitute a majority in all but one of the possibilities, and that is the title of Coordinator in the state of Wisconsin. Clearly, if these positions constitute the critical mass of administration, men have an advantage in determining the administrative culture of these agencies. The titles of Administrator and Manager seem more amenable to women than most others. Nearly one-third of Alabama administrators are women and in Wisconsin women constitute over a quarter of these titles. Perhaps this means that these two terms are becoming transgendered.

Since the proportion of women in the work force, the work of the agency, and the gender ethos of an agency are inextricably linked, a question arises as to which comes first. Table 8.3 provides a look at how much the work of an agency contributes to the proportion of women in key positions. It lists the proportion of respondents who have the title of Administrator, Chief, Commissioner, Director, Manager, or Supervisor from select agencies. Of 315 known titles among the 317 Alabama respondents, these six titles account for 66 percent of all respondents' titles. Of the 85 titles for the 714 individuals in Wisconsin, the titles that are roughly equivalent to those in Alabama account for 37 percent of individuals in top positions. These positions were selected because they are more likely to represent line positions with supervisory responsibility, as compared with staff positions with no supervision. Table 8.3 was compiled using two counts. The percentage of top posts represents the proportion of all the administrative posts filled by women or by men in each of the agencies. The percentage holding any one of the six selected titles is shown in the second line. (Alabama titles could only be derived from responses to the survey so they may not be representative of the population of titles held.) The table includes a selection of eleven of the largest Alabama state agencies. Wisconsin agencies have been matched by function as closely as possible with the Alabama agencies listed.

The proportions compared in Table 8.3—the top posts in contrast with generic titles—shed a somewhat different light than earlier data on gender ethos and the structural power of positions in these agencies. In Alabama, we find a general pattern (eight of eleven agencies) of women holding proportionally more generic titles than top posts; two others are about equal. The difference is pronounced in five of eleven cases.

A closer examination, however, reveals that in six agencies the pro-

Table 8.3

Administrators, Chiefs, Commissioners, Directors, Managers, or Supervisors: Alabama and Wisconsin

	Women	Men
Alabama		
Attorney General		
% of top posts	15	85
% holding selected titles	33	67
Conservation & Natural Resources		
% of top posts	9	91
% holding selected titles	30	70
Industrial Relations		
% of top posts	11	89
% holding selected titles	16	84
Human Resources		
% of top posts	42	58
% holding selected titles	48	52
Education		
% of top posts	24	76
% holding selected titles	18	82
Corrections		
% of top posts	14	86
% holding selected titles	23	77
Finance		
% of top posts	13	87
% holding selected titles	33	67
Medicaid		
% of top posts	50	50
% holding selected titles	50	50
Public Health		
% of top posts	30	70
% holding selected titles	29	71
Revenue		
% of top posts	5	95
% holding selected titles	12	88
Highway		
% of top posts	2	98
% holding selected titles	50	50

(continued)

Table 8.3 *(continued)*

	Women	Men
Wisconsin		
Justice		
% of top posts	6	94
% holding selected titles	0	100
Natural Resources		
% of top posts	16	84
% holding selected titles	16	84
Industry, Labor, Human Relations		
% of top posts	23	77
% holding selected titles	18	82
Health & Human Services		
% of top posts	32	68
% holding selected titles	12	88
Public Instruction		
% of top posts	30	70
% holding selected titles	31	69
Administration		
% of top posts	14	86
% holding selected titles	15	85
Revenue		
% of top posts	13	87
% holding selected titles	18	82
Transportation		
% of top posts	10	90
% holding selected titles	8	92

portions are about the same (within six percentage points), and some show the opposite arrangement, with women holding more top posts than generic titles. Interestingly, five of these six agencies are associated with traditional feminine tasks. This suggests that in the Alabama system greater power resources likely reside with nongeneric positions, as women find rough parity in feminine-associated agencies but are over-represented in the generic positions of the masculine-associated agencies. In other words, women administrators in Alabama might be wise to seek nongeneric positions if they want to tap into the positions with the most structural power.

The Wisconsin data reveal a different condition. Only one of eight agencies—Health and Social Services—shows a disparity greater than six percentage points, and then women are over-represented in top posts. While this likely reflects in part the nature of the data, Wisconsin's centralized personnel system seems to foster more consistent positional power resources. Wisconsin women can be advised to follow a strategy of filling the pipeline of standard positions, unlike in Alabama, because generic titles indeed appear to be the backbone of agencies and symbolize the structural resources such positions warrant.

Still, the agency level may not be the best suited for analysis of gender proportion. Especially in traditional male bastions, such as highway departments and agriculture departments, women who hold high positions are most often found in staff rather than line positions. Or they are even more invisible by holding "line" positions, but for administrative services or operations. In other words, they make the organization work rather than doing the work of the organization. They serve an advisory and/or maintenance function rather than having authority over substantive policy implementation. But Duerst-Lahti (1986) found that the fact that women occupy such staff positions is not necessarily automatically weakening. Some agencies use staff units as the most powerful controllers of the agency. Regardless, they are often the most likely means for women to gain a toehold into a top-level position.

3. There is a greater likelihood that women will gain top-level positions in agencies that have had women in those posts than in those agencies that have not placed women at the top

Most agencies have a velvet ghetto of jobs that are seen as being appropriate for women. These are usually positions that are subordinate, supportive positions in personnel departments, accounting, management information systems, public relations, and staff positions that often report to a male director. And the agencies that hire more women, such as social service departments, do so in positions that are "gender-appropriate." Women disproportionately hold positions that are supportive and helping in nature, with little discretion compared with those to which men have access. Thus, structural determinants of power are absent in many of the positions held by women.

Warner, Steel, and Lovrich (1989) find that the representation of women on city councils is associated with progress in the hiring of women police officers, and suggest that cities that elect women to city council positions constitute a favorable environment for employing women in policing. They speculate that the impact could be a direct effect of the setting of policy, or an indirect effect resulting from the image of women working successfully in occupations that have been historically male-dominated ones. For women to make headway into very male-dominated environments, it takes strong action by those with similar interests and stakes in the issue. In other words, it takes more women in positions of power for gender integration to occur.

When Duerst-Lahti studied the culture and gender ethos in eight of the largest Wisconsin agencies, she found that the proportion of women in an agency's work force over time, and in agencies' upper-management ranks, corresponded with the agencies' conduciveness for women (Duerst-Lahti 1986). Furthermore, the four agencies that she found to be most conducive to women had all had a female secretary at some point since the late 1970s. In fact, the Department of Industry, Labor, and Human Relations and the Department of Health and Social Services had been headed by women twice.

In an expansion of earlier work, Duerst-Lahti traced the progress of women in the eight most prominent agencies in Wisconsin from 1973 to 1989. In 1973, only two agencies of the eight listed any women as administrators! They were the Department of Health and Social Services (DHSS) and the Department of Industry, Labor, and Human Relations (DILHR). The Department of Administration (DOA) then had a few women on boards that were later incorporated into the agency. A brief history of each of these agencies is instructive.

By 1977, the Department of Natural Resources (DNR) introduced women in three positions of the secretary's staff—executive assistant, special assistant, and legislative liaison. With a brief exception, the executive assistant position has been held by a woman since then. A woman had filled the position of the division administrator for administrative services from 1979 until recently, and two of the four bureaus in that division "belong" to women.

Also in 1977, DOA had women in six top jobs, including the deputy secretary and the division administrator for administrative services. Again, with a brief exception, the latter position has been held by a woman since then. Unlike DNR, however, women have held a variety of division administrator–level jobs in the Department of Administration, with women generally constituting 30 to 40 percent of positions at the bureau director level and above. The agency has had a woman secretary, but the powerful executive budget division has never been headed by a woman.

In 1977, Virginia Hart served as commissioner and Chair of DILHR. At the time, only one other woman held an administrator position, in a bureau of the Division of Administrative Services. The commission was diminished in stature in 1979 when a secretary was named to head it. Ms. Hart stayed with the commission. With a change in governors in 1983, the deputy secretary and executive assistant jobs, as well as three of seven division administrator jobs were filled by women. By 1985, two of the divisions had become known as pockets of male resentment that perpetuated their networks. Unlike most agencies, men dominate(d) the Division of Administrative Services. Even though men filled the three top posts in 1989, the agency currently has a female secretary and the number of female division administrators has stayed generally constant. The proportion of bureau directors has risen steadily.

Barbara Thompson had been elected State Superintendent of the Department of Public Instruction (DPI), the equivalent to secretary by 1977. DPI moved from having no women administrators in 1973, to seven. Three were attached to the secretary's office, one in the division of Management and Planning—a staff division—and two in the library services division. From 1983 onward, the division has been headed by a woman, and most bureaus in it are as well. Women also fare well in the management division, with a few positions, including a prominent one, being headed by a woman. Women currently hold about half the administrator positions, doing comparatively well throughout, except that men dominate the top jobs.

The Department of Health and Social Services (DHSS) moved to five (of nearly sixty) female administrators by 1977, including the bureau director for its cafeteria. Several reorganizations have since ensued, which perhaps helped redefine the department's gender ethos. Women have served as administrators for five of its seven divisions. Interestingly, of those two never headed by a woman, the Division of Corrections was recently made into a department of its own, and the other, Policy and Budget, was downgraded to an office. Linda Reivitz served as the agency's first female secretary beginning in 1983, and another woman has held the post since. Only about 30 percent of the agency's administrators were women in 1989. Like DILHR, but unlike other agencies, the Division of Management Services remained a male bastion until 1987—perhaps a reflection of the enormous structural resources to manage here.

The Department of Revenue, a relatively small agency in this group, had only three female administrators in 1989, with none in the top three posts. From 1979 until quite recently, a woman has served as deputy secretary and as administrator for the Division of Administrative Services. A woman also served a short stay as secretary. The agency has never cracked the 20 percent proportion despite a continuing female presence. In 1989, a woman became administrator of the influential Division of Research and Analysis.

Women administrators first appeared in the Department of Transportation in 1981 with a woman administrative assistant to the secretary. Women served as executive assistant for about four years since, but no others served in the top three posts, or even as a division administrator. Several of the divisions—State Patrol, Transportation Assistance, and Planning and Budget—have no women administrators. Women here are widely dispersed, with one or two scattered in other divisions—Motor Vehicles, Highway Services, and Business Management. Notice that men dominate the staff functions for budget, while a few women penetrate "business management" where data entry, personnel, and accounting are found.

The Department of Agriculture, Trade, and Consumer Protection (DATCP) first admitted women to administrator ranks in 1979. A research veterinarian directed the animal research bureau, and a woman headed the newly created division of consumer protection. The latter division was quickly downgraded to a bureau, and the director of the animal research bureau went on to be administrator of the Division of Animal Health. Little changed in the agency until 1987 with the appointment of a woman as deputy secretary. In a pattern consistent with six of these eight agencies, by 1989 women populated the Division of Operations—the division handling staff functions.

While the proportion of women in an agency's work force does not fully determine its conduciveness for women, work force structure generally does predict where women make it to the top and seems to shape the prevailing culture or gender ethos. In Alabama, the one agency that is most representative of the population in terms of having approximately equal numbers of men and women is the Alabama Medicaid Agency, which has had women directors for over a decade. Clearly, too, women seem to populate first and most consistently the division whose functions maintain the organization, rather than line functions. The exceptions to this are two agencies in which women do relatively well throughout the rest of the agency. We have seen that women are clustered inside agencies; perhaps they are also clustered in particular agencies, as the following discussion shows.

4. Because of the combined effects of propositions 1 through 3, women in top-level positions are concentrated in a few agencies while men are found in virtually all of them

In Alabama, managers were polled in forty-eight agencies. Of those, 80 percent of the managers in Alabama state government were concentrated in the fourteen agencies listed in Table 8.4. The population of women and men in managerial positions at the time the survey was conducted are listed.

The concentration of women respondents in these fourteen agencies means that 87 percent of the women respondents from all the state agencies are in these agencies. The men who hold managerial positions in these fourteen agencies represent 80 percent of the men in managerial positions in Alabama state government. Twenty-three, or almost half, of the agencies had no women in managerial positions, while only two agencies had no men in managerial positions. Thus, men are found throughout state government agencies while women are localized in only half of them.

We considered twenty-seven Wisconsin agencies in all (not all are shown in Table 8.4). Six, or 22 percent, had no women administrators, so the exclusion of women is less pronounced in Wisconsin than in Alabama, but another eight agencies had three or fewer women administrators. In other words, more than half of the agencies had fewer than three female administrators—three would seem to be the absolute minimum to move beyond pure token conditions in the select group at the top of an agency. Also like Alabama, 83 percent of all administrators are concentrated in thirteen of the twenty-seven agencies. And again similarly but to a lesser degree, we find a clustering with 79 percent of female managers and 82 percent of male managers found in these thirteen agencies. Surely, such clustering shapes agency culture and gender ethos within the entire state picture.

Table 8.4

Total Number of Administrators in Agencies

	Women	Men
Alabama		
Agriculture and Industry	0	28
Alcoholic Beverage Control Board	2	22
Attorney General's Office	18	35
Conservation & Natural Resources	3	31
Corrections	8	50
Education	9	29
Finance	6	27
Highway	6	19
Human Resources (Welfare)	44	61
Industrial Relations	5	40
Medicaid	8	8
Public Health	21	49
Revenue	4	78
State Docks	0	18
Wisconsin		
Agriculture, Trade, Consumer Protection	9	19
Administration	7	43
Banking	1	5
Credit Union	0	2
Development	4	22
Educational Communications Board	0	10
Elections Board	3	3
Employee Trust Funds	8	11
Health and Human Services	27	57
Higher Education Aid Board	1	3
Industry, Labor, Human Relations	12	41
Insurance	3	8
Justice	2	31
Lottery Board	14	16
Military Affairs	0	33
Natural Resources	7	35
Public Defender	2	3
Public Instruction	24	56
Public Service Commission	8	7
Racing Board	0	3
Regulation and Licensing	5	6
Revenue	3	20
Savings and Loan	0	5
Securities	2	6
Transportation	7	63
Veteran's Affairs	4	27
Vocation, Technical, Adult Education	0	13

What are the consequences of clustering? Is the result isolated and disparaged ghettos, or constructive concentrations? With enough women, a "tipping point" is crossed, and women managers are no longer treated as tokens. Their presence becomes normal. Under such conditions, women, and their ways of being in an organization, are no longer perceived by the majority of managers (men) as deviant from the culture. Critical norms of an agency or unit are likely to change, however subtly, as was suggested in the previous chapter. Women managers probably will feel more comfortable and more free to behave in their preferred ways. The concentration of women becomes constructive if numbers tip far enough to form a critical mass and women become equal players under all circumstances. We know that tokens can be thought of as isolated individuals or in terms of a critical mass. Kanter places the critical mass at 15 percent; Rita Mae Kelly and Jane Bayes suggest 20 percent as a sizable enough share of a group to affect change. The most constructive condition would be for the game itself to become more friendly toward women, and to be played on an equitable—rather than equal—playing field (Chafetz 1990). The culture would then incorporate women, and their needs and styles, into the agencies' preferred modes of action, rituals, and ceremonies. Clusters of women could germinate a changed culture and a changed gender ethos.

A countervailing possibility, however, is that when the tipping point is passed, men resist further advances of women into administration (Yoder 1991). To some extent any cluster of women within state bureaucracy inevitably leads to some aspects of ghetto existence so long as women operate within a larger system that privileges masculine outlooks and men. Even when women constitute a majority of top posts, this cluster of women still must intersect with the larger system where men predominate. Organizations perpetuate themselves by promoting those who exemplify the prized norms, norms that have largely been established by men. The apparent equal treatment of women then means that women must exemplify men to be prized. Should women, especially those in a cluster, not fully share these norms, their differences are easily marked as deviance, which in turn readily becomes disparaged, diminished, or otherwise undervalued. The cluster of women becomes isolated rather than included in the whole, and any differences in outlook they might hold can easily and uncritically be dismissed rather than integrated.

Women who move into traditional male agencies are pioneers. Their performance is watched carefully and they believe they must be better and work harder than men to be accepted (Bayes 1987; Duerst-Lahti 1987). The work of pioneers can begin a transformation process, even though it is hard for them to make substantial and lasting change unless a critical mass of women come into professional ranks also. Too often pioneer women are excluded from, or at least not fully integrated into, critical managerial networks. The voices of pioneer women often are not seen or heard because they are viewed through the lens of gender, and the extant culture assumes male managers. As if they are impostors in the managerial world, pioneer women must choreograph their moves. Because they are highly visible, they live in the spotlight and face a lonely walk on a managerial tightrope.

A main problem perpetuating the managerial tightrope is homo-phyly—a resemblance due to commonality. Token managerial women are enough like their male counterparts to have been promoted into top ranks, yet they are also women and must live with themselves and others in a culture that structures options by gender. We do not know what organizational culture would be like if women predominated in systems of public power.

Ironically, mentoring has the effect of maintaining the status quo even though some women have entered top ranks. People arrive in senior positions because they represent the values that the organization wants to promote. They then mentor subordinates in whom they find these values, usually others like themselves. Thus, homophyly is perpetuated into the present by promoting the same sorts of people into power positions. In the process, organizations perpetuate themselves and their culture. Although pioneer women have traveled around or through the glass ceiling, they have not appreciably disrupted the male lineage of organizational ancestry, perhaps because these women are more like their male counterparts than they are like most women. A more persuasive explanation, however, is that their numbers remain too small to make much change, and this condition is unlikely to change because men still control promotion in most organizations.

The weight of cultural traditions on agency personnel practices becomes obvious in the appointments that are made to high positions. We will know culture has changed when women as top-level state administrators are no longer remarkable, when the sexuality of organization derives more of its center from women.

Conclusion

What are the structural or systematic explanations for the findings of this chapter? We found that agencies have particularistic cultures that encompass a gender ethos. The gender ethos, and its meaning for women, can be revealed through the pairing of conventional gender roles and the work of the agency; access to positions with structural power resources; the history of women in agency management; and the concentration of women within the work force. The configuration of culturally rooted expectations and agency norms explains the prevailing pattern. Culture helps structure when and where women enter top administrative posts. Predictably, women enter most often those agencies whose functions are consistent with conventional feminine gender roles.

The ways women have entered top positions over time proves important and largely predictable by gender stereotypes. In most agencies women have entered through the "administrative services" route. This is by far the most common pattern, and is especially true in "male bastions." However, in a few agencies, women come routinely to hold many of the management slots atop the substantive divisions. Under those circumstances, men seem to control the administrative services area. This process might be more consistent in states with a greater centralization of personnel management.

Women at the very top have made a difference by promoting women and, maybe most important, by acting as pioneers who have begun to "normalize" the presence of women in management. Nonetheless, nearly thirty years past the rebirth of feminism, when women work, their tasks are discussed in stereotypical terms. Perceptions are filtered through gendered lenses. And, even though they may have little relationship to individual people, stereotypes nevertheless are used to form judgments. Some stereotypes emerge from the ecological fallacy observed by Kanter (1977): gender stereotypes intersect with work norms and create new stereotypes derived from observations in one situation that are then assumed to be accurate across the board. An example is that men are usually described as influential and women as more easily influenced. Such a perception results from people's experience with "reality": men more often hold positions with structural power that enables influence, while women more often are in weak structural positions. Structural arrangements are erroneously attributed to gender. Structures mediate culture and culture shapes behavior.

More insidious is the gendered nature of cultural understandings of organizational life. Commonly, organizational tasks are discussed in terms of sports analogies or military metaphors. One might be expected to behave like a "team player." Language affects one's expectations about the appropriate sex of decision makers. For example, leaders "quarterback," employees are "coached," and "timeouts" are called. Such metaphors are based on childhood understandings and youth experiences that are far more common to men than to women. Yet they pervade organizational life and somehow come to be understood as "normal" and universal. One might even argue that many aspects of organizations—preoccupation with rules and hierarchies, along with gaming, other competitions, and a dysfunctional focus on territory—derive from a masculine world view. These aspects can be found in most large complex organizations. Agency culture is a primary vehicle for transmitting the gender ethos of an agency. When it is understood in terms imbued with manliness, women are closed out of major portions of it. When it is understood as normal even though it is imbued with masculinity, women confront the problem of making the nonconscious conscious before they can even begin to transform the organization in transgendered ways.

Unfortunately, even today, too few women hold positions to undertake the process of transformation. Organizations reflect the styles of those in leadership positions and both shape and are shaped by members. Women need to be in management if they are to behave managerially. Roles define behavior and implicit cultural rules govern both. If women are largely excluded from such roles, then they lack the opportunity to be "managerial." In a circular fashion, without such an opportunity, cultural expectations reinforce the absence, thereby illustrating that women are incapable of being managerial. Such a pattern then leads to a tradition that does not expect women to be in management, and once this pattern becomes traditional, values in the organization tend to correspond with the arrangement. And, again in a circular fashion, values guide behavior and the justification for a behavior too often is, "That's the way it has always been done." The absence of women in top ranks then becomes embedded in culture.

In the end, women will not become full participants in state agency life until the culture of these organizations *accepts* rather than *excepts* women managers. Ultimately, organizational culture hinges on the social construction of reality and meaning. Not until women's "deviance" in organization culture changes to the norm will women be fully integrated into organizations. Unless organizations incorporate women's vantage points, and the "reality" of organizations includes and incorporates norms, practices, and policies that suit women as well as they suit men, little will change. Transformation will not occur. Much like our discussion in chapter 7, where we found that perception was the key to women's style, the symbols and symbolism associated with top positions will have to change before women will be full participants. To achieve this, we must begin by recognizing gender within the culture of organizations.

—————————————————— **9**

Policy Preferences on Workplace Reform

Mary M. Hale and M. Frances Branch

Policies affecting workplace reform, such as affirmative action programs, prohibitions against discrimination, pay equity, and childcare, affect women and men differently. Thus, policies preferred by one sex may not be well received by the other. This chapter surveys policy preferences regarding workplace reforms and discusses how changes in these policies would alter the workplace and level the playing field for women and men in public administration. — Editor's Note

Most public policies aim to balance market forces with the general welfare of the community. The delicate balance that is sought attempts to reconcile the interests of government, business, and the environment. In order to achieve this balance, choices must be made regarding conflicting interests, values, and objectives, along with varying degrees of desire for reform. With each policy, weight has to be given to cost savings, what we *ought* to do, and how we produce and justly distribute our benefits and burdens. The choices that result from this weighting reflect the priorities upon which Americans have agreed.

Differential Impact of Workplace
Policies on Women and Men

Instead of being gender-neutral, many public policies often have a differential impact on women and men. This has much to do with the fact that policies often regulate the lives of women differently than they regulate the lives of men (Muncy 1991). Policies also produce unintended consequences, such that solving the problems of one group creates problems for other groups. Examples include policies dealing with family structure, economic development, employment, housing, civil rights enforcement, crime prevention, and the environment. In these areas, policies designed to remediate or prevent problems for government, business, or society disadvantage one sector to advantage another. Policies that promise to produce a win–win solution usually produce a win–draw–lose situation. Policies attempting to promote workplace reform have the same effect.

In the past three decades, American women and men, particularly women, experienced major changes in family structure, career choices, political influence, and economic development roles. It is commonly known that women and men sometimes view, approach, and address issues differently. Such gender differences are reflected in their different views of the world based upon their role in it and how it affects them. Differences show up in women's and men's biases about economic status, their views on competition, and their political preferences.

In this chapter, gender preferences regarding workplace policies important for human resources management are examined. These policies are of interest because they have the potential for promoting individual opportunities for career growth as well as providing a means for public agencies to capitalize on the abilities of capable employees. They are also important because they shine a spotlight on inequalities in benefits and governing power, and they limit, both directly and indirectly, opportunities for employment and advancement.

Trends in Gender Preferences

In response to the changing labor force, human resources management has become increasingly interested in policies involving economic issues such as those revolving around equal employment opportunity, pay equity, and alternative work options such as flex-time, job sharing, work sharing, child care, and leave options. Reflecting the changing circumstances of the work force, these policies are intended to enable organizations to manage their people, time, and space resources more effectively, and to enhance individual opportunities to pursue career development and enrich work experiences.

Gender and policy preferences are linked because contemporary workplace policies differentially advantage one sex over another. In this particular body of research, three research questions are of interest in determining what gender differences, if any, exist among high-level administrators in state government regarding their preferences for various workplace policies:

1. Is there a difference between female and male administrators' support for policies that advance the reality of representative bureaucracy, affirmative action, and prohibitions against discrimination?

2. Is there a difference between female and male administrators' support for policies that advance child care, pay equity, job sharing, and flexible work schedules?

3. Is there a difference between female and male administrators' degree of support for "adaption" (doing things better) or innovation (doing things differently)?

Administrators' Preferences

The surveys of public administrators included several workplace policy items pertaining to equal employment opportunity issues and support for child care, pay equity, job sharing, and flexible work schedules. The administrators were asked to indicate a score from 1 to 5 showing their degree of agreement with certain statements. Responses indicated the following: 1 = strongly disagree; 2 = disagree; 3 = neither agree nor disagree; 4 = agree; and 5 = strongly agree.

Table 9.1 shows how women and men differ in their views about representative bureaucracy. The numbers reported represent the mean responses for women and for men. Significance tests were performed to identify statistically significant differences between the sexes.

In all cases, women showed more support for a representative bureaucracy than men did. In fact, all comparisons were in the same direction. On only the first question, about a representative bureaucracy in terms of its ethnic/racial composition, did one state, Alabama, fail to reach significance. It is noteworthy that in each state men showed more support for the representation of ethnic/racial groups than they did for gender representation. Women, on the other hand, rated both similarly.

Table 9.1

Attitudes toward Representative Bureaucracy

	Women		Men
Statement 1: Employees in state government should reflect the ethnic/racial makeup of the population.			
Alabama	2.95		2.70
Arizona	4.05	*	3.16
Texas	3.20	*	3.10
Utah	3.91	*	3.22
Wisconsin	3.80	*	3.10
Statement 2: Employees in state government should reflect the gender makeup of the population.			
Alabama	2.87	*	2.13
Arizona	4.02	*	2.98
Texas	3.30	*	2.90
Utah	3.99	*	2.94
Wisconsin	3.80	*	3.00

*$p < 0.05$

Table 9.2 shows how women and men differ in their attitudes toward affirmative action. Notice that, across the board, women favor affirmative action more than men. And men favor affirmative action more for minorities than they do for women in each state except Alabama. The differences reach statistical significance in all comparisons except in Texas with regard to the question about preferential treatment for minorities. The direction of the difference, though, is consistent with that found in the other states.

The uniformity in responses across the states is remarkable. These policy issues, representative bureaucracy and affirmative action, fall along gender lines. Women favor both to a higher degree than do men. The status quo currently favors white men. Obviously, as a group, they stand to lose the most if these two policies were to be fully implemented and this point is not lost on the respondents. These responses are consistent with those appearing in Table 9.3, which presents responses first to a question that inquired into respondents' perception of the status of white males in the work force, and second, to a question that asked them for a report of their personal experience. Keep in mind that, from the standpoint of an objective observer, all respondents are

Table 9.2

Attitudes toward Affirmative Action

	Women		Men

Statement 3: Females should receive preference where female and male applicants are of equal ability and females are under-represented on a department's work force.

	Women		Men
Alabama	2.90	*	2.58
Arizona	3.74	*	3.01
Texas	3.40	*	2.90
Utah	3.41	*	2.72
Wisconsin	3.80	*	3.00

Statement 4: Minorities should receive preference where applicants are of equal value and minorities are under-represented on a department's work force.

Alabama	2.81	*	2.31
Arizona	3.79	*	3.18
Texas	3.30		3.10
Utah	3.65	*	2.85
Wisconsin	3.80	*	3.20

$*p < 0.05$

Table 9.3

Attitudes toward Personal Discrimination

	Women		Men

Statement 5: White males are sometimes discriminated against in either hiring or promotion.

Alabama	2.43	*	3.37
Arizona	2.50	*	3.04
Texas	2.40	*	3.40
Utah	1.88	*	2.68
Wisconsin	3.00	*	3.80

Statement 6: I personally believe that I have been discrimated against in either hiring or promotion.

Alabama	2.08		2.01
Arizona	2.69	*	1.88
Texas	2.60	*	2.20
Utah	2.71	*	1.87
Wisconsin	2.20		2.40

$*p < 0.05$

those "who have made it." They have reached managerial positions that only a small proportion of employees in state agencies ever reach. Also, keep in mind that perceptions, whether or not they reflect reality, have a substantial impact on policy debates.

The scores reveal that while women tend to disagree mildly that white males are sometimes discriminated against, men tend toward agreeing with the statement. Across all states, this difference reached statistical significance. However, when asked whether they believed they personally had been discriminated against, men disagreed fairly strongly compared with their response to the prior perceptual question. In three states, Arizona, Texas, and Utah, women reported significantly more discrimination than men did.

We believe these results send a loud message about the diminishing likelihood of men speaking for women and advancing women's opportunities for equal opportunities for job advancement. These male administrators, who are in decision-making positions and who far outnumber the women, report that, even in the face of personal experience to the contrary, men are discriminated against in hiring or promotion. Since perceptions, with or without facts at hand, color policy debates, this is an omen with which women must reckon.

Now we turn to attitudes on workplace reform. The policy areas include child care, pay equity, job sharing, and flexible work schedules; these are issues that are usually framed as "women's issues." Table 9.4 shows the level of support for these reforms among women and men who have made it into administrative ranks most likely without benefit of these.

As Kawar (1989, p. 100) has noted, "these issues have been unsuccessful in receiving legislative consideration at either the state or federal levels. Pay equity and child care have occasionally been placed on the federal agenda but no national policy has evolved." While both women and men demonstrated support for all four policies related to workplace reform, women were substantially more supportive, suggesting that as decision makers, they would make a difference in the outcome of policy debates over these issues if their voices were to be heard.

The importance of child care is generally agreed upon by both women and men, although women support it significantly more than men. Women and men in all states were most supportive of pay equity, although there were significant differences between the sexes in each

Table 9.4

Support for Workplace Reform

	Women		Men
Statement 7: I personally support issues related to child care.			
Alabama	3.96	*	3.56
Arizona	4.40	*	3.76
Texas	4.30	*	3.40
Utah	4.43	*	3.77
Wisconsin	3.50	*	3.10
Statement 8: I personally support issues related to pay equity.			
Alabama	4.58	*	4.12
Arizona	4.69	*	4.23
Texas	4.80	*	4.40
Utah	4.76	*	4.41
Wisconsin	3.60	*	3.00
Statement 9: I personally support issues related to job sharing.			
Alabama	3.84		3.56
Arizona	4.25	*	3.56
Texas	4.10	*	3.60
Utah	4.50	*	3.99
Wisconsin	3.90		3.70
Statement 10: I personally support issues related to flexible work schedules.			
Alabama	4.13	*	3.71
Arizona	4.38	*	3.97
Texas	4.30	*	3.40
Utah	4.65	*	4.20
Wisconsin	4.20		4.00

*$p < 0.05$

state surveyed. Perhaps support for this policy is strong because if it were to be enacted, everybody would win. Women would be helped personally by pay equity since their pay would increase, and married men would be helped indirectly by the increased salaries that their wives would bring home. Job sharing was favored more strongly by women than by men to the point that a statistically significant difference occurred between the sexes in their degree of support for it in Arizona, Texas, and Utah. Women favored flexible work schedules significantly more than men did in Alabama, Arizona, Texas, and Utah.

In spite of the fact that women tended to favor these reforms significantly more than men did, men nevertheless showed support across the board. Perhaps this is a sign that these reforms are becoming less of a "women's issue" and more of a "family issue" across the states. The consistent and statistically significant differences shown in Tables 9.1 through 9.4 provide evidence that gender patterns exist with regard to support for various policies. We are led to speculate, then, that with more women gaining entrance to decision-making posts in state government, it is more likely that these policies will be seriously discussed and will find their way onto the legislative agenda in the near future.

These gender differences inevitably reflect different views on the best way to bring about change. Since government is the engine that drives change in this nation, we can anticipate that, as the demand for workplace reform increases, the role of government in making it happen will increase. And since the respondents to this survey are already in the engine, it is even more likely that such changes will take place.

There are indications that the policies that will eventually be adopted will represent less "adaption" and more "innovation." The survey data show that there is strong support among women for workplace reforms that would decrease the negative impact that family responsibilities have on their careers. Because of this, there is a likelihood that women will reject slower modes of change and insist upon innovation. The fact that men also favor these policies further heightens this likelihood. And, finally, the fact remains that these issues are already bubbling to the surface and are being discussed. For example, alternative work options have been experimented with in several settings and this interest, coupled with the fact that more and more women are entering the labor force, promises to leave the door open to more innovations. We turn now to a discussion of how flexibility can be built into the workplace.

Labor Economics and Workplace Reforms

Economic, social, and demographic changes are forcing many organizations to implement alternative work options that deviate from the eight-hour-a-day, five-day-a-week standard. Some of those options include flex-time (also called flexitime), job splitting, and job sharing. Flex-time allows employees to set their own starting and quitting times within limits set by management. Often, all workers are required to be present during the "core" mid-day hours. Thus, the employer is able to offer extended service hours since some workers may come as early as 7:00 A.M. and others may leave as late as 8:00 P.M. The primary goals of flex-time are to offer a low-cost work benefit, to boost employee morale, and to address the changing work force, focusing particularly on women and their families (Olmsted and Smith 1989).

Job sharing was first discussed in the mid-1960s but was not put into practice until a decade later. Simply put, the program involves two employees who share one full-time position, prorating the salary along with the fringe benefits. This should not be confused with job splitting. Job sharing requires the interaction and coordination of talents and skills of two employees. Job splitting, on the other hand, occurs when the workload can be easily divided such that there is little if any inter-dependence between the two participants. This latter arrangement is more common in lower-level positions (Olmsted and Smith 1983).

Verespej (1989) estimated that in 1989 less than 1 percent of all workers shared jobs and that no more than 15 percent of all organizations offered such a program. But the popularity of job sharing seems to be increasing. Studies of the Administrative Management Society show a 6 percent increase in usage among 500 organizations from 1981 to 1987 (Olmsted and Smith 1989). And a 1985 study by the American Management Association (AMA) reported that, of the user firms, 65 percent make the option available to clerical/secretarial workers, 46 percent to hourly workers, 25 percent to professional/technical staff, 15 percent to supervisors, 9 percent to middle managers, and 5 percent to senior managers. The AMA report indicated that job sharing plans had shown significant growth since their original implementation (Olmsted and Smith 1989).

Job sharing is used in both the private and the public sectors (Lussier 1990). A 1986 survey of state personnel offices shows that thirty-five states permit job sharing. Of these, eighteen have written policies and twelve have written legislation. Workers in New York State take advantage of the Part-time/Shared Job Program: in 1988, over 7,000 salaried employees were working part-time and 87 percent of those were sharing jobs.

The adoption of alternative work options is a result of increased competition and demand, and a shrinking labor pool. For instance, a 1980 White House Conference on Families Gallup poll indicated that 54 percent of all workers surveyed felt flexible work hours, including job sharing, was a number one priority (Olmsted and Smith 1983). The problem is certainly serious: in 1988, one organization had 27 percent fewer job applications than in 1987, and 44 percent fewer for jobs involving typing and word processing (Verespej 1989). A supervisor noted, "companies will be hard pressed to find the employees they need. More and more people—both women and men—want this flexibility to balance work and family life. Instead of losing good people, we'd rather create work schedules so we can retain them" (Verespej 1989, p. 12).

Job Sharing Participants

Even though a majority of job sharers are women, a significant number of other workers are participating in this alternative work option, including men, senior employees, individuals with health problems, and part-time students. Take, for example, the case of Jess Rios and Terry Collins. On a temporary basis they shared an Auditor III position with the Franchise Tax Board of the State of California. This came about because at mid-career, Collins decided he wanted to pursue a law degree but quickly realized he could not continue working on a full-time basis. After discussing a job sharing partnership with forty-six-year-old Rios, one of his department colleagues, they presented and had their plan approved by the Board administration. Says Rios, "The American work ethic says go, go, go. You're supposed to go at full speed. I'm going at half speed. I think it's good to have something to look back on, to be able to say, 'That was a magnificent year' " (Olmsted and Smith 1983, p. 78).

The popularity of job sharing has also extended into the senior population. Often the older worker who desires additional leisure time wants to continue working beyond retirement without sacrificing job status. Job sharing is not only beneficial to the retiree, but to the organization as well, since it retains the seasoned, experienced worker who can train junior employees (Meier 1979). It is likely more seniors will participate in job sharing for two reasons. First, this segment of the population is rapidly growing, and second, supplemental income will become increasingly important due to dwindling social security benefits and inflation. Patricia Lee, president of Workshare, Inc., noted that "you have to find meaningful ways to put older people to work. You can't just put them out to pasture—they're too useful" (Bahls 1989, p. 29).

Alternative work options have grown in popularity in other nations as well. The Dutch government began a pilot job sharing program in response to an increased demand for more and better part-time positions. Social scientists in Japan, France, and Germany have studied and conducted research on the feasibility of implementing job sharing in their countries (Olmsted and Smith 1983). England's Stock Exchange offers the program for all of its workers, but is particularly well known for its successful operation at the executive level, where employees accept joint responsibility for their work objectives (Chapman 1983).

Advantages of Workplace Reforms

Alternative work options, such as flex-time and job sharing, are often selected by management because of their multiple benefits to the organization: improved employee retention, increased flexibility, reduced absenteeism, higher employee morale, increased quality and productivity, wider range of skills for one position, and lower training and recruitment costs. Because job sharers have more free time, they are less likely to use working hours for personal errands. One manufacturing company that offered such a program for its shift workers found that absenteeism for job sharers was less than 1 percent, compared to the 7.6 percent rate for all workers (Nollen 1982).

Both employers' and employees' interests are promoted by flexible work options. When job sharers are sick or on vacation, their partners can cover for them. Although many job sharers have personal reasons for not wanting full-time work, many will agree to serve a stint on a full-time schedule now and then in a dire situation. Thus, the employer is virtually guaranteed that the position will be filled almost year-round (Bahls 1989; Lussier 1990).

Alternative work option policies are conducive to good morale also. MONY's vice president of staff management operations, Jan Folta, believes job sharers are happier, more energetic, more creative, and less prone to burnout. And because they do not want to risk losing their job sharing positions, they are often more enthusiastic and productive (Verespej 1989). Furthermore, working shorter hours serves to decrease job-related stress. This relatively stress-free work environment often results in workers who are more dedicated, driven, and aggressive. Job sharer Hal Smith noted, "My editorial position was one of those 'knowledge jobs' in which there is an additional productivity bonus. Because inspiration and creativity have little respect for the clock, knowledge workers often get insights into their work when they are off duty" (Smith 1989, p. 70). Employers also benefit from the combination of two workers' skills, particularly if they are complementary. For example, an administrative assistant's job may require good oral and written communication skills. Employees can be matched to cover both of these requirements. Martha and Casa Sanchez are sisters who share a bookkeeping position with a Mexican food wholesaler in California. One sister is particularly skilled with client contact; the other handles the monthly financial statement preparations (Bahls 1989). Between them, all tasks are accomplished and both the employer and the employees benefit from their capitalizing on the strengths of each other while compensating for one another's weaknesses.

Other benefits for employees include having more free time to pursue leisure interests, family interests, and schooling. One job sharer wrote, "I could never shake off the nagging suspicion that life was passing me by. . . . Why can't we return to college or spend time with our children during their formative years or build a house or write a novel and then return to our full-time jobs without irreparably damaging our careers?" (Smith 1989, p. 70).

Similar comments from job sharers were noted in a study by Gretl Meier in 1979. One social worker commented, "What I like best is that I'm not always tired, but able to come back to work refreshed rather than always being under pressure" (Meier 1979, p. 75). Others noted the benefits of sharing decision-making duties, having the support of a partner and the opportunity to exchange ideas. Many felt that job sharing gave them a greater sense of belonging to an organization, and also added to their self-esteem and confidence. A teacher noted, "The energy of two sources means that a balance may ultimately be better struck which is much more stable than one individual's energy alone" (Meier 1979, p. 77).

Felice Schwartz (1989) maintains that in the traditional work world, today's working women have only two choices: to be career-primary or to be career-and-family women. Their job paths (commonly known as the "career" and "mommy" tracks) lead to different degrees of job success. The majority of women are career-and-family driven and are often not afforded the same job opportunities as those provided to career-primary women. Work options such as job sharing offer an alternative to this procrustean bed. They offer a third career track for those women and men with heavy family obligations or nontraditional life-styles. The job sharer is not only more able to balance conflicting obligations but also retains the position and career advancement potential of a full-time employee. Innovations such as these do not come free. They require that organizations have enough slack to afford an increase in administrative costs, benefit expenses, and training fees. Other costs may accrue from the rental of additional office space and equipment, although a number of job sharers schedule their time so that these can be shared (Olmsted and Smith 1989). The extension of supervision is also necessary, especially during the performance appraisal period (Lee 1984; Lussier 1990). As the numbers of qualified job seekers decreases, however, and retention becomes more of a challenge, these costs may be a small price to pay compared to the continual costs of hiring, training, and supervising new staff. As the survey data outlined in the tables show, both women and men favor workplace reforms, but women favor them more intensely than men. The following discussion sheds light on why women and men view such reforms differently.

The Influence of Gender on Policy Preferences

There are two explanations that provide a foundation for understanding how gender affects workplace policy preferences. The first, in which gender is viewed as a dependent variable, is socialization. Previous studies have shown that socialization likely explains men's concerns and preferences for individual rights and self-interest and women's concerns for interdependence, responsibility, and compassion (Gilligan 1982; McClelland 1975).

The second explanation, using gender as an intervening variable, has to do with differences in prior work experiences. The data in chapter 8 show that the female administrators are more likely to have had experience in the helping agencies. Having direct work and life experience dealing with peoples' problems with daily living is likely to allow women to be more sensitive to the needs of people as compared with their male counterparts, who may be more accustomed to dealing with impersonal concerns such as highway construction or tax collection.

This difference in work experience is likely to lead to gender differences in the preferences or priorities for various workplace agenda items. As Kingdon (1984, p. 101) notes, topics sometimes become prominent agenda items "partly because important policy makers have personal experiences that bring the subject to their attention." While strategies that facilitate child care, pay equity, job sharing, and flex-time, are important in addressing and confronting the responsibilities facing both women and men, they will have the most salience for women who fit either of the following categories:

1. women who have historically had to choose between obligating themselves to family responsibilities or work in ways men have not;
2. women whose potential for full-time employment and career advancement has been affected by barriers erected because of their sex.

There are several implications of gender differences regarding policy preferences. The first has to do with the relationship between gender recruitment into educational and employment settings and agenda change. In the agenda-setting stage of the policy process, women and men may differ over whether and to what degree a problem should become a concern for government. As Kingdon (1984, p. 160) notes, agenda change occurs either because "incumbents in positions of authority change their priorities and push new agenda items; or the personnel in those positions changes, bringing new priorities onto the agenda by virtue of the turnover." As the number of women and their visible participation in decision-making positions (Kingdon's "visible cluster") increases, the chances of particular subjects being given a higher priority on a governmental agenda are enhanced.

Similarly, women's growing presence in graduate public administration programs that turn out trained female administrators is likely to influence long-term agenda setting. As their careers develop, graduates achieve influential decision-making posts in government and are able to affect policy choices. Agencies that hire and promote women as administrators in significant numbers are likely to recognize different policy agendas and outcomes than those that remain dominated by men. The support for decisions made regarding these policies, including which alternatives and solutions are aired, is affected by who the participants are and which problems are on their minds (Kingdon 1984).

The second implication of gender differences has to do with their potential political importance in the workplace. Over the past thirty years, women have developed powerful social and political voices. Their voices and votes play a critical role in mass opinion, politics, and government. With women's continuing move into administrative positions, it is likely that their "preference power," combined with their knowledge of the policy process and their skills for mentoring and coalition building can be used to advance workplace reform. Their influence can make a difference both in the types of policies proposed and in the outcome of these policies.

The third implication is that organizations with more flexible workplace policies will be better able to facilitate the recruitment and retention of valuable employees. They will also be able to enhance overall morale and thereby increase their vitality. Unlike changes to provide pay equity and child care, which are more adaptive in nature, options such as flex-time and job sharing require organizational innovation. While men appear to support the innovative policies more than the adaptive policies, it is important to realize that the innovations they support are more applicable to men than are the adaptations.

Organizational advantages to both flex-time and job sharing have been reviewed earlier. To repeat, flex-time is a low-cost employee benefit that allows organizations to increase their coverage, extend service hours, and reduce tardiness. The improved conditions of part-time employment and reduced work time offered by job sharing also improve continuity, aid retention, enhance opportunities for flexible scheduling and skill development, and still meet human resources management objectives (Olmsted and Smith 1989, p. 107).

Conclusion

These research findings are offered with three caveats. First, while the number of state agencies with a significant number of women in the upper grade levels is increasing, there are still agencies and departments with no women in these top grades. Until women become, and are recognized as, powerful actors in the policy arena, their ability to influence the allocation process will continue to lag significantly behind that of men. Second, while public administrators are able to influence the policy process by direct involvement (that is, allocate public resources and guide implementation), they may or may not be direct policy makers (in the form of elected officials or political appointees). To understand the full impact of gender preferences on policies, this research should be replicated with other policy makers and political elites in elective, judicial, and appointive offices. Third, it is important to consider the many constraints bounding the policy stream. Participants in the policy process, including administrators, are not free or neutral actors; rather, "their actions are limited by the mood of the mass public and the preferences of specialized publics and elected politicians" (Kingdon 1984, p. 217).

Despite the fact that women still have a long way to go in achieving their rightful place in state government, sufficient progress has been made to allow us to ask whether female administrators make a difference. The support of the majority of administrators reported in this chapter for policy issues of child care, pay equity, job sharing, and flexible work schedules is sufficient to suggest optimism for future workplace reforms. The findings suggest that, among these decision makers, concern about these issues currently exists. Women's greater degree of support is likely to continue for two reasons: the historical view that these are "women's issues" has assisted women's success in building a strong political base, and women show no signs of giving up on promoting their interests. Since women are comprising a growing proportion of the work force, their continued involvement will make a difference on the outcome of these issues.

The link between gender and policy preferences observed in this research shows that gender differences exist and there is the potential to shape workplace policies of the future. Attention to these differences may allow workplace policies to be more inclusive in consideration of both societal segments—women and men—and may indeed be the driving force behind changes in workplace alternatives. The financial and economic impact of the policy areas examined in this research directly affect all members of society. In recognizing the importance of family and personal responsibilities faced by both women and men in the work force, we must attend to finding alternatives. Public work and private lives must inevitably blend to a greater degree than they currently do.

10

Summing Up What We Know

Mary E. Guy

This chapter summarizes how women's and men's status differs in decision-making posts in state agencies. The differences are described in terms of opportunity, power, and numbers. The author suggests levers that can be pulled to lower the barriers that prevent women from having an equal footing with men in terms of their ability to secure leadership positions. — Editor's Note

I think the most important lesson to be learned from this work is that gender predominates over geographic boundaries or political traditions when it comes to affecting one's status in public management. Although the substrate upon which women's and men's experiences are based is generally the same, it is the differences that are most visible. Thus, even though differences show up as only one point or a fraction of a point on a Likert-type scale, the direction of the differences persists across the states. The patterns are inescapable and haunting. They appear in regard to career advancement, personal background, family obligations, access to mentors, exposure to sexual harassment, fitting into the organizational culture, management style, and policy preferences.

Women and Men Are Different

To interpret differences and commonalities between women and men by means of scale scores is like studying icebergs. While six-sevenths of the iceberg are submerged, only one-seventh is above the water line and visible. The differences between the sexes that are reported in these chapters are the visible part of women and men in public management. The invisible part is the commonality that arises from being socialized in the same culture, living in the same communities, working in similar surroundings, and sharing the same overriding views about American government and democracy in general. Thus, what women and men have in common is much greater than what they do not have in common. This is why the differences that occur are so remarkable. Even with all the homogenizing influences of socialization and similar job experiences, a consistent pattern of differences showed up in all the states over most of the issues included in the survey.

Women are different from men and men are different from women. These differences matter in terms of workplace issues. And they matter in terms of representation in the work force. Women constitute over half of the population in each state, and they constitute over half of the work force in many agencies. Yet they hold only a small fraction of decision-making posts. These chapters indicate that if women were to hold decision-making posts in proportion to their representation in the work force (to say nothing of their representation in the population), many decisions now being made would be made differently. Even if the end result were to be the same, the inclusion of women in the decision-making process would enfranchise a currently disenfranchised majority of the population.

State agencies are designed to implement policies, and implementation is conducted by gendered instruments, women and men. The data show us that there is a persistent social presence of sexuality in the workplace. People are assigned to positions within the organization in sexually coded positions and locations. In 1954 Kate Mueller wrote that "Girls will be girls, or at least 90 percent of them will be girls, and the other 10 percent may find themselves in *Who's Who*" (in Powell 1988, p. 179). This sentiment is confirmed by the data, which show that women who get ahead are likely to be nontraditional, that is, they are unmarried, and if they are married, they do not have children. Being female in the traditional sense of marrying and playing the supportive roles of wife and mother is incompatible with having what it takes to be in *Who's Who*. A woman can either be feminine, or be an achiever in the world of work. Those who accomplish both are extremely rare.

Opportunity, Power, Numbers

Opportunity, power, and numbers are three significant features that differentiate men from women in the workplace. And the consequences of high or low opportunity, high or low power, and high or low numerical representation affect public administration and program implementation. Rosabeth Moss Kanter (1977) generated a rich set of hypotheses related to opportunity, power, and numbers, all of which are structural determinants of behavior in organizations. These factors help to reveal and explain women's status in public administration. For example, Kanter hypothesized that people low in career opportunity behave differently than people high in career opportunity. Opportunity relates to expectations and future prospects for mobility and growth. Those with high opportunity have high aspirations, are more attracted to high-power people, are competitive, and are more committed to the organization and to their careers. They value their competence, and become impatient or disaffected if they do not keep moving. On the other hand, those in low-opportunity positions limit their aspirations, seek satisfaction in activities outside of work, and have a horizontal orientation rather than a vertical orientation. They find ways to create a sense of efficacy and worth through personal relationships, they resign themselves to staying put, and they are concerned with basic survival and extrinsic rewards.

Kanter also developed notions about power, which she defined as the capacity to mobilize resources. People low in organizational power tend to foster lower group morale, behave in more directive, authoritarian ways, use coercive rather than persuasive power, and are more insecure. They are more controlling and more critical. People high in organizational power foster higher group morale, behave in less rigid, directive, authoritarian ways, and delegate more control. They allow subordinates more latitude and discretion and are more often seen as helping rather than hindering.

Kanter called a third characteristic "proportions." This concept relates to the composition of people in approximately the same situation. It is a numerical matter of how many people of a kind are present, so that differentness is, or is not, noticeable. People whose type is represented in very small proportion tend to be more visible, that is, they are "on display." They feel more pressure to conform and to make fewer mistakes, they find it harder to gain credibility, they are more isolated and peripheral, and they are more likely to be excluded from informal peer networks. Thus, they are limited in their source of power-through-alliance. Furthermore, they face more personal stress, are stereotyped, and are placed in role traps that limit effectiveness. People whose type is represented in very high proportion tend to "fit in," are preferred for high-communication managerial jobs, and find it easier to gain credibility in positions beset by high uncertainty. They are more likely to be accepted into the informal network, to form peer alliances, and to learn the ropes from peers. They are also more likely to be sponsored by higher-status organization members and to acquire mentors easily.

These three possessions—opportunity, power, and numbers—combine to produce self-perpetuating cycles. Thus, those with high opportunity behave in ways that generate more opportunity, which in turn produces further inducement for the behavior. High opportunity is accompanied by more power. Both opportunity and power coincide with being a member of a group that constitutes a large enough proportion of the work force so that any one member of the group is not immediately noticeable as "different." The confluence of opportunity, power, and proportion, then, produces upward cycles of advantage or downward cycles of disadvantage. The cycle of high opportunity, power, and numbers is very difficult to break into by newcomers to the managerial work force, such as women. The cycle of low opportunity, powerlessness, and tokenism is also difficult to break because of its self-perpetuating nature. Other than the occasional individual who is fortunate enough to escape its grasp, the cycle can only be broken by intervention in the form of structural change.

The status quo for managers in the states is different for men and for women: it is one of high opportunity, power, and numbers for men, and low opportunity, powerlessness, and tokenism for women. Systemic change is in process with the changing demographics of the work force and the fact that a large portion of new entrants to the labor force are women. Structural change is slowly in process as well, with workplace policies of the past giving way to accommodate women and their family obligations. But to watch the systemic and structural changes is like watching the leaves change in fall. One knows they are changing, but the pace is imperceptible if one holds a steady gaze. Only in retrospect is it obvious that substantial changes have occurred.

Changing demographics will probably serve as the foundation for a significant tempering of gendered roles in organizations. In a lagged fashion, the changes trigger, ever so slowly, unintentional change. Chafetz (1990) argues that as long as there is a sufficient number of working-age men available to meet the demand for the work they have traditionally performed, no change in the gender division of labor will occur. Of course, the converse of this is that when there are too few men entering the work force to fill existing managerial positions, more women will thereby gain access by default. But Chafetz (1990, p. 231) warns that if serious economic decline occurs, the clock is likely to be set back and gender relations in the workplace will resemble those of the 1950s rather than those of the 1970s and 1980s:

> Until women consolidate their power, they constitute an expendable labor force to be used according to the perceived needs and interests of mostly male elites. The key to the consolidation of power is the continued presence of most women in the labor force and their movement in more than token numbers into the ranks of elite gatekeepers, resource and opportunity distributors, and social definition makers.

If a structural approach to understanding behavior of men and women in management is useful, it is because it informs us about behavior in terms of opportunities, requirements, and rewards of the very real roles that women and men are scripted to play. The prevailing patterns observed in all the states surveyed can be explained by the structure of cultural expectations, societally imposed barriers, personnel system requirements, the role of work in peoples' lives, the breach/bridge between personal lives and public work, and agency norms versus sex-role norms. The chapters on career advancement, demographic characteristics, family obligations, mentoring, sexual harassment, management style, culture, and workplace policies speak to structurally related features. A brief review of each serves to uncover the components that influence gender roles in the managerial workplace.

Career Development

The career paths of women and men are different. Larwood and Gutek (1987) remind us that the modal pattern of men's careers is unlikely ever to fit the modal pattern of women's careers. Women are expected to interrupt their careers for pregnancy and child care. Those women who take extended breaks in service and return to the work force after their children are old enough to fend for themselves re-enter the work force and find their promotion opportunities limited because colleagues who have continuous service are the more likely candidates for promotion. Thus, timing and age enter into women's career paths.

While more women have steadily joined the work force since the 1960s, proportionately few have attained upper-management positions. Surveys indicate that this is the case in both the public and the private sectors. Women managers encounter a number of obstacles blocking their advancement, including family responsibilities, lack of acceptance in leadership positions, multiple roles with mutually exclusive demands, and built-in barriers within the promotion system.

The pattern in the states is for women to tend to move into management at a younger age than their male counterparts. And the women who make it are promoted from one position to another in less time than men are. Thus, the very small portion of women in the public work force who break into the high-opportunity cycle break into it early. But women managers receive lower pay than men in each state surveyed. They also continue to be under-represented in traditionally "male" occupations. Women tend to be clustered in public welfare, health care, and employment security agencies; they are under-represented in highways, corrections, and transportation departments.

Portions of this pattern are evident in public management positions with the federal government. Despite the fact that women represent 31 percent of all federal government managerial workers, the median salary for female managers is only about 60 percent of the median salary for males. Women are three times as likely as men to be concentrated in clerical positions while men are much more likely than women to shift from clerical work into professional, administrative, or technical occupations.

Responses in the surveys of women and men managers in state government reported here also revealed that women attributed greater interference from domestic responsibilities of housework, family commitments, and child care than did men. In addition, more women than men were divorced or never married. For instance, about 50 percent of the women managers are married, while over 80 percent of the men are married. This indicates that women who do not have family obligations are more likely to advance in management than if they have such obligations.

Based on the research reported here, one can conclude that while women are experiencing organizational barriers that stymie their career advancement to the upper levels of management, they are concurrently coping with domestic responsibilities of childbearing, child care, housework, and other family obligations. This clearly distinguishes the female manager from the male. The male manager not only experiences fewer organizational barriers in his career progression, but he has a wife who can handle child care and other family commitments while he works.

Only through a process of significant change and reform can we expect to see a more equitable balance between the numbers of female and male managers in state agencies. What can be done in order that more significant progress may be made in moving women into higher management levels in greater numbers in the future? Within agencies, agency directors can provide job enrichment experiences for aspiring women managers that will expose them to management experiences heretofore closed to them. For example, management rotation serves to cross-train managers, exposes them to work units with which they would otherwise have little experience, and qualifies them for promotion to assignments that require broad exposure to agency operations. By paving the way for constructive mentoring experiences and collegial networks, agency directors smooth the path that aspiring managers must travel to be noticed and groomed for advancement. Insisting upon a workplace environment that will not tolerate sexual harassment prevents the psychological warfare that dissuades women from pursuing higher posts. Directors can also restructure jobs and position classification systems so that employees who have family obligations can take advantage of flexitime and job sharing responsibilities without jeopardizing their chances for promotion. By facilitating child care and parental leave, employers remove a major obstacle for employees whose family obligations interfere with their promotion potential.

Practicing affirmative action means much more than merely adhering to the letter of the law in terms of considering applicants for promotion. It means promoting qualified women into positions even though there may never have been a woman who held that position before. It means making reasonable accommodations to the workplace so that women who are qualified for promotion are not penalized for being female. It means *affirmatively* reinforcing equal opportunity in the workplace by actions as well as words. Only when such measures are taken can an unfair system be altered so that women are treated as equals when they compete for management positions. In other words, it means no longer withholding opportunities from women. It means setting the stage for women to enter the high-opportunity cycle, rather than the low-opportunity cycle.

Personal Background

The positions that public managers achieve are influenced by their background. Women and men who have attained equally high positions in state government differ in their educational achievement, socioeconomic status, and, to a lesser extent, political activism. The similarity between the effects of sex across the states cannot be overstated. Regardless of political traditions, economic differences, systemic differences, and geographic differences, the same patterns prevail. Women who make it to the top managerial ranks in state agencies tend to come from more advantaged backgrounds than do the men who make it into those ranks. In the states surveyed, as many as 58 percent of the male managers held an advanced degree beyond the bachelor's degree, while as many as 76 percent of the women held such degrees. While as many as 28 percent of the women managers had mothers who held professional or managerial jobs, only as many as 13 percent of male managers' mothers had such a work history. While as many as 44 percent of female managers' fathers held professional or managerial jobs, only as many as 32 percent of the male managers' fathers held such jobs. While as many as 29 percent of the female managers reported that they had grown up in an upper-middle- or upper-class setting, only as many as 11 percent of the men reported such a background. And while as many as 32 percent of female managers said they had grown up in a lower-middle- or lower-class background, as many as 59 percent of male managers reported such a background. And, women are more likely to have achieved their position through their political connections than are men.

What does this information tell us? I think it says that, while the average man is able to climb the bureaucratic ladder, the average woman is shut out. She needs to be above-average in order to make it. It seems that the networks provided by one's socioeconomic status, family connections, education, and political activities apparently help women to crack the barriers that they face and gain a toehold where those without such networks would fail. What this means is that the women who make it to the top are different from the men, not so much because of their sex, but probably more because of a social distance that creates an even deeper chasm across which they must struggle to communicate with their male peers. When the women and the men perceive a lack of homogeneity between themselves, it is not only a sex difference but also a social and perhaps a political difference. The downside of this is that the differentness associated with being female is exaggerated by the differentness associated with social background. This differentness is responsible for a social distance that is attributed to gender when, in fact, it is produced by socioeconomic differences. Each sex expects the other to behave in ways they are accustomed, and each sex is disappointed. People like to associate with those whom they perceive to be like themselves. These men and women do not perceive one another like this. There is a social distance that gets translated into a gender difference, or perhaps exaggerated as a gender difference.

When women are promoted into management posts, they bring with them diversity. In this case, at the least, diversity is manifested in differing backgrounds and levels of educational achievement. As a consequence, the traditional homogeneity of the managerial roundtable is disturbed. Women have to work doubly hard to "fit in" because they are different not only by gender but by life-style habits. Their differentness diminishes their power, since they must first concentrate on forming coalitions with their peers and overcoming their "differentness" in order to be accepted as partners in organizational life. Power is derived from the ability to form coalitions of support. But before a coalition will form, its members must feel a kinship through common interests, affiliations, goals, or identification. In this regard, diversity hampers power for women.

Family Obligations

Public work and private lives intersect in the careers of top-level public servants. The personal is political here because conventional career patterns assume a particular relationship to family/private life obligations that pose problems for women pursuing careers. The fact is that men in top-level positions tend to live traditional family lives, while women disproportionately live nontraditional lives. Women who lead traditional lives carry an extra burden of family obligations and are less likely to be promoted into management ranks. Women who do not lead traditional lives carry an extra burden of being "different" from most women. As many as 71 percent of female managers reported they had no dependents, while only as many as 48 percent of male managers reported this. Women are caught in a catch-22: a woman's power is diminished by being "different" once she arrives in a management post; on the other hand, if she is not different, then she will have family obligations that are likely to prevent her from even being promoted to management.

Conventional ideology does not do a good job of describing the nexus between private lives and public work. Family arrangements, particularly those of women, do not fit the stereotype of organization man and family woman. These professional women are more likely than men not to be married and not to live with dependents, and most women have considerable responsibility for breadwinning. Despite these characteristics, women more than men believe that their private lives interfere with their careers. Women's "other orientation"—their concern for family—continues to constrain their public work. Yet we also know that men, too, are concerned with others and that their responsibilities, especially for dependents, limit their careers. The surveys showed that these successful public managers had work histories that deviated from the norms of full-time, continuous employment. Many had worked part-time at some point in their careers, and career interruptions were not uncommon. Life circumstances, and not simply gender, shaped work histories.

Career structures fit a particular kind of man, a man whose family responsibilities other than breadwinning are handled by a wife. While the system is changing slowly, the career structure remains, and it is a structure that limits women and suits many men poorly. Declining birth rates and increasing female labor force participation rates make urgent the adjustment of organizations to workers' lives. Contemporary career structures and dynamics must shift from a base that assumes organization man and family woman.

Mentoring

In addition to differences in career development, personal and social characteristics, and family obligations, there are also differences in mentoring that men and women report. Mentoring provides potential benefits to all involved participants: mentors and protégés, as well as organizations. A mentor not only offers friendship, support, and career advice, but also can provide help in promotion and in gaining access to key organizational leaders. Along with identification with role models, encouragement, and network development, protégés gain increased self-confidence, growth opportunities, familiarity with organizational politics, motivation to achieve career goals, support and cooperation of co-workers and peers, and visibility. These benefits, in turn, increase their probability of succeeding in organizations.

Because there are so few women in top posts, women who aspire to such posts find few mentors to turn to for advice. Although many women receive mentoring from senior men, there are some barriers women confront that men never do, and a man's ability to mentor a women through such barriers can be limited. While as many as 57 percent of the men reported having a male mentor at the agency-director level, only as many as 35 percent of the women reported having a woman mentor at that level. There are so few women who hold management positions that aspiring women looking for senior women to serve as their mentors have trouble finding them. Although women benefit from having male mentors, they also need mentors who have successfully forded the barriers that confront women but that men may not even be aware exist. Men, on the other hand, have many senior men from whom to select mentors.

The problem of numbers that Kanter talks about comes into play here. Because there are so few women in top positions, women who aspire to reach that level must rely on male mentors, who may be oblivious to the barriers that confront women as they struggle to move up the career ladder. The fact that there are so few women to help other women contributes to the continuing shortage of women in top posts. This cause–effect–cause cycle is tough to break.

Sexual Harassment

Sexual harassment is a very real problem for women in the workplace. While as many as 16 percent of women managers had experienced unwelcome sexual advances, only as many as 1 percent of male managers had experienced this. And while as many as 24 percent of women managers had experienced requests for sexual favors, only as many as 7 percent of male managers reported such requests. And the higher women go in the ranks, the more likely they are to experience harassment. Not only is the target of sexual harassment victimized and humiliated, but the agency suffers from productivity loss, negative publicity, and litigation fees. Such harassment affects work style, self-perception, and a woman's ability to perform her job functions, especially in regard to interpersonal relations.

Sexual harassment remains a contributor to the "glass ceiling effect," which keeps women out of upper levels of management and even discourages them from seeking entrance to those levels. Sexual harassment is also a factor in the power differential between women and men. The fact that such harassment continues in the public service reflects negatively on the perception that state governments are dedicated to ending sex discrimination and gender power differentials. As long as dominance in the workplace is allowed to be played out in sexual terms, men will prevail and women will remain in subordinate positions. Once again, we see women occupying the powerless positions while men occupy those with power.

Management Style

Organizations are gendered, and one way of exploring their gendered dimensions is through stereotypes and style. We have learned that "equal" treatment too often leads to an enshrining of what men have conventionally done. And approaches that deviate from the norm are deemed "lesser" rather than "different." So it is not unusual for women to stumble off the career ladder when they do not fit the "normal" behavior style, which, of course, is the traditional male model.

We know that bureaucratic stereotypes are largely masculine, yet the data showed that respondents in the Wisconsin sample believed gender-neutral traits to be of the greatest consequence, with feminine and masculine traits being similarly valued in top administrators. Perhaps the best way to think about style is to make our concepts more sophisticated by granting any number of combinations of behaviors to both women and men. To consider gender an advantage, however, we clearly must move beyond style. Such change begins with "a turn of the heart" in thinking about gender and advantage in organizations. Style explains far less than structures of power and the gendered processes that are integral to organizations.

When differences are found in the effectiveness of female managers compared with male managers, they tend to result from factors other than gender. Differences disappear when the contexts of the jobs are the same. But the contexts of the jobs are rarely the same. Women are found in positions that have less discretion and in cultures that will tolerate women in management positions. This fact is the basis of sex segregation.

The critical task facing those who work in public bureaucracies is to recognize that we engender the behavior of managers. We must explore structures of power coupled with an examination of the ways gender infuses organizational processes and shapes our interpretations of behaviors and events. Knowledge of gender, styles, and advantage can help agencies to function optimally while simultaneously overcoming institutionalized, and largely invisible, male advantage.

Women and men use mostly the same style of management, even though we find different clusters of behaviors for each gender. The reason there are so few women in top levels of state administrative positions flows from the innumerable small influences that shape the way we organize, along with who decides how we do it. With so few women in top spots, it is hard to know whether organizations might benefit from a "female advantage" in style *if* more women were to enter top ranks. It seems more evident that we can say public organizations will benefit from more women managers, and only more women managers will make apparent the ways in which organizations are gendered.

Agency Culture

Sex segregation has been a remarkably stable feature of the American workplace during the twentieth century (Powell 1988). State agencies are no exception. Powell (1988) notes that in 1900, 67 percent of the work force would have had to change jobs for sex segregation to be eliminated. Not much changed over the course of the century. By 1981, 62 percent of the work force would have had to change jobs for sex segregation to be eliminated. Diamond (1987) says that the proportion of women and men employed in professional and technical jobs is roughly the same for both sexes, but that women are more likely to be employed in traditional female job areas such as nursing, health technology, elementary or secondary education, librarianship, and social work. Men, on the other hand, are more likely to be bankers, engineers, architects, lawyers, physicians, and business executives. While we cannot determine the extent to which a self-selection process occurs in socialization to particular professions and agencies, we can see that women are clustered in those agencies whose missions are consistent with stereotypical "women's" concerns, such as health, welfare, and human resources.

Duerst-Lahti (1986) studied the culture and gender ethos in eight of Wisconsin's largest agencies. She concluded that the proportion of women in an agency's work force, and in an agency's upper management, corresponded with the agency's conduciveness for women. Furthermore, the four agencies found most conducive to women had all had a female secretary at some point since the late 1970s. While the proportion of women in an agency's work force does not fully determine its conduciveness for women, work force structure helps to predict where women do or do not make it to the top, and seems to shape the prevailing gender ethos of the culture.

Organizations reflect the styles of those in leadership positions and are transformed by all members. Women need to be in management if they are to behave managerially because roles prescribe behavior. If women are excluded from such roles, then they never have the opportunity to be "managerial" and thus are never given the opportunity because there are no examples to point to, showing that women are capable of being "managerial."

In what ways is the concentration of women constructive? Concentration is constructive when it provides a means for women to enter the system and change it; when women can attain resources of power accompanying such positions; when women are visible and serve as role models for women and men; when such concentration challenges traditional stereotypes; when it reveals use of inequity as justification for male privilege; and when it celebrates those constructive qualities that women bring to the work setting. Ghettoization, on the other hand, implicitly and explicitly affirms male norms. It delimits women's scope of influence; perpetuates tradition and/or convention; undervalues what women have done; and perpetuates a fear of "emasculation" for men so that it gives men an incentive to perpetuate gender difference and then to couple difference with dominance.

Structures mediate culture and culture shapes behavior. This means that structures are created that promote culturally valued behavior and impede behaviors that are not valued. And the stronger the values are, the more resistant they are to change, even when they risk obsolescence. For example, the disregard for women's leadership skills is perpetuated when barriers prevent women from gaining top posts and proving their skills. Agencies deprive themselves of a rich pool of talent when they fail to promote skilled women in order to continue doing what they have always done. Furthermore, they perpetuate the low-power, low-opportunity, low-numbers cycle that plagues women.

Policy Preferences

Policies affecting workplace reform, such as affirmative action programs, prohibitions against discrimination, and moves toward pay equity and child care, affect women and men differently. Changes in these policies would alter the workplace and level the playing field for women and men in public administration. As one might expect, workplace policies that treat all workers as if they were men get the most support from men. And policies that favor advancing women's interests receive the most support from women. In the surveys, women expressed a greater preference for workplace reforms related to proportionate representation of women, and issues related to child care and pay equity. Across the states the results are always in the same direction. There is something about being male that causes respondents to view the questions one way and there is something about being female that causes respondents to view the questions another way.

Women and men disagree over whether or not there is equal opportunity for both sexes. While men believe that discrimination against women is diminishing, women believe that it is increasing (Simon and Landis 1989). More specifically, when asked about employment discrimination in general, the percentage of women perceiving discrimination increased from 46 percent to 56 percent between 1975 and 1987; but the percentage of men perceiving discrimination decreased from 50 percent to 46 percent. In terms of their views about women being able to achieve executive positions, both women and men are becoming less optimistic: in 1985, working women were more optimistic than men about their chances for promotion and advancement in their positions, but by 1987 a smaller percentage of both men and working women agreed that women have an equal chance of becoming an executive (Simon and Landis 1989).

Despite the fact that women still have a long way to go in achieving their rightful place in state government, sufficient progress has been made to allow us to ask whether female administrators make a difference. The support of the majority of administrators for policies related to child care, pay equity, job sharing, and flexible work schedules is sufficient to suggest optimism for future workplace reforms. Concern about these issues currently exists and a greater degree of support by women is likely to continue for two reasons: (a) the historical view that these are "women's issues" has assisted women's success in building a strong political base; and (b) women show no signs of giving up on promoting their interests. Since women are comprising a growing proportion of the work force, their continued involvement will make a difference on the outcome of these issues.

The link between gender and policy preferences observed in this research shows that gender differences exist but that there is the potential to shape workplace policies of the future. Attention to these differences may allow workplace policies to be more inclusive in consideration of both societal segments—women and men—and may indeed be the driving force behind changes in workplace alternatives. The financial and economic impact of the policy areas examined in this research directly affect all members of society. It seems clear that as women are needed in the work force, child care and parental leave will be seen as necessary benefits. All three factors that combine to impede women's progress in management—meaning power, opportunity, and numbers—stand to be affected by workplace reforms. As reforms are put in place, the playing field becomes more level and women come closer to competing on an equal footing for promotions.

The Gendered Workplace

In 1980 the median salary for men who were in administrative positions in state and local government around the United States was $23,150; for women it was $17,493—a gap of $5,657. Ten years later, the median salary for men in the same type of positions was $40,469; for women it was $32,686, a gap of $7,783. If salary is a windsock for indicating progress, then this is a grim indicator. Salary figures reflect not only the lack of pay equity between the sexes but also the fact that women are often relegated to working in lesser-valued missions that pay lower wages. The results of the structural barriers that confront women show themselves in limited opportunity compared to what is available for men, limited power compared to what is exercised by men, and limited numbers compared to those of men.

We know that women are making advances into management posts but there is a long way to go before women will hold management positions proportional to their representation in the work force, let alone their representation in the population. We know that women in management in state and local government earn only 80 percent to 90 percent of what men earn. We know that women who live traditional lives are not nearly as likely to progress up the career ladder as are nontraditional women. We know that both women and men rely on mentors to assist their advancement, but that women have few senior women to look to for mentoring. We know that the higher a woman goes in the organization, the more likely it is that she has not only heard about sexual harassment happening to those around her but that she has actually experienced it. For her male colleagues, we know that they have heard about it but are unlikely to have experienced it. In terms of management style, we know that sex-role stereotypes seem to sculpt what are thought to be appropriate styles for women and men. When we closely examine styles, however, we see that what is thought to be real often fades into fantasy. We know that women in management ranks are concentrated in only a few agencies. The structure of the workplace mitigates against women having opportunities equal to those of men when it comes to attaining management positions. But these structures are not immutable and it is within the reach of states to adjust these structures to accommodate the needs of the changing work force and to breathe life into the ideal of a representative bureaucracy.

Although individuals make choices, institutional patterns shape alternatives and make one choice more likely than another. The case of the gendered workplace provides an example. Gender differentiation in subsequent generations stems from that of the current generation. One generation learns its behavior from its parent generation. The greater the gendered division of labor in this generation, the greater will be the gender differentiation in the next generation as a result of modeling. Thus, one can conclude that female managers are more likely to experience structural barriers (whether employed in the state, federal, or private sector) than are men. These barriers include sex-segregated jobs, sex bias and stereotyping of women evidenced by the opportunity channels for advancement being closed more often to women than to men, and pay inequities. If change is to happen, it will do so slowly over the generations, with gradually diminishing differentiation in the workplace between men and women.

Women have a difficult time making it beyond the mid-level management plateau. Top-level management and key decision-making positions are still predominantly reserved for men. Very few women make it to and remain in "mainstream" line management. Instead, women dominate the staff and personnel management functions while the top management positions remain male-dominated. Even though women go into management for the same reasons men do, females encounter sex discrimination and problems associated with stereotyping of women once they get there. The confluence of bureaucracy and gender equity has been the focus of this book. The findings reported herein shine a bright light on the status quo.

Let these chapters be a call for thinking "out of the box" about new leadership styles and new structures for classifying positions. We need to rest our career structures on assumptions that go beyond simple gender dualisms. Many details of the life and behavior inside state agencies reflect the culture, language, and style of mainstream American public administration as it approaches the end of the twentieth century. Opportunity, power, and numbers within the context of an agency, given its structural and systemic features, earmark the status of women in public administration in the states and serve to impede women's advancement.

Toward a More Equitable System

What levers would have to be pulled to ameliorate the differences between the sexes in public management? Four come to mind readily. They pertain to loosening rigid position classifications to accommodate women's career paths, encouraging agencies to be representative bureaucracies vertically as well as horizontally, overcoming the reluctance to promote women, and finally, promoting affirmative action in deed as well as in word.

First of all, position classification systems need to be adjusted. They need to be constructed so that they take into account the fact that career development for women is different than it is for men. Systems that use broad-band classifications to signify skill levels without the lock-step progression that inheres in more rigid systems provide at least some degree of flexibility toward this end. The incorporation of flexi-time and job sharing opportunities also expands opportunities for women to continue working and accruing experience even though their family obligations cannot accommodate a standard forty-hour work schedule. A theory of career development, Larwood and Gutek (1987) remind us, needs to be "roomy" enough to allow for breaks in service for women to accommodate child care responsibilities.

Second, the goal of a representative bureaucracy should be treated more seriously. Vertical representation is missing. Women should hold decision-making posts in far greater numbers than they do. Currently, women occupy the lower rungs on the agency ladders and men occupy the upper rungs. Although giving the appearance of being representative in terms of sheer numbers, the agency is anything but representative in its decision-making processes.

As participants in the policy process, administrators are not entirely neutral actors. They are able to influence the policy process by direct involvement, that is, by allocating public resources and guiding implementation. Until women become, and are recognized as, powerful actors in the policy arena, their ability to influence the allocation process will continue to lag significantly behind that of men. While the number of state agencies with a significant number of women in the upper grade levels is increasing, there are still agencies and departments with no women in these top grades. Keeping tabs on the proportion of women to men in decision-making posts in state government is not a trivial pursuit. It is important to keep an eye on middle- and upper-level managers because of the large numbers of personnel employed at the state level, coupled with the importance of policies and programs developed and governed by the states. Policy implementation should be directed by women and men, not just by men. This is the promise, as yet unrealized, of the notion of representative bureaucracy.

Third, the agencies' reluctance to change the way they have historically made promotions is hard to combat. But combat it they must if they are to put their best people in management. The changing demographics of the work force, along with the fact that economic changes are making resources ever tighter, forces agencies to work smarter to achieve their goals. Resources are tight and we must capitalize on the human potential of the work force. Windows of opportunity must be opened wider in order to identify and capitalize on the best talents, and often those best talents are women.

Fourth, taking affirmative action more seriously will also turn a lever. Simply promoting one or two women into decision-making posts may give the appearance of affirming women's presence in management but it stops short of meeting the intent of affirmative action. Integrating women into top management will introduce diversity and that is unavoidable. It is simply not sufficient to rest on one's laurels after "we have one," an expression heard all too often by directors explaining how they have met their affirmative goals. An important personnel function is to see that integration goes beyond tokenism. Being a member of a group that comprises only a small minority of those at the leadership level reduces members of that group to tokens. Until women integrate upper management to a greater degree, they largely remain tokens. Thus, their performance is always in the limelight. If a woman fails at a task, the failure is interpreted as an inadequacy of women in general. If a man fails at a task, his failure is interpreted as his personal failing, not that of all men. So women in management have two jobs: they must work not only at doing their jobs but at trying to increase the level of comfort that others have with them. Not until they are represented in numbers large enough to remove them from the status of tokens will they have the privilege of having only one job, that is, performing the tasks they are hired to do.

What do we know now that we did not know before these surveys were conducted? We know that we need more women managers for simple demographic reasons. We know, too, that if men who lead organizations continue to ignore questions of gender, their inactivity fosters suspicion about the extent to which they consciously, rather than inadvertently, perpetuate male advantage. We know that the entire system of organizing must be considered for its genderedness. We know also that public organizations have the greatest imperative to do so. The government establishes standards for other workplaces, so when it functions as an employer, the government ought to provide a model of the equal opportunities it mandates elsewhere. Public bureaucracies are a powerful branch of government. The interpretation of law and the legitimacy of governmental action depend upon broadening the scope of vision in order to understand the advantages offered by opportunity, power, and numbers.

Appendix A

Questionnaire Development

This six state study began as a spinoff of a cross-national project initiated within the Committee on Sex Roles of the International Political Science Association (Col 1985; Bayes 1991). This committee was concerned about the absence of information on women elites in civil service around the world. American scholars saw the fifty U.S. states as a useful testing ground for exploring how and why women advance in the public sector. Surveying employees in state governments permitted systematic comparison across organizational and political units.

Using the more qualitative analyses and interview results completed in the international project, several U.S. scholars (Jane Bayes, Dail Neugarten, Dorothy Riddle, Nancy Felipe Russo, Beverly Springer, and Jeanie Stanley) joined with Mary M. Hale and Rita Mae Kelly to develop a survey instrument applicable to the state level of government. The instrument was designed to obtain data on several topics. One major topic was gender similarities and differences in career patterns of public service elites. Other concerns encompassed perceptions of career success and satisfaction; employment behavior, including job functions, competencies, and behavioral styles; perceptions of structural barriers, including promotional opportunities and discrimination patterns; sources and types of mentoring support; domestic responsibilities and constraints; attitudes related to employment policy; and childhood and professional socialization.

The questionnaire (reproduced in Appendix B) was pretested by three groups: the first was a group of public servants at a federal training center in Colorado; the second was a randomly selected group of public administrators in Arizona; and the third was a focus group of public administrators in the State of Arizona. Since permission to conduct a systematic survey of upper-level public administrators required political approval in each state, the final questionnaire used in each state varied. Sensitivity to questions varied from state to state. In addition, the researchers had slightly varying research agendas and concerns. Hence, the questionnaires used in each of the six states overlap on most, but not all, of the items. These variations determine whether or not each state's data are included in the tables found in the text.

Sampling

Various sample designs were used. Arizona, the state in which the study was first conducted, Texas, Alabama, and Wisconsin used systematic probability samples. In Utah, a quota sample was used. In California, all top-level women in the Department of Social Services and Finance were studied. The California study also differed from the others in that it relied on more in-depth interviews and focused more on strategies used by individual women to attain career success. The California study followed the interview rather than survey approach of the international project and was used as a counterpart in that project to data collected by Bayes (1987) for comparable federal departments.

All six studies sought to distinguish upper-level from middle-level managers. This was done using criteria based on salary levels, duties performed, and personnel grade schedules as described below. Due to the different personnel systems in each state, the precise definition of the upper-echelon managers varied slightly from state to state.

In Alabama, all persons in positions paying $60,000 and above in spring 1989 were selected, except for physicians and other high-paid professionals who clearly were not managers. Individuals in the lower-paying levels III, IV, and V were selected *if* the job being performed was managerial regardless of salary. These criteria resulted in a universe of 806. Only 796 surveys reached their destination; 317 were returned, for a response rate of 40 percent. The final sample consisted of 229 male respondents out of a population of 618 (37 percent), 83 females out of a population of 151 (55 percent), and 5 of 27 (19 percent) questionnaires from individuals who did not indicate their sex.

In Arizona, the grade schedule extends from 1 to 30. Although distinctions are made by classification rather than grade, those in GS

23–30 generally are considered management, have more responsibilities, more authority, make more autonomous decisions, and supervise more employees. These grades include the exempt political
appointees and upper-level public sector managers. Exempt positions
are all policy-making positions or those directly responsible to a person in
a policy-making position. For example, all directors are exempt, deputy directors might be exempt, and assistant directors are exempt. The
Arizona universe of upper-level administrators was 478 in January
1987. Of these, 87 percent ($n = 414$) were males and 13 percent ($n = 64$) were females. All the 53 women who could be reached and who
were still in their positions at the time of the survey in spring of 1987
were included in the sample. Of these, 79 percent ($n = 42$) responded.
Of the 414 men, a systematic probability sample of 305 was drawn;
208 responded for a response rate of 68.2 percent.

In California, only two departments were studied: the Department of
Social Services, which is associated with traditional women's occupations, and the Department of Finance, which is associated more with
traditional male occupations concerning finance, money, and accounting. Due to the small numbers of women in the very top positions, all
women making over $40,000 a year were included in the sample.
Hence, this study blurs the top and middle management levels more
than the others. The individuals finally included in the California study
were 20 of 26 women in the eligible universe in the Department of
Social Service and all eleven women in the Department of Finance. At
the time of the study in 1986, 79 men were in the universe in the
Department of Social Services, and 57 percent of them ($n = 45$) were
interviewed. In the Department of Finance, 41 men were eligible and
27 percent (11) were interviewed.

The Texas state personnel system is highly decentralized, with over
200 relatively independent state agencies. Less than 25 percent of all
state employees are included in a state merit employment system.
Grades 19–21 appear to be those where most upper-level managers
fall. Hence, for this study a random sample of the 400 state employees
in these grades was selected. Of these, 130 men and 117 women responded, producing an overall response rate of 61.8 percent.

The Utah quota sample was drawn from those 495 individuals who
in 1986–87 were in Category One, "Officials and Administrators."
Individuals holding technical rather than managerial positions, such as
civil engineers, physicians, and accountants, were removed from the

universe so as to enhance the probability that those selected would actually perform policy-making and managerial functions. Of the 495, 13 percent ($n = 64$) were women. After removing the technical group, 62 women remained. All were sampled. A systematic probability sample was then completed of 50 percent of the men ($n = 87$). The return rate was 74 percent for the women ($n = 46$) and 62 percent for the men ($n = 116$).

The Wisconsin universe consisted of 640 professional and executive employees in pay ranges 13 and up. The response rate was 61 percent, yielding a sample of 389. For the purposes of this study, only those falling in pay ranges 16 to 24 and in the Executive Salary Group (ESG denotes political appointees) are included as they are the upper-level elite corps of the state's civil service. Women were oversampled to yield sufficient cases for analysis. All men and women in the ESG were surveyed, resulting in a sample of 16 women and 36 men; and 125 men and 125 women in ranges 16 to 24 were surveyed, with a resulting response of 84 women and 95 men. The final sample used for this study consisted of 100 women and 131 men.

Appendix B

Survey Questions

The following pages list the questions that were asked in the surveys conducted in the states. The questionnaires were accompanied by a cover letter that explained the purpose of the survey and told respondents where to return the completed survey form.

1. Current position:

   a. Position title: _____
   b. Years in this position: _____
   c. Approximate salary................$_____
   d. Age when you took this position/job.._____
   e. Number of persons directly supervised.._____
   f. Is your present position (check one):

       _____ (1) nonexempt (covered) position
       _____ (2) exempt (uncovered) position/appointment

2. Compared to your most previous position, did this position represent:
   (Please check)

   a. _____ (1) a range increase   b. _____ (1) a salary increase
       _____ (2) no change in range   _____ (2) no change in salary
       _____ (3) a range decrease   _____ (3) a salary decrease

   c. a position title change reflecting greater responsibility
       _____ (1) yes   _____ (2) no

3. Motivation in seeking this position: (Using the scale below, circle the number which best indicates the
   extent to which each was significant in your search for this position.)

	VERY UNIMPORTANT				VERY IMPORTANT
a. Greater responsibility...............	1	2	3	4	5
b. More enjoyment.......................	1	2	3	4	5
c. More power...........................	1	2	3	4	5
d. Higher salary........................	1	2	3	4	5
e. More status..........................	1	2	3	4	5
f. More autonomy........................	1	2	3	4	5
g. More authority.......................	1	2	3	4	5
h. Greater interest and challenge.......	1	2	3	4	5
i. More job security....................	1	2	3	4	5

4. Where did you hear about this position: (Please check as many as apply)

_____ (a) **Newspaper**
_____ (b) Professional journal
_____ (c) Friend employed in same agency
_____ (d) Friend employed in other state agency
_____ (e) Friend employed outside the agency
_____ (f) Executive search firm
_____ (g) Professional colleague in same agency
_____ (h) Professional colleague in another state
_____ (i) Internal announcement/supervisors

5. Second most recent position: (If you do not have a second most recent position, skip to item 17)

a. Position title _____

b. Years in this position.......................... _____ /yr.

c. Approximate salary......................... $ _____

d. Age when you took this position/job......... _____

e. Number of persons directly supervised....... _____

f. Was this position (please circle):

   1. Full-time   1. Public sector   1. Career position   1. In this state
   2. Part-time   2. Private for profit   2. Exempt appointment   2. Outside this state
                       3. Private non-profit   (specify_____)

6. Did this position represent: (Please check)

a. _____ (1) a range increase   b. _____ (1) a salary increase
   _____ (2) no change in range   _____ (2) no change in salary
   _____ (3) a range decrease   _____ (3) a salary decrease
   _____ (4) non-applicable   _____ (4) non-applicable

c. a position title change reflecting greater responsibility
   _____ (1) yes   _____ (2) no   _____ (3) N/A

7. Motivation in seeking this position: (Using the scale below, circle the number which best indicates the extent to which each was significant in your search for this position.)

	VERY UNIMPORTANT				VERY IMPORTANT
a. Greater responsibility............	1	2	3	4	5
b. More enjoyment....................	1	2	3	4	5
c. More power........................	1	2	3	4	5
d. Higher salary.....................	1	2	3	4	5
e. More status......................	1	2	3	4	5
f. More autonomy.....................	1	2	3	4	5
g. More authority....................	1	2	3	4	5
h. Greater interest and challenge....	1	2	3	4	5
i. More job security.................	1	2	3	4	5

8. Where did you hear about this position: (Please check as many as apply)

_____ (a) Newspaper
_____ (b) Professional journal
_____ (c) Friend employed in same agency
_____ (d) Friend employed in other state agency
_____ (e) Friend employed outside the agency
_____ (f) Executive search firm
_____ (g) Professional colleague in same agency
_____ (h) Professional colleague in another state
_____ (i) Internal announcement/supervisors

9. Third most recent position: (If you do not have a third most recent position, skip to item 17)

a. Position title_____
b. Years in this position.................._____
c. Approximate salary....................$_____/yr.
d. Age when you took this position/job......_____
e. Number of persons directly supervised......._____
f. Was this position (please circle):

1. Full-time	1. Public sector	1. Career position	1. In this state
2. Part-time	2. Private for profit	2. Exempt appointment	2. Outside this state
	3. Private non-profit		(specify_____)

10. Did this position represent: (Please check)

a.
_____ (1) a range increase
_____ (2) no change in range
_____ (3) a range decrease
_____ (4) non-applicable

b.
_____ (1) a salary increase
_____ (2) no change in salary
_____ (3) a salary decrease
_____ (4) non-applicable

c. a position title change reflecting greater responsibility
_____ (1) yes _____ (2) no _____ (3) N/A

11. Motivation in seeking this position: (Using the scale below, circle the number which best indicates the extent to which each was significant in your search for this position.)

	VERY UNIMPORTANT				VERY IMPORTANT
a. Greater responsibility...........	1	2	3	4	5
b. More enjoyment...................	1	2	3	4	5
c. More power.......................	1	2	3	4	5
d. Higher salary....................	1	2	3	4	5
e. More status......................	1	2	3	4	5
f. More autonomy....................	1	2	3	4	5
g. More authority...................	1	2	3	4	5
h. Greater interest and challenge...	1	2	3	4	5
i. More job security................	1	2	3	4	5

12. Where did you hear about this position: (Please check as many as apply)

_____ (a) Newspaper
_____ (b) Professional journal
_____ (c) Friend employed in same agency
_____ (d) Friend employed in other state agency
_____ (e) Friend employed outside the agency
_____ (f) Executive search firm
_____ (g) Professional colleague in same agency
_____ (h) Professional colleague in another state
_____ (i) Internal announcement/supervisors

234

13. Fourth most recent position: (If you do not have a fourth most recent position, skip to item 17)

a. Position title _____

b. Years in this position.............. _____

c. Approximate salary................ $ _____ /yr.

d. Age when you took this position/job....... _____

e. Number of persons directly supervised....... _____

f. Was this position (please circle):

    1. Full-time   1. Public sector   1. Career position   1. In this state
    2. Part-time   2. Private for profit   2. Exempt appointment   2. Outside this state
                 3. Private non-profit   (specify _____)

14. Did this position represent: (Please check)

a. _____ (1) a range increase   b. _____ (1) a salary increase
    _____ (2) no change in range   _____ (2) no change in salary
    _____ (3) a range decrease   _____ (3) a salary decrease
    _____ (4) non-applicable   _____ (4) non-applicable

c. a position title change reflecting greater responsibility

          _____ (1) yes   _____ (2) no   _____ (3) N/A

15. Motivation in seeking this position: (Using the scale below, circle the number which best indicates the extent to which each was significant in your search for this position.)

	VERY UNIMPORTANT				VERY IMPORTANT
a. Greater responsibility.............	1	2	3	4	5
b. More enjoyment...................	1	2	3	4	5
c. More power......................	1	2	3	4	5
d. Higher salary...................	1	2	3	4	5
e. More status.....................	1	2	3	4	5
f. More autonomy...................	1	2	3	4	5

g. More authority................... 1 2 3 4 5
h. Greater interest and challenge..... 1 2 3 4 5
i. More job security................ 1 2 3 4 5

16. Where did you hear about this position: (Please check as many as apply)

_____ (a) Newspaper
_____ (b) Professional journal
_____ (c) Friend employed in same agency
_____ (d) Friend employed in other state agency
_____ (e) Friend employed outside the agency
_____ (f) Executive search firm
_____ (g) Professional colleague in same agency
_____ (h) Professional colleague in another state
_____ (i) Internal announcement/supervisors

17. Often, key people play an important role in shaping one's career. These individuals are mentors and may have supported, trained, "taught you the ropes," provided advice, or endorsed you in your career development. Please PLACE A NUMBER in the space indicating how many mentor(s) you have/had of each gender.

a. LOCATION	MALE	FEMALE
1. Peers in workplace organization.......	_____	_____
2. Supervisor in workplace organization......	_____	_____
3. CEO/Other higher level executive......	_____	_____
4. Professor/educator.......	_____	_____
5. Spouse/other family member.......	_____	_____
6. Friend/colleague in other profession......	_____	_____

7. Parent...

8. Other (specify: _____)

b. ETHNICITY   MALE   FEMALE

1. Black........................ _____   _____

2. White........................ _____   _____

3. Native American.............. _____   _____

4. Hispanic..................... _____   _____

5. Asian........................ _____   _____

6. Other........................ _____   _____

18. During the average week, how much time do you spend at work and on work-related activities?

a. ____ 32 hrs. or less b. ____ 33-40 hrs. c. ____ 41-50 hrs. d. ____ 51-60 hrs. e. ____ 61+ hrs.

19. With regard to your present position, how often do you believe you are left out of informal discussions with colleagues where important decisions are made? (Please check)

(a) Often	(b) Sometimes	(c) Occasionally	(d) Rarely	(e) Not at all
_____	_____	_____	_____	_____

20. Using the following scales, indicate how successful and how satisfied you feel in your career. (Circle your response.)

a. Not successful   1   2   3   4   5   Very successful
b. Extremely dissatisfied   1   2   3   4   5   Extremely satisfied

21. With regard to the competencies and functions listed in items a though v, please indicate the extent to which (a) each is important in your performance evaluation, (b) each is important to you in terms of your effectiveness in your present position, and (c) the extent to which you would like additional training in each area.

	(a) Important in Performance Evaluation (circle answer)		(b) Important for Your Effectiveness (circle answer)		(c) I want Additional Training in This Area (circle answer)	
	NOT IM-PORTANT	VERY IM-PORTANT	VERY UNIM-PORTANT	VERY IM-PORTANT	NOT AT ALL	VERY MUCH
a. Communication abilities	1 2 3	4 5	1 2 3	4 5	1 2 3	4 5
b. Coalition formation/conflict management	1 2 3	4 5	1 2 3	4 5	1 2 3	4 5
c. Specialized expertise (e.g., engineering, law)	1 2 3	4 5	1 2 3	4 5	1 2 3	4 5
d. Adaptability/flexibility	1 2 3	4 5	1 2 3	4 5	1 2 3	4 5
e. Ability to balance short- and long-term considerations	1 2 3	4 5	1 2 3	4 5	1 2 3	4 5
f. Collect/assess/analyze information; anticipate outcome, make judgments	1 2 3	4 5	1 2 3	4 5	1 2 3	4 5
g. Sensitivity to the environment	1 2 3	4 5	1 2 3	4 5	1 2 3	4 5
h. Focus on results/goal achievement	1 2 3	4 5	1 2 3	4 5	1 2 3	4 5
i. Taking initiative/ showing creativity	1 2 3	4 5	1 2 3	4 5	1 2 3	4 5
j. Leadership	1 2 3	4 5	1 2 3	4 5	1 2 3	4 5
k. Interpersonal relations/ sensitivity	1 2 3	4 5	1 2 3	4 5	1 2 3	4 5
l. Personnel management	1 2 3	4 5	1 2 3	4 5	1 2 3	4 5
m. Affirmative action/EEO management	1 2 3	4 5	1 2 3	4 5	1 2 3	4 5

n. Budgetary resource management	1 2 3 4 5	1 2 3 4 5	1 2 3 4 5
o. Keeping up with agency policies/priorities, external issue/trends	1 2 3 4 5	1 2 3 4 5	1 2 3 4 5
p. Keeping subordinates informed re: agency policies, issues, and trends	1 2 3 4 5	1 2 3 4 5	1 2 3 4 5
q. Selling/defending work activities to supervisor and external groups	1 2 3 4 5	1 2 3 4 5	1 2 3 4 5
r. Coordinating and integrating work activities with those of other organizations	1 2 3 4 5	1 2 3 4 5	1 2 3 4 5
s. Identifying policy and program alternatives	1 2 3 4 5	1 2 3 4 5	1 2 3 4 5
t. Managing programs (planning, coordinating, guiding staff)	1 2 3 4 5	1 2 3 4 5	1 2 3 4 5
u. Monitoring program compliance/program evaluation	1 2 3 4 5	1 2 3 4 5	1 2 3 4 5
v. Research and program development	1 2 3 4 5	1 2 3 4 5	1 2 3 4 5

22. Circle the number indicating the extent to which each activity listed below contributed to your career.

	HINDERED MY CAREER			HELPED MY CAREER	N/A
a. Working on political campaigns.........	1	2	3 4	5	6
b. Being an aide to legislator or elected official..	1	2	3 4	5	6
c. Continuous employment in one state agency........	1	2	3 4	5	6
d. Employment in several state agencies.............	1	2	3 4	5	6
e. Employment in different levels of government (federal, state, local).................	1	2	3 4	5	6
f. Employment in different branches of government (executive, legislative, judicial).............	1	2	3 4	5	6
g. Lateral moves in state agencies..........	1	2	3 4	5	6
h. Moves between public and private sectors..........	1	2	3 4	5	6
i. Continuous full-time employment.............	1	2	3 4	5	6

23. Have you lost an opportunity for promotion (within the last five years) because of: (Check as many as apply)

a. _____ Unable/unwilling to relocate
b. _____ Time required to be away from home/family
c. _____ Supervisor's biased attitude
d. _____ Spouse/family not supportive

e. _____ Veteran's preference
f. _____ Age discrimination
   (specify: _____ too young _____ too old)
g. _____ Ethnic discrimination
h. _____ Gender discrimination
i. _____ Not applicable

24. Has there been any particularly critical incident(s) that has influenced your career development?
(1) _____ yes   (2) _____ no
If YES, please specify: _____

_____

(if more space is needed, please use comments section on last page)

25. Success is due to a combination of factors: Think about a male colleague in a comparable position in your organization whom you consider a success and indicate the extent to which you think the following were/are important. Then think about a successful female colleague. Indicate the extent to which the items were/are important to her. Then think about yourself and indicate the extent to which the items were/are important to you. Using the scale, circle the most appropriate response.

1	2	3	4	5
Not Important		Important		Very Important

MALE COLLEAGUE

a. Ability..........................	1 2 3 4 5
b. Hard work.......................	1 2 3 4 5
c. Whom I know (family, spouse, friends)..	1 2 3 4 5
d. Whom I know (political connections)....	1 2 3 4 5
e. Professional contacts..............	1 2 3 4 5
f. Luck............................	1 2 3 4 5
g. Other (specify: _____)...........	1 2 3 4 5

FEMALE COLLEAGUE

1 2 3 4 5
1 2 3 4 5
1 2 3 4 5
1 2 3 4 5
1 2 3 4 5
1 2 3 4 5
1 2 3 4 5

MYSELF

1 2 3 4 5
1 2 3 4 5
1 2 3 4 5
1 2 3 4 5
1 2 3 4 5
1 2 3 4 5
1 2 3 4 5

240

26. Think about the behavioral style(s) utilized within your organization. Using the scale below, indicate the extent to which you think the following characterize your style. (Circle the number of your response.)

	1	2	3	4	5
	Not Very Characteristic		Characteristic		Very Characteristic

a. Competitive........ 1 2 3 4 5
b. Creative........ 1 2 3 4 5
c. Process-oriented........ 1 2 3 4 5
d. Predictable........ 1 2 3 4 5
e. Task-oriented........ 1 2 3 4 5
f. Loyal........ 1 2 3 4 5
g. Willing to use
   intimidation........ 1 2 3 4 5
h. Independent........ 1 2 3 4 5
i. Dominant........ 1 2 3 4 5
j. Managerial........ 1 2 3 4 5
k. Ambitious........ 1 2 3 4 5

l. Trusting........ 1 2 3 4 5
m. Assertive........ 1 2 3 4 5
n. Attractive........ 1 2 3 4 5
o. Affectionate........ 1 2 3 4 5
p. Opportunistic........ 1 2 3 4 5
q. Risk-taking........ 1 2 3 4 5
r. Skilled in interpersonal
   transactions........ 1 2 3 4 5
s. Straightforward and frank.. 1 2 3 4 5
t. Team-oriented........ 1 2 3 4 5
u. Do things "by the book".... 1 2 3 4 5

27. Place a check by the three items you feel have been most important for your career success.

a. My attitude/self-concept/motivation........ _____
b. My education........ _____
c. My skills and abilities........ _____
d. My work style........ _____
e. Promotional opportunities offered to me........ _____
f. Financial support from others........ _____
g. Training opportunities........ _____
h. Mentor(s) or sponsorship........ _____
i. Emotional support of others........ _____
j. Having distinct career goals........ _____
k. Whom I know........ _____

241

28. Indicate the extent to which you agree that the following have interfered with your career. (Using the scale below, circle the most appropriate response.)

	1	2	3	4	5	
	Strongly Disagree				Strongly Agree	

	1	2	3	4	5
a. Military service	1	2	3	4	5
b. Health: Personal	1	2	3	4	5
c. Health: Spouse's	1	2	3	4	5
d. Health: Children's	1	2	3	4	5
e. Health: Parents	1	2	3	4	5
f. Spouse's Career	1	2	3	4	5
g. Age: Too young	1	2	3	4	5
h. Age: Too old	1	2	3	4	5
i. Family's attitude toward your work	1	2	3	4	5
j. Housework tasks (cleaning, grocery shopping, laundry, etc.)	1	2	3	4	5
k. Other family commitments (e.g., planning organizing, and coordinating)	1	2	3	4	5
l. Childbearing	1	2	3	4	5
m. Child care	1	2	3	4	5
n. Parent care	1	2	3	4	5

29. In the column on the right, please check those behaviors that you have personally experienced in your career. In the second column, please check those behaviors that you have heard occurred to someone else in your organization.

	EXPERIENCED	HEARD ABOUT
a. Unwelcome sexual advances in exchange for an employment opportunity by a superior	___	___
b. Requests for sexual favors from work colleagues	___	___
c. Other offensive physical conduct of a sexual nature	___	___
d. Offensive verbal behavior such as jokes and snide comments	___	___

30. During your past four positions, indicate the significant types and sources of support you have received. Place a check in the appropriate boxes.

TYPES OF SUPPORT	SIBLING	PARENT	SPOUSE	PERSONAL FRIENDS	PROFESSIONAL COLLEAGUES Out- side my agency	In- side my agency	SUPERVISOR	PROFESSORS/ EDUCATORS	EMPLOYING INSTITUTION
a. Educational loan									
b. Living expenses									
c. Tuition support									
d. Administrative leave for skill development									
e. Career-related advice									
f. Introduction to helpful people									
g. Explanation of the way things get done									
h. Moral support & encouragement									
i. Public endorsements									
j. Access to otherwise unreachable resources									
k. Childbearing									
l. Child care									
m. Parent care									
n. Housework tasks									

o. Other family
   commitments
   (e.g., planning,
   organizing,
   scheduling,
   coordinating)

p. Health care
   (own or family)

31. Using the scale, circle the most appropriate response.

	STRONGLY DISAGREE				STRONGLY AGREE
a. Employees in state government should reflect the ethnic/racial makeup of the population.	1	2	3	4	5
b. Employees in state government should reflect the gender makeup of the population.	1	2	3	4	5
c. Females should receive preference where female and male applicants are of equal ability and females are under-represented on a department's work force.	1	2	3	4	5
d. Minorities should receive preference where applicants are of equal value and minorities are under-represented on a department's work force.	1	2	3	4	5
e. White males in this state are sometimes discriminated against in either hiring or promotion.	1	2	3	4	5
f. I personally believe that I have been discriminated against in either hiring or promotion.	1	2	3	4	5
g. I personally support issues related to:					
(a) Child care.	1	2	3	4	5
(b) Pay equity.	1	2	3	4	5
(c) Job sharing.	1	2	3	4	5
(d) Flexible work schedules.	1	2	3	4	5

BACKGROUND

32. SEX: Female _____ Male _____

33. AGE: _____

34. PRIMARY RACIAL IDENTITY:

a. Black.....   c. Asian........   e. American Indian.... _____
b. White.....   d. Hispanic....   f. Alaskan Native..... _____

35. MARITAL STATUS:

a. Never married....   c. Divorced.....   e. Widowed...... _____
b. Married..........   d. Separated....   _____

36. LIVING SITUATION:

a. Living alone....   b. Living with other adult(s) with dependents... _____
c. Sole adult living
   with dependents.   d. Living with one other adult only............. _____
e. Other (specify: _____).....

37. NUMBER OF DEPENDENTS LIVING AT HOME:

a. Children under 2 yrs. of age..   d. Parents or grandparents..... _____
b. Children aged 2-6..............   e. Other adult(s) relatives.... _____
c. Children aged 7-18............   f. Other adult(s) unrelated.... _____

38. EDUCATION COMPLETED: (Check the levels of education you and your spouse have completed. Indicate for yourself its type and location.)

BY SELF   BY SPOUSE

                        WAS IT:

                        (1)Public _____ In state _____
                        (2)Private _____ Out-of-state _____

a. High school _____

b. Some college

        (1)Public   In state
        (2)Private   Out-of-state

c. Undergraduate degree

        (1)Public   In state
        (2)Private   Out-of-state

d. Masters/ professional degree

        (1)Public   In state
        (2)Private   Out-of-state

e. Doctorate

        (1)Public   In state
        (2)Private   Out-of-state

f. Are you employed in a job concerned with the subject matter in which you specialized for your highest degree?   (1) yes   (2) no

39. MILITARY STATUS

a. Awarded veteran's preference status in this state government?   (1) yes   (2) no   b. Retired from the military   (1) yes   (2) no

40. POLITICAL PARTY PREFERENCE

   (1) Democrat   (2) Republican   (3) Independent   (4) Other

41. RELIGIOUS AFFILIATION

   (1) Protestant   (3) Jewish   (5) Latter Day Saints   (7) None
   (2) Catholic   (4) Moslem   (6) Other

42. What portion of your total household income from all sources is represented by your salary?

   (1) Less than 1/3   (3) 1/2 to 2/3   (5) 100%
   (2) 1/3 but less than 1/2   (4) More than 2/3 but less than 100%

43. In the family in which I was reared, I was ____ of ____ children. (indicate birth order).

246

44. Father's highest level of formal education: (circle number)
0=Less than high school   2=Some college   4=Bachelor's   6=Doctorate
1=High school   3=A.A.   5=Master's   7=Other Professional Degree
                                                              (specify: _____)

45. Mother's highest level of formal education: (circle number)
0=Less than high school   2=Some college   4=Bachelor's   6=Doctorate
1=High school   3=A.A.   5=Master's   7=Other Professional Degree
                                                              (specify: _____)

46. Father's major profession/occupation during your childhood: (circle one number)

1=Professional/technical   5=Craftsman/foreman   9=Service work

2=Manager or administrator   6=Laborer, except farm   10=Transport
                                                                  equipment operator

3=Sales   7=Farmwork/agriculture   11=Operative,
                                                                  except transport

4=Clerical   8=Not employed outside home

47. Mother's major profession/occupation during your childhood: (circle one number)

1=Professional/technical   5=Craftsman/foreman   9=Service work

2=Manager or administrator   6=Laborer, except farm   10=Transport
                                                                  equipment operator

3=Sales   7=Farmwork/agriculture   11=Operative,
                                                                  except transport

4=Clerical   8=Not employed outside home

48. How would you characterize the social class of your family while you were growing up? (circle number)

1=Upper   2=Upper-middle   3=Middle   4=Lower-middle   5=Lower

THANK YOU FOR YOUR TIME AND PARTICIPATION

References

Acker, J. 1990. Hierarchies, jobs, bodies: A theory of gendered organizations. *Gender and Society* 20(5–6): 139–58.

Adler, N.J., and Izraeli, D.N., eds. 1988. *Women in Management Worldwide.* Armonk, NY: M.E. Sharpe.

Almquist, E.M., and Angrist, S.S. 1971. Role model influences on college women's career aspirations. *Merrill-Palmer Quarterly* 17(3): 263–79.

Arkkelin, D., and Simmons, R. 1985. The good manager: Sex-typed, androgynous or likable? *Sex Roles* 12(11–12): 131–42.

Arnott, N. 1988. Should you manage like a man? *Executive Female* (March/April): 20–24.

Austin, M. 1972. The Lord's definition of woman's role as He has revealed it to His prophets of the Latter Day. Master's Thesis, Brigham Young University, Provo, Utah.

Bacharach, S.B., and Lauer, E.J. 1988. *Power and Politics in Organizations.* San Francisco: Jossey-Bass.

Backhouse, C., and Cohen, L. 1981. *Sexual Harassment on the Job.* Englewood Cliffs, NJ: Prentice Hall.

Bahls, J.E. 1989. Two for one: A working idea. *Nation's Business* 77: 28–30.

Bancroft, G. 1958. *The American Labor Force.* New York: John Wiley and Sons.

Barclay, L. 1982. Social learning theory: A framework for discrimination research. *Academy of Management Review* 7: 587–94.

Barnier, L.A. 1982. A study of the mentoring relationship: An analysis of its relation to career and adult development in higher education and business. *Dissertation Abstracts International* 42(7-A): 3012–13.

Bartol, K.M. 1974. Male versus female leaders. *Academy of Management Journal* 17: 225–33.

———. 1978. The sex structuring of organizations: A search for possible causes. *Academy of Management Review* 3: 805–15.

Basil, D.C. 1972. *Women in Management.* New York: Dunellen.

Basow, S.A. 1980. *Sex-role Stereotypes: Traditions and Alternatives.* Monterey, CA: Brooks/Cole.

Bayes, J. 1987. Do female managers in public bureaucracies manage with a different voice? Paper presented at the Third International Congress on Women, Trinity College, Dublin.

————. 1989. Women in the California executive branch of government. In *Gender, Bureaucracy, and Democracy: Careers and Equal Opportunity in the Public Sector*, ed. M.M. Hale and R.M. Kelly. Westport, CT: Greenwood.

————. 1991. Women in public administration: A comparative perspective. A Special Symposium. *Women and Politics* 11:3.

Beckman, G.M. 1976. Legal barriers, what barriers? *Atlanta Economic Review* 26(2): 15–20.

Bennis, W. 1969. Changing organizations. In *Organizational Concepts and Analysis*, ed. W. Scott. Belmont, CA: Dickenson.

Berelson, B.R.; Lazarsfeld, P.R.; and McPhee, W.N. 1954. *Voting*. Chicago: University of Chicago.

Berger, P.L., and Luckman, T. 1966. *The Social Construction of Reality*. Garden City, NY: Doubleday.

Bergmann, B.R. 1986. *The Economic Emergence of Women*. New York: Basic.

Berk, S.F. 1985. *The Gender Factory: The Apportionment of Work in American Households*. New York: Plenum.

Berry, P. 1983. Mentors for women managers: Fast-track to corporate success. *Supervisor Management* 28(8): 36–40.

Beyer, J.M., and Trice, H.M. 1988. The communication of power relations in organizations. In *Inside Organizations: Understanding the Human Dimension*, ed. M.O. Jones, M.D. Moore, and R.C. Snyder. Newbury Park, CA: Sage.

Bielby, D.D., and Bielby, W.T. 1988. Women's and men's commitment to paid work and family. In *Women and Work*, ed. B.A. Gutek, A.H. Stromberg, and L. Larwood. Newbury Park, CA: Sage.

Blackburn, R.T.; Chapman, D.W.; and Cameron, S.M. 1981. Cloning in academe: Mentorship and academic careers. *Research in Higher Education* 15(4): 315–27.

Blank, R.M. 1988. Women's paid work, household income, and household well-being. In *The American Woman*, ed. S. Rix. New York: W.W. Norton.

Blau, F.D., and Ferber, M.A. 1987. Occupations and earnings of women workers. In *Working Women: Past, Present, Future*, ed. K.S. Koziara, M.H. Moskow, and L.D. Tanner. Washington, DC: Bureau of National Affairs.

Bolton, E.B. 1980. Conceptual analysis of the mentor relationship in the career development of women. *Adult Education* 30(4): 195–207.

Bolton, E.B., and Humphreys, L.W. 1977. A training model for women—An androgynous approach. *Personnel Journal* 56(5): 230–34.

Bowen, D.D. 1985. Were men meant to mentor women? *Training and Development Journal* 39(2): 31–34.

Bowers, A.G. 1984. Mentors and protégés in male-dominated corporate cultures: The experience of top-level women executives. *Dissertation Abstracts International* 45(9): 3103B.

Bowman, G.W.; Worthy, N.B.; and Greyser, S.H. 1965. Are women executives people? *Harvard Business Review* 43: 164–78.

Branson, H., and Branson, R. 1988. The supervisor and sexual harassment. *Supervision* 50(2): 10–12.

Brass, D.J. 1985. Men's and women's networks: A study of interaction patterns and influence in an organization. *Academy of Management Journal* 28(2): 327–43.

Bremer, K., and Howe, D.A. 1988. Strategies used to advance women's careers in the public service: Examples from Oregon. *Public Administration Review* 48(6): 957–61.

Broverman, I.K.; Broverman, D.M.; Clarkson, F.E.; Rosenkrantz, P.; and Vogel, S.R. 1970. Sex-role stereotypes and clinical judgments of mental health. *Journal of Consulting Psychology* 34: 1–7.

Brown, D.A. 1985. The role of mentoring in the professional lives of university faculty women. *Dissertation Abstracts International* 47(1): 160A.

Brown, L.K. 1988. Female managers in the United States and in Europe: Corporate boards, M.B.A. credentials, and the image/illusion of progress. In *Women in Management Worldwide*, ed. N.J. Adler and D.N. Izraeli. Armonk, NY: M.E. Sharpe.

Brown, W. 1987. Where is the sex in political theory? *Women and Politics* 7(1): 3–24.

———. 1988. *Manhood and Politics: A Feminist Reading in Political Theory.* Totowa, NJ: Rowman and Littlefield.

Brownmiller, S. 1984. *Femininity.* New York: Linden.

Bularzik, M. 1978. *Sexual Harassment at the Workplace—Historical Notes.* Somerville, MA: New England Free Press.

Bullock, C.S., and MacManus, S.A. 1991. Municipal electoral structure and the election of councilwomen. *Journal of Politics* 53(1): 75–89.

Burke, R.J. 1984. Mentors in organizations. *Group and Organizational Studies* 9(3): 353–72.

Burrell, G., and Hearn, J. 1989. The sexuality of organization. In *The Sexuality of Organization*, ed. J. Hearn, D.L. Sheppard, P. Tancred-Sheriff, and B. Burrell, 1–28. London: Sage.

Buss, D. 1981. Sex differences in the evaluation and performance of dominant acts. *Journal of Personality and Social Psychology* 40(1): 147–54.

Cann, A., and Siegfried, W.D., Jr. 1987. Sex stereotypes and the leadership role. *Sex Roles* 17(7/8): 401–408.

Cardozo, A.R. 1986. *Sequencing.* New York: Atheneum.

Carroll, S.M. 1989. The personal is political: The intersection of private lives and public roles among women and men in elective and appointive office. *Women and Politics* 9: 51–68.

Carr-Ruffino, N. 1985. *The Promotable Woman: Becoming a Successful Manager.* Belmont, CA: Wadsworth.

Cayer, N.J., and Sigelman, L. 1980. Minorities and women in state and local governments: 1973–1975. *Public Administration Review* 40(5): 443–50.

Chafetz, J.S. 1990. *Gender Equity: An Integrated Theory of Stability and Change.* Newbury Park, CA: Sage.

Chapman, R. 1983. Jobsharing: Fad or fixture? *Personnel Management* 15:3.

Chodorow, N. 1978. *The Reproduction of Mothering.* Berkeley: University of California.

Christian Science Monitor. 1986. The new professional majority. March 20, p. 19.

Clarke, L.W. 1986. Women supervisors experience sexual harassment, too. *Supervisory Management* 31(4): 35–36.

Clawson, J.G., and Kram, K.E. 1984. Managing cross-gender mentoring. *Business Horizons* 27(3): 22–32.

Clegg, S. 1981. Organization and control. *Administrative Science Quarterly* 26: 545–62.

Col, J.M. 1985. Barriers to women's advancement in administration and management. Unpublished manuscript. Springfield, IL: Sangamon State University.

Coles, F.S. 1986. Forced to quit: Sexual harassment complaints and response. *Sex Roles* 14(1): 81–95.

Collins, G.C., and Scott, P. 1979. Everyone who makes it has a mentor. *Harvard Business Review* 56: 89–101.

Collins, N.W. 1983. *Professional Women and Their Mentors*. Englewood Cliffs, NJ: Prentice Hall.

Cook, M.F. 1979. Is the mentor relationship primarily a male experience? *The Personnel Administrator* 24(11): 82–86.

Costain, A.N. 1988. Women's claims as a special interest. In *The Politics of the Gender Gap: The Social Construction of Political Influence*, ed. C.M. Mueller. Newbury Park, CA: Sage.

Coyle, A. 1989. Women in management: A suitable case for treatment? *Feminist Review* 31(Spring): 117–25.

Crompton, R., and Sanderson, K. 1986. Credentials and careers: Some implications of the increase in professional qualifications amongst women. *Sociology* 29(1): 25–41.

Crozier, M. 1964. *The Bureaucratic Phenomenon*. Chicago: University of Chicago.

Cussler, M. 1958. *The Woman Executive*. New York: Harcourt and Brace.

Daley, D. 1984. Political and occupational barriers to the implementation of affirmative action: Administrative, executive and legislative attitudes toward representative bureaucracy. *Review of Public Personnel Administration* 4(3): 4–15.

Dalton, G.W.; Thompson, P.H.; and Price, R.L. 1977. The four stages of professional careers: A new look at performance by professionals. *Organizational Dynamics* 69(1): 19–42.

Dandekar, N. 1990. Contrasting consequences—Bringing charges of sexual harassment compared with other cases of whistle blowing. *Journal of Business Ethics* 9(2): 151–58.

Dandridge, T.C. 1988. Work ceremonies: Why integrate work and play? In *Inside Organizations: Understanding the Human Dimension*, ed. M.O. Jones, M.D. Moore, and R.C. Snyder. Newbury Park, CA: Sage.

Darcy, R.; Welch, S.; and Clark, J. 1987. *Women, Elections, and Representation*. New York: Longman.

Davis, S.M. 1984. *Managing Corporate Culture*. Cambridge, MA: Ballinger.

Deal, T.E., and Kennedy, A.A. 1982. *Corporate Cultures: The Rites and Rituals of Corporate Life*. Reading, MA: Addison-Wesley.

Denhardt, R., and Perkins, J. 1976. The coming death of administrative man. *Public Administration Review* 36(July): 379–84.

Denmark, F.L. 1977. Styles of leadership. *Psychology of Women Quarterly* 2: 99–113.

Derthick, M. 1987. American federalism: Madison's middle ground in the 1980s. *Public Administration Review* 47(1): 66–74.

DeWine, S., and Casbolt, D. 1983. Networking: External communication systems for female organizational members. *Journal of Business Communication* 20(2): 57–67.

Dexter, C. 1985. Women and the exercise of power in organizations: From ascribed to achieved status. In *Women and Work: An Annual Review*, ed. L. Larwood, A.H. Stromberg, and B.A. Gutek. Newbury Park, CA: Sage.

Diamond, E.E. 1987. Theories of career development. In *Women's Career Development*, ed. B.A. Gutek and L. Larwood. Newbury Park, CA: Sage.

Diamond, I. 1977. *Sex Roles in the State House*. New Haven, CT: Yale University.

DiIulio, J.J., Jr. 1989. Recovering the public management variable: Lessons from schools, prisons, and armies. *Public Administration Review* 49(2): 127–33.

Dipboye, R.L. 1987. Problems and progress of women in management. In *Working Women: Past, Present, Future*, ed. K.S. Koziara, M.H. Moskow, and L.D. Tanner. Washington, DC: Bureau of National Affairs.

Donnell, S.M., and Hall, J. 1980. Men and women as managers: A significant case of no significant difference. *Organizational Dynamics* 8(4): 60–77.

Douvan, E. 1976. The role of models in women's professional development. *Psychology of Women Quarterly* 1(1): 5–20.

Downs, Anthony. 1967. *Inside Bureaucracy*. Boston: Little, Brown.

Dreher, G.F.; Dougherty, T.W.; and Whitely, W. 1989. Influence tactics and salary attainment: A gender-specific analysis. *Sex Roles* 20(9/10): 535–50.

Driscoll, J.B., and Bova, R.A. 1980. The sexual side of enterprise. *Management Review* 69(7): 51–54.

Dubno, P. 1985. Attitudes toward women executives: A longitudinal approach. *Academy of Management Journal* 28(1): 235–39.

Duerst-Lahti, G. 1986. Organizational ethos and women's power capacity: Perceived and formal structure in state administrative organizations. Paper presented at the annual meeting of the American Political Science Association, Washington, D.C.

———. 1987. Gender power relations in public bureaucracies. *Dissertation Abstracts International* 49(3): 605A–606A.

———. 1990. But women play the game too: Communication control and influence in administrative decision making. *Administration and Society* 22(2): 182–205.

Duerst-Lahti, G., and Johnson, C.M. 1990. Gender and style in bureaucracy. *Women and Politics* 10(4): 67–120.

Duncan, G.J., and Corcoran, M.E. 1984. Do women 'deserve' to earn less than men? In *Years of Poverty, Years of Plenty*, ed. G.J. Duncan. Ann Arbor, MI: Institute for Social Research.

Dye, T.R. 1990. *American Federalism: Competition among Governments*. Lexington, MA: Lexington Books.

Eagly, A.H., and Steffen, V.J. 1984. Gender stereotypes stem from the distribution of women and men into social roles. *Journal of Personality and Social Psychology* 46: 735–54.

Eccles, J.S. 1987. Gender roles and women's achievement-related decisions. *Psychology of Women Quarterly* 11: 135–72.

The Economist. 1990. How the other half works. June 30, pp. 21–24.

Elazar, D.J. 1987. *Exploring Federalism*. Tuscaloosa: The University of Alabama.

————. 1988. *The American Constitutional Tradition.* Lincoln: University of Nebraska.

Ellison v. *Brady.* 59 Law Week 2455 (9th cir). Jan. 23 (1991).

Elshtain, J.B. 1981. *Public Man, Private Woman.* Princeton, NJ: Princeton University.

Engstrom, R.L.; McDonald, M.D.; and Chou, B. 1988. The desirability hypothesis and the election of women to city councils: A research note. *State and Local Government Review* 20(Winter): 38–40.

Epstein, C.F. 1988. *Deceptive Distinctions: Sex, Gender, and the Social Order.* New Haven, CT: Yale University.

Falbo, T.; Hazen, M.D.; and Linimon, D. 1982. The costs of selecting power bases or messages associated with the opposite sex. *Sex Roles* 8: 147–57.

Farley, L. 1978. *Sexual Shakedown: The Sexual Harassment of Women on the Job.* New York: McGraw-Hill.

Farren, C.; Gray, J.D.; and Kaye, B. 1984. Mentoring: A boon to career development. *Personnel* 61(6): 20–24.

Farris, R., and Ragan, L. 1981. Importance of mentor–protégé relationships to the upward mobility of the female executive. *Mid-South Business Journal* 1(4): 24–28.

Ferguson, K. 1985. *A feminist Case against Bureaucracy.* Philadelphia: Temple University.

Firefighters Local Union No. 1784 v. *Statts.* 104 S.Ct. 2576 (1984).

Fisher, A.B. 1990. *Wall Street Women.* New York: Alfred A. Knopf.

Fitt, L.W., and Newton, D.A. 1981. When the mentor is a man and the protégée is a woman. *Harvard Business Review* 59: 56–60.

Frost P.J.; Moore, L.F.; Louis, M.R.; Lundberg, C.C.; and Martin, J. 1985. *Organization Culture.* Beverly Hills, CA: Sage.

Gacioch, L. 1987. Employing fear. *Arizona View*, pp. 1–9.

Garvey, M.S. 1986. The high cost of sexual harassment suits. *Personnel Journal* 65: 75–78.

Gilder, G. 1981. *Wealth and Poverty.* New York: Basic.

Gillespie, D.L., and Leffler, A. 1987. The politics of research methodology in claims-making activities. *Social Problems* 34(5): 490–98.

Gilligan, C. 1982. *In a Different Voice.* Cambridge, MA: Harvard University.

Glass, J. 1990. The impact of occupational segregation on working conditions. *Social Forces* 68(3): 779–96.

Governing. 1991. Yardsticks. February, pp. 70–71.

Graddick, M.M. 1984. Organizational correlates of advancement. In *The Successful Woman Manager: How Did She Get There?*, ed. R. Richie. Symposium conducted at 92nd Annual Meeting of the American Psychological Association, Toronto.

Grant, J. 1988. Women as managers: What they can offer to organizations. *Organizational Dynamics* 16(Winter): 56–63.

Griggs v. *Duke Power Company.* 401 U.S. 424, 915 S.Ct. 849 (1971).

Grove City College v. *Bell.* 104 S.Ct. 1211 (1984).

Gruber, J.E. 1989. Sexual harassment research: Problems and proposals. Paper presented at the American Sociological Association Annual Meeting, August 1989.

Gutek, B.A. 1985. *Sex and the Workplace*. San Francisco: Jossey Bass.

Gutek, B.A., and Bikson, T.K. 1985. Differential experiences of men and women in computerized offices. *Sex Roles* 13(3): 123–37.

Gutek, B.A., and Larwood, L., eds. 1987. *Women's Career Development*. Newbury Park, CA: Sage.

Gutek, B.A., and Morasch, B. 1982. Sex-ratios, sex-role spillover, and sexual harassment. *Journal of Social Issues* 38(4): 33–54.

Gutek, B.A.; Nakamura, C.Y.; and Nieva, V. 1981. The interdependence of work and family roles. *Journal of Occupational Behavior* 2: 1–16.

Guy, M.E. 1985. *Professionals in Organizations: Debunking a Myth*. New York: Praeger.

Hackett, G., and Betz, N.E. 1981. A self-efficacy approach to the career development of women. *Journal of Vocational Behavior* 18: 326–39.

Hale, M.M., and Kelly, R.M., ed. 1989a. *Gender, Bureaucracy, and Democracy: Careers and Equal Opportunity in the Public Sector*. Westport, CT: Greenwood.

Hale, M.M., and Kelly, R.M. 1989b. Women in management and public sector careers. In *Gender, Bureaucracy, and Democracy: Careers and Equal Opportunity in the Public Sector*, ed. M.M. Hale and R.M. Kelly. Westport, CT: Greenwood.

Hale, M.M.; Kelly, R.M.; and Burgess, J. 1989. Women in the Arizona executive branch of government. In *Gender, Bureaucracy, and Democracy: Careers and Equal Opportunity in the Public Sector*, ed. M.M. Hale and R.M. Kelly. Westport, CT: Greenwood.

Hammond, V. 1988. *Women in Management*. New York: Ashridge Management College.

Hanson, C. 1991. Fitness for leadership. *Christian Science Monitor*. February 15, p. 12.

Hardesty, S., and Jacobs, N. 1986. *Success and Betrayal: The Crisis of Women in Corporate America*. New York: Franklin Watts.

Harlan, A., and Weiss, C.L. 1981. Moving up: Women in managerial careers final report. Working paper No. 86. Wellesley, MA: Wellesley College Center for Research on Woman.

———. 1982. Sex differences in factors affecting managerial career advancement. In Women in the Workplace, ed. P.A. Wallace. Boston: Auburn House.

Harrigan, B.L. 1977. *Games Mother Never Taught You: Corporate Gamesmanship for Women*. New York: Warner Books.

Harriman, A. 1985. *Women–Men–Management*. New York: Praeger.

Hart, P.B. 1988. Organizational barriers to women administrators in selected four-year institutions of higher learning in Alabama. *Dissertation Abstracts International* 50(8): 2326-A.

Hartmann, S.M. 1989. *From Margin to Mainstream: American Women and Politics since 1960*. Philadelphia: Temple University Press.

Harvard Business Review. 1981. *When the Executive Is a Woman*. Boston: The Harvard Business School.

Hays, S.W., and Kearney, R.C., eds. 1983. *Public Personnel Administration: Problems and Prospects*. Englewood Cliffs, NJ: Prentice Hall.

Hearn, J., and Parkin, P.W. 1983. Gender and organizations: A selective review and a critique of a neglected area. *Organizational Studies* 4(3): 219–42.

————. 1987. *Sex at Work: The Power and Paradox of Organization Sexuality.* New York: St. Martin's.

————. 1988. Women, men and leadership: A critical review of assumptions, practices, and change in the industrialized nations. In *Women in Management Worldwide*, ed. N.J. Adler and D. Izaeli. New York: M.E. Sharpe.

Hearn, J.; Sheppard, D.L.; Tancred-Sheriff, P.; and Burrell, B., eds. 1989. *The Sexuality of Organization.* London: Sage.

Heilman, M.E.; Block, C.J.; Martell, R.F.; and Simon, M.C. 1989. Has anything changed? Current characterizations of men, women, and managers. *Journal of Applied Psychology* 74(6): 935–42.

Helgesen, S. 1990. *The Female Advantage.* New York: Doubleday.

Hemming, H. 1985. Women in a man's world: Sexual harassment. *Human Relations* 38(1): 67–79.

Henderson, D.W. 1985. Englightened mentoring: Characteristics of public management professionalism. *Public Administration Review* 45: 857–63.

Hendricks, J.J. 1984. The prognosis for affirmative action at the state level: A study of affirmative action implementation in Delaware. *Review of Public Personnel Administration* 4(3): 57–70.

Hennig, M., and Jardim, A. 1977. *The Managerial Woman.* New York: Pocket Books.

Herbert, C. 1989. *Talking of Silence: The Sexual Harassment of Schoolgirls.* London: Falmer.

Hewlett, S.A. 1986. *A Lesser Life.* New York: William Morrow.

Hill, M.S. 1980. Authority at work: How men and women differ. In *Five-Thousand American Families: Patterns of Economic Progress*, vol. 7, ed. G.J. Duncan and J.N. Morgan. Ann Arbor, MI: Institute for Social Research, University of Michigan.

Hochstedler, E.; Regoli, R.M.; and Poole, E. 1984. Changing the guard in American cities: A current empirical assessment of integration in twenty municipal police departments. *Criminal Justice Review* 9: 8–14.

Hofstede, G. 1984. *Culture's Consequences.* London: Sage.

Humphreys, L.W., and Shrode, W.A. 1978. Decision-making profiles of female and male managers. *Michigan State University Business Topics* 26(4): 45–51.

Hunt, D.M., and Michael, C. 1983. Mentorship: A career training and development tool. *Academy of Management Review* 8: 475–85.

Hyde, J.S., and Essex, M.J. 1991. *Parental Leave and Child Care: Setting a Research and Policy Agenda.* Philadelphia: Temple University.

Hymnowitz, C., and Schellhardt, T.D. 1986. The glass ceiling: Why women can't seem to break the invisible barrier that blocks them from the top. *The Wall Street Journal.* March 24, sec. 4:1.

Ilgen, D.R., and Youtz, M.A. 1986. Factors affecting the evaluation and development of minorities in organizations. In *Research in Personnel and Human Resources Management*, vol. 4., ed. K.M. Rowland and G.R. Ferris. Greenwich, CT: JAI.

Jacobs, J., and Powell, R. 1985. Occupational prestige: A sex-neutral concept? *Sex Roles* 12: 1061–73.

Jaggar, A.M., and Bordo, S.R., eds. 1989. *Gender/Body/Knowledge.* New Brunswick, NJ: Rutgers University.

Jay, A. 1972. *Corporate Man*. London: Cape.

Johnson, C.M., and Duerst-Lahti, G. 1990. Comparing career paths for women and men in state civil service: Data from Wisconsin. Paper presented August 30–September 2 at the Annual Meeting of the American Political Science Association, San Francisco.

————. Private lives and public work: Professional careers in state civil service. Unpublished manuscript.

Johnson, M.C. 1980. Speaking from experience: Mentors—The key to development and growth. *Training and Development Journal* 57(July): 55.

Kadushin, C. 1983. Networking: No panacea. *Social Policy* 13(4): 59–60.

Kamerman, S.B. and Kahn, A.J. 1987. *The Responsive Workplace: Employers and a Changing Labor Force*. New York: Columbia University.

Kanter, R.M. 1977. *Men and Women of the Corporation*. New York: Basic.

————. 1979. Power failure in management circuits. *Harvard Business Review* 57(July/August): 65–75.

————. 1980. *A Tale of "O": On Being Different in an Organization*. New York: Harper and Row.

————. 1987. Men and women of the corporation revisited. *Management Review* 76: 14–16.

————. 1989a. The new managerial work. *Harvard Business Review* 67(6): 85–92.

————. 1989b. Place and power: Men and women of the corporation revisited. *The World* 3(2): 8–9.

————. 1989c. *When Giants Learn to Dance*. New York: Simon and Schuster.

Kaplan, R. 1984. Trade routes: The manager's network of relationships. *Organizational Dynamics* 12(4): 37–52.

Katz, E., and Lazarsfeld, P.F. 1955. *Personal Influence*. Glencoe: Free Press.

Kawar, A. 1989. Women in the Utah executive branch of government. In *Gender, Bureaucracy, and Democracy: Careers and Equal Opportunity in the Public Sector*, ed. M.M. Hale and R.M. Kelly. Westport, CT: Greenwood.

Kelly, R.M. 1991. *The Gendered Economy: Work, Careers, and Success*. Newbury Park, CA: Sage.

Kelly, R.M., and Bayes, J., eds. 1988. *Comparable Worth, Pay Equity and Public Policy*. Westport, CT: Greenwood.

Kelly, R.M., and Boutilier, M. 1978. *The Making of Political Women: A Study of Socialization and Role Conflict*. Chicago: Nelson-Hall.

Kelly, R.M.; and Guy, M.E.; with Bayes, J.; Duerst-Lahti, G.; Duke, L.L.; Hale, M.M.; Johnson, C.; Kawar, A.; and Stanley, J.R. 1991. Public managers in the states: A comparison of career advancement by sex. *Public Administration Review* 51(5): 402–12.

Kelly, R.M.; Hale, M.M.; and Burgess, J. 1991. Gender and managerial/leadership styles: A comparison of Arizona public administrators. *Women and Politics* 11(2): 19–39.

Kemper, T.D. 1968. Reference groups, socialization and achievement. *American Sociological Review* 33(1): 31–45.

Keown, C.F., and Keown, A.L. 1982. Success factors for corporate woman executives. *Group and Organizational Studies* 7(4): 445–56.

Kessler-Harris, A. 1981. *Women Have Always Worked*. New York: Feminist Press.

Kiechel, W. 1987. The high cost of sexual harassment. *Fortune* 116: 147–48.

Kingdon, J.W. 1984. *Agendas, Alternatives, and Public Policies*. Glenview, IL: Scott, Foresman.

Kipnis, D.; Schmidt, S.; and Wilkinson, I. 1980. Intraorganizational influence tactics: Explorations in getting one's way. *Journal of Applied Psychology* 65(4): 440–52.

Knight, P.A., and Saal, F.E. 1984. Effects of gender differences and selective agent expertise on leader influence and performance evaluations. *Organizational Behavior and Human Performance* 4: 225–43.

Kohn, M.M. 1971. Bureaucratic man: A portrait and an interpretation. *American Sociological Review* 36(3): 461–74.

Konrad, W. 1990. Welcome to the woman-friendly company where talent is valued and rewarded. *Business Week*, August 6, pp. 48–55.

Kram, K.E. 1980. Mentoring processes at work: Developmental relationships in managerial careers. Ph.D. dissertation, Yale University, New Haven.

———. 1983. Phases of the mentor relationship. *Academy of Management Journal* 26(4): 608–25.

———. 1985. *Mentoring at Work: Developmental Relationships in Organizational Life*. Glenview, IL: Scott, Foresman.

Kram, K.E., and Isabella, L.A. 1985. Mentoring alternatives: The role of peer relationships in career development. *Academy of Management Journal* 28: 10–132.

Lamis, A.P. 1984. *The Two-Party South*. New York: Oxford University Press.

Larwood, L., and Blackmore, J. 1978. Sex discrimination in manager selection: Testing predictions of the vertical dyad linkage model. *Sex Roles* 4: 359–67.

Larwood, L., and Gutek, B.A. 1987. Toward a theory of women's career development. In *Women's Career Development*, ed. B.A. Gutek and L. Larwood. Newbury Park, CA: Sage.

Larwood, L., and Lockheed, M. 1979. Women as managers: Toward second generation research. *Sex Roles* 5(5): 659–66.

Lazarsfeld, P.F.; Berelson, B.R.; and Gaudet, H. 1944. *The People's Choice*. New York: Duell, Sloan and Pierce.

Lean, E. 1983. Cross-gender mentoring—Downright upright and good for productivity. *Training and Development Journal* 37(5): 60–65.

Lee, P. 1984. Job sharing—A concept whose time has come. *Office Administration and Automation* 45: 28–30.

Lewis, G.B. 1988a. Clerical work and women's earnings in the federal civil service. In *Comparable Worth, Pay Equity, and Public Policy*, ed. R.M. Kelly and J. Bayes. Westport, CT: Greenwood.

———. 1988b. Progress toward racial and sexual equality in the federal civil service? *Public Administration Review* 48(3): 700–707.

Lewis, G.B., and Park, K. 1989. Turnover rates in federal white-collar employment: Are women more likely to quit than men? *American Review of Public Administration* 19(1): 13–28.

Lewis, S., and Cooper, C. 1988. Stress in dual-earner families. In *Women and Work*, ed. B.A. Gutek, A.H. Stromberg, and L. Larwood. Newbury Park, CA: Sage.

Lipman-Blumen, J. 1984. *Gender Roles and Power*. Englewood Cliffs, NJ: Prentice Hall.

Liscum, B., and Guy, M.E. 1991. Job change decisions for managers in state government: A comparison by sex. Unpublished manuscript.

Loden, M. 1985. *Feminine Leadership: Or How to Succeed in Business without Being One of the Boys.* New York: Times Books.

————. 1986. A machismo that drives women out. *New York Times*, February 9, sec. 3, p. 2.

Lott, A.J. 1973. Social psychology. In *Handbook of General Psychology*, ed. B. Wolman. Englewood Cliffs, NJ: Prentice Hall.

Lowi, T.J. 1979. *End of Liberalism.* 2d ed. New York: W.W. Norton.

Lunding, F.J.; Clements, G.L.; and Perkins, D.S. 1978. Everyone who makes it has a mentor. *Harvard Business Review* 56(4): 89–101.

Lunneborg, P. 1990. *Women Changing Work.* New York: Bergin and Garvey.

Lussier, R.N. 1990. Should your organization use job sharing? *Supervision* 52: 9–11.

Maccoby, E.E. and Jacklin, C.N. 1974. *The Psychology of Sex Differences.* Stanford, CA: Stanford University.

MacKinnon, C.A. 1987. Sexual harassment: Its first decade in court. In *Feminism Unmodified: Discourses on Life and Law*, ed. C.A. MacKinnon. Cambridge: Harvard University.

Maital, S. 1989. A long way to the top. *Across the Board*, December 26, pp. 6–7.

Markham, W.T.; South, S.J.; Bonjean, C.M.; and Corder, J. 1985/1986. Gender and opportunity in the federal bureaucracy. *American Journal of Sociology* 91(1): 129–50.

Marshall, J. 1984. *Women Managers: Travelers in a Male World.* New York: John Wiley and Sons.

Massengill, D., and DiMarco, N. 1979. Sex-role stereotypes and requisite management characteristics: A current replication. *Sex Roles* 5: 561–70.

McClelland, D.C. 1975. *Power: The Inner Experience.* New York: Irvington.

McGlen, N.E., and Sarkees, M.R. 1990. Leadership styles of women in foreign policy. Paper presented at the Annual Meeting of the American Political Science Association, San Francisco, August 30–September 2.

McIlhone, M. 1984. Barriers to advancement: The obstacle course. In *The Successful Woman Manager: How Did She Get There?* ed. R. Ritchie. Symposium conducted at 92nd Annual Meeting of the American Psychological Association, Toronto.

McIntyre, D.I., and Renick, J.C. 1982. Protecting public employees and employers from sexual harassment. *Public Personnel Management Journal* 11: 282–92.

Meier, G.S. 1979. *Job Sharing—A New Pattern for Quality of Work and Life.* Kalamazoo, MI: W.E. Upjohn Institute for Employment Research.

Melia, J., and Lyttle, P. 1986. *Why Jenny Can't Lead: Understanding the Male Dominant System.* Saguache, CO: Operational Politics.

Miller, J. 1986. *Pathways in the Workplace: The Effects of Gender and Race on Access to Organizational Resources.* New York: Cambridge University.

Mills, A.J. 1989. Gender, sexuality and organization theory. In *The Sexuality of Organization*, ed. J. Hearn, D.L. Sheppard, P. Tancred-Sheriff, and G. Burrell. London: Sage.

Mintzberg, H. 1973. *The Nature of Managerial Work.* New York: Harper and Row.

Missirian, A.K. 1982. *The Corporate Connection: Why Women Need Mentors to Reach the Top*. Englewood Cliffs, NJ: Prentice Hall.

Moore, G. 1987. Women in the old-boy network: The case of New York State government. In *Power Elites and Organizations*, ed. G.W. Domhoff and T.R. Dye. Newbury Park, CA: Sage.

Moore, L.M., and Rickel, A.U. 1980. Characteristics of women in traditional and non-traditional managerial roles. *Personnel Psychology* 33: 317–33.

Moore, P., and Mazey, M.E. 1986. Minorities and women in state and local government: 1973–1980. *Journal of Urban Affairs* 8(3): 1–13.

Morrison, A.M., White, R.P., and Van Velsor, E. 1987. Executive women: Substance plus style. *Psychology Today*, August, pp. 18–26.

Morrison, A.M.; White, R.P.; Van Velsor, E.; and the Center for Creative Leadership. 1987. *Breaking the Glass Ceiling*. Reading, MA: Addison-Wesley.

Mortimer, J.T., and London, J. 1984. The varying linkages of work and family. In *Work and Family*, ed. P. Voydanoff. Palo Alto, CA: Mayfield.

Mueller, K.H. 1954. *Educating Women for a Changing World*. Minneapolis: University of Minnesota.

Muncy, R. 1991. *Creating a Female Dominion in American Reform*. New York: Oxford University Press.

National Commission on the Public Service. 1990. *Leadership for America: Rebuilding the Public Service*. Lexington, MA: Lexington Books.

National Manpower Council. 1957. *Womanpower*. New York: Columbia University.

Nemec, J. 1988. Give salespersonship a high priority. *American Salesman* 33(9): 20–23.

Neugarten, D.A., and Miller-Spellman, M. 1983. Sexual harassment in public employment. In *Public Personnel Administration: Problems and Prospects*, ed. S.W. Hays and R.C. Kearney. Englewood Cliffs, NJ: Prentice Hall.

New York Conference Board. 1985. The working woman progress report. *World Work Report* 10: 3–4.

Nicholson, N., and West, M.A. 1988. *Managerial Job Change: Men and Women in Transition*. New York: Cambridge University.

Nieva, V.F. 1985. Work and family linkages. In *Women and Work*, ed. L. Larwood, A. Stromberg, and B. Gutek. Newbury Park, CA: Sage.

Nieva, V.F., and Gutek, B.A. 1981. *Women and Work: A Psychological Perspective*. New York: Praeger.

Noe, R.A. 1988. Women and mentoring: A review and research agenda. *Academy of Management Review* 13(1): 65–78.

Nollen, S.D. 1982. *New Work Schedules in Practice*. New York: Van Nostrand Reinhold.

Nyquist, L.V., and Spence, J.T. 1986. Effects of dispositional dominance and sex role expectations on leadership behaviors. *Journal of Personality and Social Psychology* 56: 87–93.

O'Connell, A.V., and Russo, N.F., eds. 1988. *Models of Achievement: Reflections of Eminent Women in Psychology*. Vol. 2. Hillsdale, NJ: Lawrence Erlbaum Associates.

O'Leary, V.E. 1974. Some attitudinal barriers to occupational aspirations in women. *Psychological Bulletin* 81: 139–47.

Olmsted, B., and Smith, S. 1983. *The Job Sharing Handbook*. Berkeley, CA: Ten Speed.

————. 1989. *Creating a Flexible Workplace: How to Select and Manage Alternative Work Options*. New York: American Management.

Orth, C.D., and Jacobs, F. 1971. Women in management: Pattern for change. *Harvard Business Review* 49: 139–47.

Ortner, S.B. 1974. Is female to male as nature is to culture? In *Woman, Culture, and Society*, ed. M.Z. Rosaldo and L. Lamphere. Stanford, CA: Stanford University.

Ott, J.S. 1989. *Classic Readings in Organizational Behavior*. Pacific Grove, CA: Brooks/Cole.

Ouchi, W. 1981. *Theory Z: How American Business Can Meet the Japanese Challenge*. Reading, MA: Addison-Wesley.

Papanek, H. 1973. Men, women, and work: Reflections on the two-person career. *American Journal of Sociology* 78: 857–72.

Pear, R. 1982. Advocates fear for autonomy of Civil Rights Commission. *New York Times*, October 3, p. E5.

Pereia, J.L. 1988. Women allege sexist atmosphere in offices constitutes harassment. *Wall Street Journal*, February 10, sec. 2, p. 23.

Perman, F. 1988. The players and the problems in the EEO enforcement process: A status report. *Public Administration Review* 48(4): 827–33.

Personnel Policies Forum. 1987. Sexual harassment: Employer's policies and problems (PPF Survey no. 144). Washington, DC: Bureau of National Affairs.

Peterson-Hardt, S., and Perlman, N.D. 1979. *Sex-segregated Career Ladders in New York State Government: A Structural Analysis of Inequality in Employment*. Working Paper No. 1. Albany: Center for Women in Government, State University of New York.

Phillips-Jones, L. 1982. Establishing a formalized mentoring program. *Training and Development Journal* 37(2): 38–42.

Pleck, J.H. 1985. *Working Wives/Working Husbands*. Newbury Park, CA: Sage.

Plimpton, B.W. 1984. Senior careerists: Strategies for using their skills. *Public Administration Review* 44(July/August): 451.

Powell, G.N. 1980. Career development and the woman managers: A social power perspective. *Personnel* 57(3): 22–32.

————. 1986. What do tomorrow's managers think about sexual intimacy at work? *Business Horizons* 29(4): 30–35.

————. 1988. *Women and Men in Management*. Newbury Park, CA: Sage.

Presley, S.; Weaver, J.; and Weaver, B. 1986. Traditional and nontraditional Mormon women: Political attitudes and socialization. *Women and Politics* 5(4): 51–77.

Preston, M.B. 1986. Affirmative action policy: Can it survive the Reaganites? In *Affirmative Action Theory, Analysis, and Prospects*, eds. M.W. Combs and J. Gruhl. Jefferson, NC: McFarland.

Radin, B.A. 1980. Leadership training for women in state and local government. *Public Personnel Management* 9(2): 52–60.

Ragins, B.R. 1989. Barriers to mentoring: The female manager's dilemma. *Human Relations* 42(1): 1–22.

Ragins, B.R., and Sundstrom, E. 1989. Gender and power in organizations: A longitudinal perspective. *Psychological Bulletin* 105(1): 51–88.

Rapoport, R., and Rapoport, R.N. 1971. *Dual earner families*. London: Penguin.

Reich, M.H. 1985. Executive views from both sides of mentoring. *Personnel* 62(3): 42–46.

———. 1986. The mentor connection. *Personnel* 63: 50–56.

Renwick, P.A. 1977. The effects of sex differences on the perception and management of superior–subordinate conflict: An exploratory study. *Organizational Behavior and Human Performance* 19: 403–415.

Reskin, B., ed. 1984. *Sex Segregation in the Workplace: Trends, Explanations, Remedies*. Washington, DC: National Academy.

Reskin, B., and Hartmann, H. 1986. *Women's Work, Men's Work*. Washington, DC: National Academy.

Revilla, V.M. 1984. Conflict management styles of men and women administrators in higher education. *Dissertation Abstracts International* 45(6): 1601-A.

Riccucci, N.M. 1986. Female and minority employment in city government: The role of unions. *Policy Studies Journal* 15: 3–16.

Richbell, S. 1976. De facto discrimination and how to kick the habit. *Personnel Management* 8: 11.

Riley, S., and Wrench, D. 1985. Mentoring among women lawyers. *Journal of Applied Social Psychology* 15: 374–86.

Rix, S. 1989. *The American Woman, 1988–89: A Status Report*. New York: W.W. Norton.

Roche, G.R. 1979. Much ado about mentors. *Harvard Business Review* 57(1): 14–31.

Roethlisberger, F.J. 1941. *Management and Morale*. Cambridge, MA: Harvard University.

Rogers v. *EEOC*. 454 Fd. 2nd. 234 (5th Cir. 1971), cert. denied, 406 U.S. 957 (1972).

Roosevelt, E., and Hickok, L.A. 1954. *Ladies of Courage*. New York: G.P. Putnam's Sons.

Rosen, B. and Jerdee, T. 1978. Perceived sex differences in managerially relevant characteristics. *Sex Roles* 4(6): 837–43.

Rosen, B.; Templeton, M.E.; and Kirchline, K. 1981. The first few years on the job: Women in management. *Business Horizons* 24(6): 26–29.

Rosener, J.B. 1990. Ways women lead. *Harvard Business Review* 68(6): 119–25.

Ross, C., and England, R.E. 1987. State government's sexual harassment policy initiatives. *Public Administration Review*, pp. 259–62.

Ruble, D.N., and Higgins, T. 1976. Effects of group sex composition on self-presentation and sex-typing. *Journal of Social Issues* 3: 125–32.

Rynes, S., and Rosen, B. 1983. A comparison of male and female reactions to career advancement opportunities. *Journal of Vocational Behavior* 22: 105–16.

Rytina, N.F., and Bianchi, S.M. 1984. Occupational re-classification and changes in distribution by gender. *Monthly Labor Review* 107(3): 11–17.

Safran, C. 1976. What do men do to women on the job? *Redbook* 149: 217–23.

Samuels, C. 1975. *The Forgotten Five Million: Women in Public Employment: A Guide to Eliminating Sex Discrimination*. Brooklyn, NY: Women's Action Alliance, Publication no. 93.68.

Sanger, M.B., and Levin, M.A. 1991. Move over, policy analysis: It's management that counts. *Governing*, February, p. 9.

Sapiro, V. 1983. *The Political Integration of Women.* Urbana: University of Illinois.

Sargent, A.G. 1983. *The Androgynous Manager.* New York: American Management Association.

Schein, E.H. 1971. Organizational socialization and the profession of management. In *Organization Psychology: A Book of Readings,* ed. D. Kolb. Englewood Cliffs, NJ: Prentice Hall.

Schein, V.E. 1973. The relationship between sex role stereotypes and requisite management characteristics. *Journal of Applied Psychology* 57(2): 95–100.

———. 1975. Relationships between sex role stereotypes and requisite management characteristics among female managers. *Journal of Applied Psychology* 60(3): 340–44.

Schwartz, F.N. 1989. Management women and the new facts of life. *Harvard Business Review* 67(1): 65–76.

Shapiro, E.C.; Haseltine, F.P.; and Rowe, M.P. 1978. Moving up: Role models, mentors, and the "patron system." *Sloan Management Review* 19: 51–58.

Shapiro, R.Y., and Mahajan, H. 1986. Gender differences in policy preferences: A summary of trends from the 1960s to the 1980s. *Public Opinion Quarterly* 50: 42–61.

Sheppard, D.L. 1989. Organizations, power and sexuality: The image and self-image of women managers. In *The Sexuality of Organization,* ed. J. Hearn, D.L. Sheppard, P. Tancred-Sheriff, and B. Burrell. London: Sage.

Shockley, P.S., and Stanley, C.M. 1980. Women in management training programs: What they think about key issues. *Public Personnel Management* 9: 214–24.

Shockley-Zalabak, P. 1981. The effects of sex differences on the preference for utilization of conflict styles of managers in a work setting: An exploratory study. *Public Personnel Management Journal* 10: 289–95.

Siegfried, W.D.; Macfarlane, I.; Graham, D.B.; Moore, W.A.; and Young, P.L. 1981. A re-examination of sex differences in job preferences. *Journal of Vocational Behavior* 18: 30–42.

Siehl, C., and Martin, J. 1988. Measuring organizational culture. In *Inside Organizations: Understanding the Human Dimension,* ed. M.O. Jones, M.D. Moore, and R.C. Snyder. Newbury Park, CA: Sage.

Sigel, R. 1975. The adolescent in politics: The case of American girls. Paper presented at the Annual Meeting of the American Political Science Association, San Francisco.

Sigelman, L., and Cayer, N.J. 1986. Minorities, women and public sector jobs: A status report. In *Affirmative Action Theory, Analysis, and Prospects,* ed. M.W. Combs and J. Gruhl. Jefferson, NC: McFarland.

Simon, R.J., and Landis, J.M. 1989. Women's and men's attitudes about a woman's place and role. *Public Opinion Quarterly* 53: 265–76.

Sinkkonen, S. 1985. Women in local politics. In *Unfinished Democracy: Women in Nordic Politics,* ed. E. Haavio-Mannila. Oxford: Pergamon.

Smeltzer, L.R., and Fann, G.L. 1989. Gender differences in external networks of small business owners/managers. *Journal of Small Business Management* 27(April): 25–32.

Smith, H. 1989. Confessions of a job sharer. *Training* 26:70.

Smith, H.L., and Grenier, M. 1982. Sources of organizational power for women: Overcoming structural obstacles. *Sex Roles* 8: 733–46.

Solomon, C.M. 1990. Careers under glass. *Personnel Journal* 69: 96–105.

Sone, P.G. 1982. The effects of gender on managers' resolution of superior–subordinate conflict. *Dissertation Abstracts International* 42(11): 4914-A.

Speizer, J.J. 1981. Moving up: Role models, mentors, and sponsors—The elusive concepts. *Signs* 6: 692–712.

Spruell, G.R. 1985. Daytime drama: Love in the office. *Training and Development Journal* 39(2): 21–23.

Stanley, J.R. 1987. Gender differences in Texas public administration. Paper presented at the annual meeting of the American Political Science Association, Chicago.

———. 1989. Women in the Texas executive branch of government. In *Gender, Bureaucracy, and Democracy: Careers and Equal Opportunity in the Public Sector*, ed. M.M. Hale and R.M. Kelly. Westport, CT: Greenwood.

Steuernagel, T. 1989. Gender neutrality: Women's friend or foe? Paper presented at the American Political Science Association meeting, September 3, Atlanta.

Stewart, D.W. 1976. Women in top jobs: An opportunity for federal leadership. *Public Administration Review* 36(4): 357–64.

Stewart, L.P., and Gudykunst, W.B. 1982. Differential factors influencing the hierarchial level and number of promotions of males and females within an organization. *Academy of Management Journal* 25: 586–97.

Stoper, E. 1988. Alternative work patterns and the double life. In *Women, Power and Policy*, ed. E. Boneparth and E. Stoper. New York: Pergamon.

Strober, M. 1982. The MBA: Same passport to success for women and men? In *Women in the Workplace*, ed. P.A. Wallace. Boston: Auburn House.

Sutton, C.D., and Moore, K.K. 1985. Probing opinions of executive women—Twenty years later. *Harvard Business Review* 63: 52–66.

Tannenbaum, A.S. 1968. *Control in Organizations*. New York: McGraw-Hill.

Taylor, A., III. 1986. Why women managers are bailing out. *Fortune*, August 18, pp. 16–23.

Taylor, M.S., and Ilgen, D.R. 1981. Sex discrimination against women in initial placement decisions: A laboratory investigation. *Academy of Management Journal* 24: 859–65.

Thompson, J. 1976. How to find a mentor. *MBA* 10: 26–32.

U.S. Code. 1992 (January). *Congressional & Administrative News*, no. 11, 102d Congress, 1st Session, P.L. 102–152 to 102–198; 105 Stat. 985 to 1627.

U.S. Commission on Civil Rights. 1987. *Federal enforcement of equal employment requirements*. Washington: Clearinghouse Publication no. 93.68.

U.S. Congress. House. Committee on Education and Labor. *A Report on the Investigation of the Civil Rights Enforcement Activities of the Office of Federal Contract Compliance Programs, U.S. Department of Labor*. 100th Cong., 1st sess., 1987.

U.S. Congress. House. Committee on Government Operations. *Overhauling the Federal EEO Complaint Processing System: A New Look at a Persistent Problem*. 100th Cong., 1st sess., 1987. Vol. 14, 6.

U.S. Congress. House. Committee on Government Operations. *Processing EEO Complaints in the Federal Sector—Problems and Solutions (Part 2)*. 99th Cong., 1st sess., 1986. Vol. 1, 44.

U.S. Congress. House. Committee on Government Operations. Subcommittee of the Committee on Government Affairs. *Processing EEO Complaints in the Federal Sector: Problems and Solutions (Part 2)*. 99th Cong., 2nd sess., 1986.

U.S. Department of Commerce, Bureau of the Census. 1980. *Census of Population. Characteristics of the Population*. Vol. 1. PC80-1-D1-A. Table 281, 1–268 and 1–271.

U.S. Department of Labor, Women's Bureau. 1983. *Time of Change: 1983 Handbook on Women Workers*. Bulletin 298.

U.S. Equal Employment Opportunity Commission. 1982. *Job Patterns for Minorities and Women in State and Local Government, 1980*. Washington, DC: Government Printing Office.

U.S. Equal Employment Opportunity Commission. 1985. *Job Patterns for Minorities and Women in State and Local Government, 1985*. Washington, DC: Government Printing Office.

U.S. Equal Employment Opportunity Commission. 1990. *Job Patterns for Minorities and Women in State and Local Government, 1989*. Washington, DC: Government Printing Office.

U.S. Merit Systems Protection Board. 1987. *Sexual Harassment in the Federal Workplace: Is It a Problem?* Washington, DC: U.S. Government Printing Office.

Van Maanen, J., and Barley, S.R. 1985. Cultural organization: Fragments of a theory. In *Organizational Culture*, ed. P. Frost, L.F. Moore, M.R. Louis, C.C. Lundberg, and J. Martin. Newbury Park, CA: Sage.

Verespej, M.A. 1989. The new workweek. *Industry Week* 238: 11–21.

Vertz, L.L. 1985. Women, occupational advancement, and mentoring: An analysis of one public organization. *Public Administration Review* 45(3): 415–23.

Wallace, P.A. 1982. *Women in the Workplace*. Boston: Auburn House.

Wall Street Journal. Labor Letter. Jan. 21, 1986, p. 1., vol. 207, no. 14, Eastern ed.

Walsh, D.C., and Kelleher, S.E. 1987. The "corporate perspective" on the health of women at work. In *Women and Work*, ed. A.H. Stromberg, L. Larwood, and B.A. Gutek. Newbury Park, CA: Sage.

Warihay, P.D. 1980. The climb to the top: Is the network the route for women? *Personnel Administrator* 25(4): 55–60.

Warner, R.L.; Steel, B.S.; and Lovrich, N.P. 1989. Conditions associated with the advent of representative bureaucracy: The case of women in policing. *Social Science Quarterly* 70(3): 562–78.

Whyte, W.H., Jr. 1956. *The Organization Man*. New York: Simon and Schuster.

Wigand, R.T., and Boster, F.J. 1991. Mentoring, social interaction and commitment: An empirical analysis of a mentoring program. *Communications: The European Journal of Communications* 16(1): in press.

Wiley, M.G., and Eskilson, A. 1982. The interaction of sex and power base on perceptions of managerial effectiveness. *Academy of Management Journal* 25(3): 671–77.

Wolf, W.C., and Fligstein, N.D. 1979. Sex and authority in the workplace: The causes of sexual inequality. *American Sociological Review* 44: 235–52.

Wong, P.T.P.; Kettlewell, G.; and Sproule, C.F. 1985. On the importance of being masculine: Sex role, attribution and women's career achievement. *Sex Roles* 12(7/8): 757–69.

Woodlands Group. 1980. Management development roles: Coach, sponsor, and mentor. *Personnel Journal* 59(11): 918–21.

Workforce 2000. 1987. Indianapolis, IN: Hudson Institute.

Yoder, J. 1991. Rethinking tokenism: Looking beyond numbers. *Gender and Society* 5(2): 178–93.

Zey, M.G. 1984. *The Mentor Connection*. Homewood, IL: Dow Jones-Irwin.

———. 1985. Mentor programs: Making the right moves. *Personnel Journal* 64: 53–57.

Index